Negro exodus from the state during the so-called "Kansas Fever" of 1879, the spread of the Farmers' Union and Alliance of the 1880's, and the rise of Populism in the 1890's.

Having crushed Greenbackism and related independent movements, Hair says, the Bourbon oligarchy proceeded to fasten upon Louisiana what was probably the most reactionary and least socially responsible regime in the history of the post-Civil War South.

Bourbonism and Agrarian Protest combines thorough scholarly research and clear, perceptive writing. It covers every issue and every event of consequence of the era and is an excellent sequel to Roger W. Shugg's *Origins of Class Struggle in Louisiana*, which treats the period from 1840 to 1875.

WILLIAM IVY HAIR is Associate Professor of History at Florida State University. A native of Winnsboro, he attended Louisiana State University where he received his B.A., M.A., and Ph.D. degrees. He has also taught at Louisiana State University.

Bourbonism and Agrarian Protest

WILLIAM IVY HAIR

Bourbonism and Agrarian Protest

LOUISIANA POLITICS
1877–1900

LOUISIANA STATE UNIVERSITY PRESS
BATON ROUGE

Copyright © 1969 by
Louisiana State University Press
Library of Congress Card Number: 70–88741
SNB Number: 8071–0908–8
Manufactured in the United States of America by
Thos. J. Moran's Sons, Inc., Baton Rouge, Louisiana
Designed by Jules B. McKee

To KAROLYN, *with love*

Preface

IN THIS BOOK I have attempted to capture the esssence
of Louisiana in the late nineteenth century, the time of
America's Gilded Age. If I have dealt in large part with politics, it is because Louisianians are, or were, among the most
political people on earth. But politics anywhere should never
be studied in a vacuum. For that reason the unessential details of the various election campaigns have been left out of
the narrative, and in their place considerable attention has
been devoted to race relations, economics, and social issues.
Everything I found which had a significant bearing upon the
drift of public affairs has been included. Thus, what I offer
the reader is something more than, and something less than, a
political history of Louisiana from 1877 to 1900.

Louisiana, in some ways so distinctive from the rest of
America, has attracted much historical interest and speculation; but hitherto, virtually nothing, outside of a few articles,
has been published about the state during the decades following Reconstruction. The romantic antebellum years, the ex-
citing era of Civil War and Reconstruction, and the dramatic
age of Huey Long have drawn most of the attention from both
scholars and journalists. But about the period of the late nineteenth century, as well as the early twentieth, vital questions
have remained unanswered and indeed unasked. Yet it was
during this time, when a repressive Bourbon oligarchy was

confronted by little more than impotent agrarian reformers, that the social forces which would help produce Huey Long were being engendered.

Many people, too numerous to mention all, have earned my gratitude for assisting or encouraging me in the preparation of this study. Some deserve a particular word of thanks. Professors Burl Noggle and John Loos of Louisiana State University gave me sound advice and inspired me during my days as a graduate student, and have helped in many ways since that time. The staff of the L.S.U. Library, especially the archivist, Mr. V. L. Bedsole, provided valuable help in locating research materials. To the staff of the Library of Congress, and of the libraries at Florida State University, Tulane University, the University of Texas, and the University of North Carolina, I am also indebted. A grant from Florida State University allowed me the time to complete the manuscript, and to my colleagues there, particularly Professors Earl R. Beck, Richard A. Bartlett, Donald D. Horward, Wallace W. Reichelt, and William W. Rogers, I wish to express my gratitude for their interest in my work. A former student of mine and a friend, Rick Nihlen, gave of his time in reading portions of the initial drafts. Appreciation is also expressed to John Price, a graduate student at L.S.U., who kindly provided photographs of Populist leaders.

My greatest indebtedness is to my family. My parents Mr. and Mrs. Walter Ivy Hair, and my sister June Hair, all of whom now live in Baton Rouge, have over the years given me wonderful inspiration and encouragement. And without the sustaining devotion of my wife Karolyn and my two little sons Steven and Walter, my work would have been infinitely more difficult.

Table of Contents

Illustrations

Maps

Bourbonism and Agrarian Protest

Reconstruction's End

C O L D   R A I N S poured down on New Orleans in February of 1877, forcing many Mardi Gras revelers indoors and spoiling the grand parade of Rex, Lord of Misrule. The Carnival season that year was further dampened by a gloomy political crisis which had hovered over Louisiana and all America since the previous November. For the presidential election of 1876 remained in deadlock. Samuel J. Tilden, Democrat, had won a popular majority. But Rutherford B. Hayes, Republican, claimed a slim electoral victory on the basis of confused returns from the three Southern states still under Reconstruction rule: Florida, South Carolina, and—most muddled of all—Louisiana. Some Americans feared the momentary outbreak of another Civil War.[1]

Three months before this unwontedly somber Carnival season, on November 7, 1876, both state and nation had balloted in what proved to be the last Reconstruction election. And for Louisiana the current gubernatorial contest did produce more excitement and anxiety than had presidential politics. Outgoing Governor William P. Kellogg hoped to deliver that office to his party's nominee, a fellow carpetbagger, Stephen B. Packard. The Democratic aspirant to the governorship was

[1] New Orleans *Daily Picayune,* February 14–16, 1877; Paul Leland Haworth, *The Hayes-Tilden Disputed Presidential Election of 1876* (Cleveland, 1906) , 168.

Francis T. Nicholls. A former brigadier general in the Confederate army, Nicholls had lost an arm and a leg on Civil
War battlefields; as a candidate, his heroically mangled body
helped compensate for his deficiencies as a public speaker.[2]
Beyond doubt, a solid majority of the white population supported the ticket of Tilden and Nicholls. But over half of Louisiana's voters, according to the registration rolls, were not
white.[3]

Most of the state passed through the pre-election activity
in 1876 with comparatively little of the violence that had previously made Louisiana a scandal to the rest of the nation.
As planned by Nicholls' campaign managers—especially the
shrewd "Major" Edward A. Burke—the Democrats generally
reversed their earlier tactics and spoke of the advent of a new
era of racial good feelings; they began persuading Negro voters with parades instead of pistols, with beef barbecues rather
than bullwhips. Even the extremist editor of the Natchitoches
People's Vindicator, a spokesman for the paramilitary White
League, proffered "the right hand of fellowship" to black
people, because "our interests are yours, yours are ours."
This appeal to the Negroes of that region closed, however,
with the less cordial information that come what may, white
Democracy was "determined" to triumph. "No compromise.
Victory or death." [4]

Naked force remained the rule only in certain of the heavily

2 New Orleans *Times,* July 28, 1876; Clarence Howard Nichols, "Francis T.
Nicholls, Bourbon Democrat" (M.A. thesis, Louisiana State University, 1959),
46–55; Hilda Mulvey McDaniel, "Francis Tillou Nicholls and the End of Reconstruction," *Louisiana Historical Quarterly,* XXXII (1949), 372–74.

3 The state registration figures for 1876 gave 115,268 colored and 92,354
white voters. However, the census figures for 1870 and 1880 indicate that the
racial division of Louisiana adult males must have been approximately equal
in 1876.

4 Natchitoches *People's Vindicator,* November 4, 1876. See also Philip D.
Uzee, "Republican Politics in Louisiana, 1877–1900" (Ph.D. dissertation, Louisiana State University, 1950), 27–30.

Negro parishes: Ouachita, Morehouse, East Baton Rouge, and East and West Feliciana. Events in these localities just prior to the Hayes-Tilden election, insisted one national periodical, "would have disgraced Turks in Bulgaria." [5] Nevertheless, the Democratic plan of selected intimidation this time usually stopped short of murder. Nor was any of the political lawlessness of 1876 conducted under the Ku Klux or the White League banner, but rather it was done by local groups named Regulators, Rifle Clubs, or, in the case of one group of apparent specialists in cabin burning, the Coal Oil Clan.[6] Midnight visitations and threats, with whippings for the stubborner blacks, accomplished the desired results in all but Ouachita, where several killings were required. On November 7, each of the above parishes turned in lopsided majorities for Tilden and Nicholls, and contributed in the process a new word to the American language: "bulldozer." The exact source and meaning of that slang expression is unclear, but it was first applied to political vigilante methods in the state during the 1876 campaign. The Louisiana "bulldozer," who coerced or slew Negroes for reasons of politics, immediately became a stock villain in Northern Republican magazines and newspapers.[7]

Tilden, on the face of the precinct returns, carried Louisiana by 7,639 votes out of a total 160,964 allegedly cast. Nicholls defeated Packard by 8,010. The Republicans, having anticipated Democratic landslides from the five "bulldozed" parishes, stood ready to cancel these votes through the return-

5 *Harper's Weekly,* XX (December 16, 1876) , 1006.
6 Fanny Z. Lovell Bone, "Louisiana in the Disputed Election of 1876," *Louisiana Historical Quarterly,* XIV (1931) , 553–55; New Orleans *Daily Picayune,* January 4, 1877.
7 Eric Partridge (comp.) , *A Dictionary of Slang and Unconventional English* (New York, 1953) , 104; Garnie W. McGinty, *Louisiana Redeemed: The Overthrow of Carpet-bag Rule, 1876–1880* (New Orleans, 1941) , 53; *Harper's Weekly,* XX (December 9, 1876) , 986; New York *Times,* July 13, 1877, January 17, 1879.

ing board at the state capitol; as in the past, the board was empowered to reject returns from precincts where there was some evidence of fraud. Yet it was soon discovered that even if the totals from the five troubled parishes were tossed out, the Republican slate would still not emerge victorious.[8] Statewide, the Democratic majority was bigger than expected.

Then came the stunning realization that Louisiana's eight electoral votes could swing the national election. The outcome in Florida and South Carolina was likewise in doubt; Tilden needed only one of the disputed states to become the next President, while Hayes must have all three. But Louisiana's votes became the most delicate and explosive question.[9] National Democratic chieftains believed that even if Hayes were awarded the electors of the other states, Tilden's claim to Louisiana was irrefutable. President Ulysses S. Grant, serving out his last months in office, dismayed the Republicans by saying that Hayes had probably lost the Pelican State, and with it the election.[10]

It was not possible, then or later, to determine which ticket should have had Louisiana in 1876. The Democratic pretense that throngs of Negroes had freely cast ballots for the party of white supremacy was transparently false, but equally mendacious were the Republican registration figures, which had been doctored prior to the election so as to show a statewide black voting majority of over twenty thousand. *Harper's*

[8] Ella Lonn, *Reconstruction in Louisiana After 1868* (New York, 1918), 438–60; Albert M. Gibson, *A Political Crime: The History of the Great Fraud* (New York, 1885), 298–99. A useful compendium of state registration figures and election returns from the 1870's to 1900 is to be found in *Report of the Secretary of State to His Excellency W. W. Heard, Governor of the State of Louisiana*, 1902, pp. 544–87.

[9] C. Vann Woodward, *Reunion and Reaction: The Compromise of 1877 and the End of Reconstruction* (Boston, 1951), 17–20, 106, 163. Louisiana in 1876 had eight electoral votes, South Carolina seven, and Florida four.

[10] Harry Barnard, *Rutherford B. Hayes and His America* (Indianapolis, 1954), 323.

Weekly, in one of its lapses from Republican orthodoxy, surmised that "one claim was as good as another, and as bad, for nobody could possibly know the truth." [11]

In the panicky days following November 7, distinguished representatives from both national parties boarded southbound trains for Louisiana's capital city which was at that time New Orleans. Upon arrival these so-called "visiting statesmen" witnessed and in some instances attempted to direct the official canvassing of the state's vote, which was now in the hands of the returning board. The hitherto good reputations of several "visiting statesmen" would be permanently smirched by their partisan meddling at the State House.[12] As for the members of the returning board, they were men of no repute anyway.

J. Madison Wells, elderly but still fiery, presided over the four-man board. "Mad" Wells, as his many foes called him, had a questionable political past which stretched back to 1839–40, when as sheriff of Rapides Parish he had defaulted over $12,000 in tax monies.[13] A Unionist during the Civil War, he was elected governor in 1865 only to be removed by General Philip H. Sheridan when military Reconstruction began two years later; the disgusted Sheridan described Wells's conduct as "sinuous as the mark left in the dust by the movement of a snake." [14] Yet by attaching himself to the Grant administration, Wells had slowly emerged from political

11 *House Miscellaneous Documents,* 44th Cong., 2nd Sess., No. 34, pp. 475–78; *Harper's Weekly,* XX (December 23, 1876), 1030.

12 William A. Dunning, *Reconstruction, Political and Economic, 1865–1877* (New York, 1907), 310–12. Among the "visiting statesmen" to Louisiana after the 1876 election were: Congressman James Garfield (R.-Ohio), who would be elected president four years later; Senator John Sherman (R.-Ohio); and Lew Wallace, a politician-author who was then writing the novel *Ben Hur.*

13 Walter McGehee Lowrey, "The Political Career of James Madison Wells," *Louisiana Historical Quarterly,* XXXI (1948), 1001.

14 Philip H. Sheridan, *Personal Memoirs of P. H. Sheridan* (New York, 1888), II, 266–67.

eclipse and in the interval, according to one melancholy observation, he had "steadily deteriorated in character." [15] The other white man on the board was Thomas C. Anderson, a state senator who had siphoned public money into a navigation company which he partly owned. The two Negro members were Louis M. Kenner and Gadane Cassanave.

Kenner owned a disreputable saloon adjacent to the State House. He had previously been indicted for larceny. Cassanave, an undertaker by trade, was thought to be somewhat more honest than his returning board colleagues, but he was also considered an ignoramus.[16] All four men were Republicans. All were also native-born Louisianians, and their devious conduct during the post-election crisis led the *Nation* to conclude that they were "probably the most depraved politicians this country has ever produced." [17] Other onlookers began to see comic opera aspects in the board's proceedings; someone suggested that the affair ought to be set to music by Gilbert and Sullivan.[18]

The board delayed its decision until early December. In the interval Wells shamelessly offered to sell Louisiana's electoral votes to the highest bidder. He appears to have negotiated with Democratic managers in Washington and New York; one of the go-betweens later testified that Wells "wanted at least $200,000 apiece for himself and Anderson and a smaller amount for the niggers." [19] Reportedly, Wells also quoted the Democratic National Committee a package price

---

[15] James F. Rhodes, *A History of the United States From the Compromise of 1850 to the McKinley-Bryan Campaign of 1896* (New York, 1920), VII, 295.
[16] Lowrey, *Louisiana Historical Quarterly*, XXXI, 1093; Gibson, *A Political Crime*, 155–56; Haworth, *The Hayes-Tilden Election*, 97–98.
[17] *Nation*, XXIX (August 21, 1879), 120.
[18] *Harper's Weekly*, XXIII (March 22, 1879), 222.
[19] Washington *National Republican*, February 2, 1877, quoted in Woodward, *Reunion and Reaction*, 155.

for all transactions necessary to count in both Tilden and Nicholls: one million dollars.[20] The Democrats spurned Wells's solicitations, perhaps because they had reason to believe he could not be trusted. Wells also importuned the leaders of the Republican Party. In a letter to United States Senator Joseph R. West he wrote that "millions have been sent here, and will be used in the interests of Tilden, and unless some counter-movement is made it will be impossible for me ... to arrest its productive results. ... A hint to the wise." [21]

As they probably intended all along, Wells and the other board members decided in favor of the Republicans. By dismissing selected precincts and whole parish returns they transformed Tilden's 7,639 lead into a Hayes majority of 3,437, thus authorizing Governor Kellogg to certify the Hayes electors. The board also declared Packard the victor over Nicholls. But this in itself settled nothing. The Democrats were in no mood to concede. As a countermove John McEnery, who claimed to have defeated Kellogg at the previous gubernatorial election in 1872, emerged from political hibernation to once again announce himself as *de jure* chief executive of the state; "Governor" McEnery then signed the certificates of the Tilden electors.[22] The impasse was thereby placed in the lap of Congress.

While the rival electoral certificates went on their way to Washington, Louisiana's two claimants to the governorship prepared for separate inaugurations in New Orleans. Similar, if somewhat less dramatic, situations existed in Florida and South Carolina. Both Packard and Nicholls took an oath of

[20] New York *Times*, February 1, 1877.

[21] J. Madison Wells to Joseph R. West, November 21, 1876, in *Nation*, XXVI (February 8, 1878) , 80.

[22] New Orleans *Daily Picayune*, December 5–6, 1876; Haworth, *The Hayes-Tilden Election*, 238–39, 301–303. For McEnery's "inauguration" as governor in 1873, see New Orleans *Times*, January 13, 1873.

office on January 8, 1877. Assisted by Kellogg, Packard's Republican legislature occupied the State House, while Nicholls and his solons bided their time in Odd Fellows Hall. A handful of federal soldiers stood by on the capitol grounds to protect Packard, but President Grant, wishing his last weeks in the White House to be as peaceful as circumstances permitted, agreed not to send troops against Nicholls' government unless there were "violent excesses."[23] As the dual state regimes continued operating, a number of Packard's solons, sensing the drift of events and, in the words of the New York *Times*, "reduced to [their] last chew of tobacco and . . . last sup of whiskey," slipped over to obtain a seat—or a monetary consolation prize—at Odd Fellows Hall.[24]

In Washington, where the Hayes-Tilden drama was being played out, Congress had created the unprecedented Electoral Commission to determine who should receive the votes of the three contested states. During February of 1877 the commission awarded Hayes all three. But angry Democratic congressmen retaliated with a filibuster which threatened to prevent the formal completion of the electoral count, block Hayes's inauguration, and thereby push the national government to the edge of anarchy.

Beneath this turbulent surface, however, certain Northern Republicans and Southern Democrats had, in private Washington meetings, been arranging the terms of one of the most significant compromises in American history. More was involved than the occupancy of the White House. Most Southern Democrats, especially the Louisianians, were supremely anxious to end the last vestiges of Reconstruction and they

---

[23] New Orleans *Times,* January 9, 1877; *Nation,* XXIV (January 11, 1877), 19; E. A. Burke to F. T. Nicholls, February 26, 1877, in *House Miscellaneous Documents,* 45th Cong., 3rd Sess., No. 31, p. 618.
[24] New York *Times,* April 24, 1877.

wanted pledges to that effect. The Southerners also desired future federal appropriations for regional railroad and waterways projects. For an understanding on these matters they were prepared to concede the Presidency to Hayes.[25]

One man from Louisiana took the lead in arranging the political part of the bargain with Hayes's authorized spokesmen. Major Burke, who had so successfully managed the recent Democratic state campaign, was sent to Washington early in 1877 as Nicholls' chief negotiator. Burke was assisted by Louisiana Congressmen Randall L. Gibson, E. John Ellis, and William M. Levy. Backed by other Southern Democrats, they obtained a promise that the Hayes administration would withdraw military support from Packard and from the carpetbagger regime in South Carolina; the one in Florida had already disintegrated in January. In return, Burke and his associates were to undercut the Democratic congressional filibuster which had been aimed at prolonging the presidential deadlock past inauguration day.[26]

Pledges were meanwhile extracted from the Nicholls government. The legislature in Odd Fellows Hall, after agreeing to seat some members from Packard's dwindling assembly, went on to promise that under Democratic rule every person in the state, regardless of race or party, would enjoy political freedom and equality under the law. Furthermore, it was resolved that Louisiana's future would be distinguished by equal education for all and "the promotion of kindly relations between white and colored citizens . . . on a basis of justice and mutual trust." Local Republican activists were assured of immunity from prosecution for "past political con-

25 Dee Brown, *The Year of the Century: 1876* (New York, 1966), 315–37; Woodward, *Reunion and Reaction,* 12–13, 191–201.
26 Lonn, *Reconstruction in Louisiana,* 495–519; McGinty, *Louisiana Redeemed,* 79–84.

duct." Governor Nicholls added his personal endorsement to these resolutions.[27]

On March 1, 1877, the national understanding began to yield its fruit. Democratic Congressman Levy dramatically arose from his seat and spoke; he pleaded for an end to the delaying tactics so that the electoral count might be completed and Hayes declared the winner.[28] Probably the filibuster would have soon collapsed anyway, but Levy's speech became the signal for other Southerners to abandon Tilden's cause. Northern Democratic congressmen now found themselves hopelessly outnumbered. Three days later the new Republican President took office without incident.

South Carolina Democrats were allowed to assume control over their State House on April 10. A few days later a special presidential commission arrived in New Orleans to help pull down the curtain on Reconstruction's final scene. Assistance of another kind came from the notorious Louisiana Lottery Company, which contributed $40,000 or more for the purpose of bribing Packard's remaining legislators, and the metropolitan police, into an acceptance of the situation.[29] On April 24, just as the clock atop St. Louis Cathedral struck the midday hour, federal troops marched away from the State House and the forsaken Packard departed its grounds. Soon Hayes would officially recognize Nicholls as the lawful governor. Reconstruction was over. For Louisiana, it had lasted fifteen years. Suddenly, spontaneously, a public celebration began that matched in boisterousness any Mardi Gras of memory.

The streets of New Orleans witnessed a Carnival-like revelry which went on all afternoon and into the night. Some

[27] New Orleans *Daily Picayune*, April 17, 1877; *Nation*, XXIV (April 19, 1877), 227.

[28] *Congressional Record*, 44th Cong., 2nd Sess., 2046–47.

[29] Berthold C. Alwes, "The History of the Louisiana State Lottery Company," *Louisiana Historical Quarterly*, XXVII (1944), 996–98.

Northerners expressed amusement at the victory jubilee; others thought it rather disgusting.[30] Yet no scene in the city could have been more grotesque than some reported from towns upriver and across the state. In Baton Rouge, for example, citizens greeted the restoration of "white home rule" in noisy fashion, and "the loudest and longest ringing . . . was the bell of the Mount Zion (Colored) Baptist Church. Long after the others had stopped, its clarion notes sounded forth, 'Nicholls is Governor! Louisiana is free!' " [31]

Even so, most Negroes were conspicuously absent from the festivities associated with Louisiana's restoration of conservative white government. Four days later the Democratic *Daily Picayune*, noting their gloom, concluded it was time to inform the "poor, misled and fear-ridden blacks" that they, too, should rejoice in the recent happenings. "Shake off the degrading prejudices," the Negroes were told. "Trust to honor, and we who bear the grand old name of gentleman will show you how great a victory your defeat has been." [32]

30 New York *Times*, April 22, 24, 28, 1877.
31 New Orleans *Daily Picayune*, April 25, 28, 1877.
32 Editorial, *ibid.*, April 28, 1877.

The "New Departure"

ONE PARTICIPANT in the compromise of 1877 hailed it as a "New Departure" in the affairs of Louisiana, the South and the nation.[1] This phrase, so widely repeated, was neither original nor, as it turned out, particularly accurate. Yet to many optimists Hayes's inauguration and the end of Reconstruction looked like foretokens of a happier, more tranquil era. Surely it was time for peace. Louisiana had suffered much during the preceding years of Republican rule; she was, suggested *Harper's Weekly*, "the most unlucky of all the States." [2] While other parts of the late Confederacy benefited from certain praiseworthy features of Reconstruction, in the Pelican State the scattered fragments of reform had barely been visible in a roily sea of corruption and hate.[3]

But in 1877 many Louisianians, like other Americans, spoke in tones that indicated a weariness with sectional chauvinism and its politically motivated "bloody shirt" oratory.

[1] New Orleans *Times*, February 24, 1877.

[2] *Harper's Weekly*, XVIII (October 31, 1874), 901.

[3] Even the conservative Southern historian E. Merton Coulter and the Negro Marxist historian W. E. B. Du Bois, whose interpretations of Reconstruction are diametrically opposed, at least agree on the proposition that Louisiana endured the most squalid aspects of Reconstruction. See Coulter, *The South During Reconstruction: 1865–1877* (Baton Rouge, 1947), 344–45; and Du Bois, *Black Reconstruction in America: An Essay Toward a History of the Part Which Black Folk Played in the Attempt to Reconstruct Democracy in America, 1860–1880* (New York, 1935), 461, 482.

The Northern public seemed to endorse the new President's "hands off" policy toward the South. Ex-Confederates found things to admire in a Republican administration which promised economic aid while leaving the states to manage their own racial and civil problems.[4] In Louisiana, momentarily, ranking Democrats prophesied a future of idyllic race relations in which black laborers would cheerfully follow the helpful advice of their white neighbors and employers. Conservative newspapers assiduously copied reports of such harmony, including one macabre example of biracial cooperation along the Bayou Teche where a "mixed crowd of negro and white" lynched a black man suspected of rape.[5]

Like a prism, the New Departure reflected light according to the vantage point of the onlooker. To President Hayes it showed the possibility of achieving respectability and new strength for his party in the South, as well as a continuation of the recent alliance between Southern Democrats and Northern Republicans in Congress. Hayes and his advisers particularly hoped that the good will generated by the removal of federal troops would prompt the "better class" of Dixie conservatives to break with the racist Democrats and even join Republican ranks; he envisioned gentlemen of property in North and South again clasping political hands as they once did in the defunct but not forgotten Whig Party.[6]

A member of the President's cabinet suggested that "the

---

4 Vincent P. De Santis, *Republicans Face the Southern Question: The New Departure Years, 1877–1897* (Baltimore, 1959), 61–87; Vidalia *Concordia Eagle*, April 7, 1877.

5 Natchitoches *People's Vindicator*, May 19, 26, 1877; Letter from "Uncle Silas" of Thibodaux, in New Orleans *Daily Picayune*, April 8, 1877. After Reconstruction, several stories reached print about Louisiana Negroes being killed by racially integrated mobs. Apparently the whites acquiesced in the Negroes' presence, so lynchings must not have been considered social occasions. For a notably gruesome "mixed lynching," see Vienna (La.) *Sentinel*, quoted in Bastrop *Morehouse Clarion*, September 10, 1880.

6 New York *Times*, April 26, 1877; H. J. Eckenrode, *Rutherford B. Hayes, Statesman of Reunion* (New York, 1930), 247–48.

prejudices existing in the South" necessitated a change in party name;[7] but Hayes, a cautious politician, refused to risk alienating Union veterans and Negro voters accustomed to the Republican label. Besides, Hayes had in hand a stack of optimistic reports from the South. One ebullient informant was James M. Comley, the President's closest personal friend, who journeyed down the Mississippi as a political evangelist for New Departure Republicanism. "I find," Comley told Hayes, "that on the River there is a sort of general feeling that . . . 'Henry Clay Whiggery' is to live again." It "seemed wonderful." [8] Later, however, Comley unhappily noted that "the 'Old Whig' sentiment I spoke of in the former letter petered out before we reached New Orleans." He indicated that most of the Louisiana whites he talked to were mainly interested in federal appointments to the Custom House.[9]

Yet some predicted that the last state freed from Reconstruction might initiate a Southern move toward neo-Whiggish Republicanism. "Louisiana is . . . peculiar," wrote John B. Robertson of New Orleans, "and . . . she contains so many heterogeneous elements that it is not at all improbable she will be the first to lead off in the reconstruction of parties in the Union.[10] Former Congressman Chester B. Darrall, a wealthy carpetbagger living in St. Mary Parish, assured Hayes that the respectable whites now realized, because of the President's conciliatory actions, that the party of Lincoln and Grant was no longer hostile toward the South; in fact, said Darrall, "I think we have reached their hearts." [11]

Efforts were also made to reach the class consciousness of

---

[7] Washington *Daily Nation,* quoted in New Orleans *Daily Picayune,* April 26, 1877.

[8] James M. Comley to Rutherford B. Hayes, April 30, 1877, in Rutherford B. Hayes Papers (Microfilm copy in Library of Congress) .

[9] James M. Comley to Rutherford B. Hayes, May 11, 1877, *ibid.*

[10] John B. Robertson to David M. Key, April 26, 1877, *ibid.*

[11] Chester B. Darrall to Rutherford B. Hayes, April 27, 1877, *ibid.*

wealthy whites. One visiting Republican officeholder from New York, Stewart L. Woodford, placed the proposition before Louisiana's gentry in blunt language: "The Republican party at the North comprises the wealth, intelligence, and respectability of the community, and it is not strange then that it should desire alliance with the same element in the South, allowing the ignorant masses to go where they belong, to the Democratic party." [12]

When Woodford and others like him scorned the South's "ignorant masses," they presumably alluded only to the poor whites. "Our colored citizens," wrote a group of Hayes's Louisiana supporters, "are *almost instinctively Republicans* and nothing will drive them into . . . the Democratic party except coercion." [13] In essence the New Departure Republicans were saying that Negroes would remain in the party because it had once been the liberal instrument of emancipation, and affluent ex-Confederates should join it because it was now a conservative bulwark for property and privilege.

Southern Democrats certainly welcomed the federal appropriations flowing out of Hayes's policy. Louisiana obtained more money for public works than any other American state during the first fiscal year after Reconstruction.[14] But a switch in party allegiance was something else. The Democratic emblem had become too deeply engraved in the twin pillars of Southern politics: states' rights and white supremacy. Republicanism, no matter how conservatively it might have evolved in the North, was still the historical disturber of Southern institutions. Another obstacle came from the Stalwart wing of the Republican Party. The Stalwarts in Congress,

12 New Orleans *Daily Picayune,* November 25, 1879.
13 John Ray and others to Rutherford B. Hayes, April 21, 1877, in Hayes Papers.
14 *Senate Executive Documents,* 45th Cong., 3rd Sess., No. 9, cited in Woodward, *Reunion and Reaction,* 233.

who more or less clung to the Radical philosophy of the Grant years, kept old fears alive by publicly denouncing the President's appeasement of the South.[15]

Moreover, Whiggish-minded Southerners were beginning to discover that a national coalition of conservatives was equally available inside the Democratic Party. By the end of Reconstruction, Northeastern business and professional men had become almost as powerful in Democratic as in Republican councils. From the 1870's until 1896 every presidential nominee of the party which most white Southerners preferred would be a Northern conservative.[16]

"From a political standpoint," a New York *Times* correspondent accurately assumed in 1877, the Republican New Departure "is almost . . . certain to be a most disastrous failure." White Louisianians, he observed, were jubilant over the return to home rule "but that they should feel any gratitude to President Hayes . . . has never entered their minds." The *Times* man added that although many "old Whigs" of 1861 had opposed secession, their wartime property losses and the social upsets of Reconstruction had made "these rich men" staunchly conservative Democrats.[17]

In this instance what was true of Louisiana applied generally to the South. Hayes's policy bore meager political fruit. Few prominent Democrats between the Potomac and the Rio Grande were induced to change parties. While in Congress the bipartisan coalition that had assisted Hayes into the White House started falling apart as early as October of 1877; at

15 De Santis, *Republicans Face the Southern Question,* 104–106; New York *Times,* December 30, 1877, March 26, 1878.

16 Thomas B. Alexander, "Persistent Whiggery in the Confederate South, 1860–1877," *Journal of Southern History,* XXVII (1961) , 325–29; Ray Ginger, *Age of Excess: The United States From 1877 to 1914* (New York, 1965) , 98–128.

17 New York *Times,* April 26, 1877.

that time Southern congressmen failed to support the President's friend James Garfield in his bid for the speakership of the House. Worse news arrived the following year. The state and congressional contests of 1878 saw a resurgence of "bloody shirt" waving by Republican candidates in the North and a repetition of Democratic terror tactics against Negroes in the South.[18]

Rank-and-file Louisiana Republicans, the vast majority of whom were black, had been apprehensive about the New Departure from the beginning. Perhaps the most naive of them at first believed, as one rural Radical paper said it did, that the state's decisive role in the 1876 election would make national politicians more sympathetic toward the needs of its Negro voters.[19] Such talk, however, was ephemeral specuation; the fact that Democrats now controlled the state government became the thing of realistic and dread concern.

A Northerner reported in June of 1877 that "a large portion of the colored people desire to leave the State. They do not care where they go, but are puzzled to know how to get away." [20] One Negro leader of Natchitoches, Rayford Blunt, urged his race to stay and resist the "white aristocratic miscreants" with labor strikes which would paralyze the farm economy of the region; this notion infuriated the *People's Vindicator,* which, with its customary lack of subtlety, warned that "some one may inaugurate a new system of agriculture by planting Blunt." [21] White Republicans in a few parishes became so disillusioned by Hayes's actions that they organized

18 *Congressional Record,* 45th Cong., 1st Sess., 797; C. Vann Woodward, *Origins of the New South: 1877–1913* (Baton Rouge, 1951) , 46–49; *Nation,* XXVII (December 12, 1878) , 358.

19 Clipping from Natchitoches *Republican,* December 23, 1876, in Breda Family Papers, Department of Archives, Louisiana State University.

20 New York *Times,* June 9, 1877.

21 Natchitoches *People's Vindicator,* April 21, 1877.

local—but feeble—"independent" parties during the autumn of 1877.[22]

Of the prominent Republicans who had occupied state offices, most of them after Reconstruction seemed unconcerned with anything except possible appointments to federal positions. J. Madison Wells and his returning board wasted no time in reminding the President of their labors on his behalf; Gadane Cassanave pointedly quoted an old Creole saying that "it is not much to give a leg to him who gave you the fowl." [23] The existence of the New Orleans Custom House made federal patronage in Louisiana greater in proportion to population than in any other state; by the summer of 1879 Hayes had placed into that building about fifty relatives and friends of the returning board members.[24] The President similarly felt obliged to assist various carpetbaggers who had been stranded in the state. Packard, for instance, received the lucrative consulship in Liverpool, England. Others accepted government jobs in the West. One such appointee wrote Hayes from Dakota Territory that he was "glad to be out of Louisiana where it was a mistake for any of us to go." [25]

Governor Nicholls faced difficulties rather like those of President Hayes. Both their titles were clouded by the compromise of 1877. The Governor, as did the President, witnessed powerful elements inside his party working against his conciliatory approach. "From the beginning," wrote Nicholls, "there were men around me trying to injure me & to break

22 For reports of embryo "independent" or "workingmen's" parties in 1877, see the rural journals quoted in New Orleans *Daily Picayune,* September 30, October 6, December 13, 1877.

23 J. Madison Wells to Rutherford B. Hayes, April 28, 1877, in Hayes Papers; *Nation;* XXIX (August 21, 1879) , 120.

24 *Nation,* XXIX (August 21, 1879) , 120.

25 Hugh Campbell to Rutherford B. Hayes, January 3, 1878, in Hayes Papers.

down my influence." [26] Republican former Governor Henry Clay Warmoth pithily observed that "Nicholls is a good man, but from the country. . . . They are running over him while they are using him." [27] The fact that the Governor appointed a handful of educated Negroes to minor posts outraged the Bourbon racists but did little to reassure the uneasy mass of freedmen. According to reports, most blacks thought that Nicholls meant well but was powerless.[28]

In 1877 and for several years thereafter the leadership of the state Democratic Party stood divided into three major factions. These were roughly identifiable as: the patrician (or *noblesse oblige*) conservatives; the Bourbon reactionaries; and the Lottery-New Orleans machine interests. There was no really liberal faction. Naturally, many active Democrats eluded a simple categorization. And no one of the three groups became strong enough to dominate either their party or Louisiana without assistance.

Nicholls personified the strengths and weaknesses of the patrician faction. In another part of the South he might be better classified as a Bourbon. His fiscal conservatism was unyielding. His official messages, though full of benign sentiments, revealed an inability or an unwillingness to understand the problems and aspirations of ordinary whites and blacks. Nicholls appeared sincere when he spoke of "kindness and strict justice to the colored people," but in his mind this meant law dispensed by the white elite for an innately inferior race. Referring to his selection of Negroes for state positions, which so angered the Bourbons, Nicholls privately

26 Barnes F. Lathrop (ed.), "An Autobiography of Francis T. Nicholls, 1834–1881," *Louisiana Historical Quarterly,* XVII (1934), 259.

27 Cincinnati *Enquirer,* quoted in New Orleans *Daily Picayune,* November 22, 1878.

28 New York *Times,* June 9, 1877.

wrote: "[I] appointed a number of them to small offices sandwiching them on Boards between white men where . . . they were powerless to do harm."[29] Relatively speaking, however, Nicholls was not a Bourbon—not by Louisiana criteria. His Republican critics usually conceded that the Governor represented the best, the most humane, among the state's ruling class.

Men of his type, although not Nicholls personally, had once during Reconstruction offered a genteel alternative to the costly, oppressive road of political racism. This was the short-lived "Louisiana Unification Movement" of 1873. The leaders of Unification—New Orleans business and professional men and some of the less hidebound rural planters— had proposed a new biracial third force in politics, one which would, under patrician direction, work toward racially liberal but economically conservative goals. Its platform urged an end to discrimination against Negroes while its spokesmen also talked of a reduction of state taxes and expenditures.[30] But Unification died in its infancy in 1873. Neither race gave it the necessary mass support. Common whites were hostile to desegregated schools and public accommodations; and the majority of Negroes, as one commentator indicated, simply refused to believe that well-to-do white men could ever be sincere in advocating rights for black people.[31] Nevertheless, something of the spirit of Unification had survived

29 *Official Journal of the Proceedings of the House of Representatives of the State of Louisiana,* hereinafter referred to as *House Journal;* 1878, pp. 7–14; *ibid.,* 1879, pp. 7–19; Lathrop (ed.) , *Louisiana Historical Quarterly,* XVII, 257.

30 New Orleans *Times,* June 17, July 1, 1873; New Orleans *Daily Picayune,* July 12, 1873. For a perceptive analysis of Unification, see T. Harry Williams, "The Louisiana Unification Movement of 1873," *Journal of Southern History,* XI (1945) , 349–69.

31 Lake Providence *Lake Republican,* August 2, 1873. For an example of the reaction of race-minded whites against Unification, see the unnamed Louisiana newspaper quoted in New York *Times,* June 26, 1873.

among the white elite and was reflected, if but dimly, by the attitude of the Nicholls administration in 1877–80.

The New Orleans *Times* furnished an editorial voice for the Nicholls patricians, as it earlier did for the Unificationists. Unlike the Bourbon organs, which preferred to blame Negroes for virtually all the evils of Reconstruction, the *Times* maintained that members of the white upper class bore a large share of guilt for much of the recent venality. "There has not been a steal in the past twelve years," this paper charged in 1877, "in which some of those who proudly enroll themselves, among the 'oldest and best' have not had their hands." [32] As did others of the Governor's friends, the *Times* deplored both the political corruption and the racist Bourbonism within the Democratic Party. The possibility that these two malignancies might combine posed a grave danger to Nicholls and to the state.

Of all the terms applied to Southern politicians after Reconstruction, that of "Bourbon" was perhaps liable to the widest misuse. A modern scholar, noting that it was applied so indiscriminately in some states during the 1870's and 1880's, proposes that it is time the expression be abandoned by historians.[33] On the other hand, as we shall see, in the politics of Louisiana the meaning of the expression—or epithet—was reasonably precise, and, indeed, Democrats who were so designated were frequently proud of it. "We must admit," said Baton Rouge's Mayor Leon Jastremski, "that we are . . . Bourbons." To the men of the extreme right, Nicholls' attitude or in fact any whisper of moderation was considered "rampant pseudo-liberalism." [34]

32 New Orleans *Times*, April 24, 1877.

33 Woodward, *Origins of the New South*, 75.

34 Baton Rouge *Daily Capitolian-Advocate*, March 7, 30, 1882. At the time Jastremski was mayor of Baton Rouge as well as editor of the city's daily newspaper. For another of several instances of pride in the designation "Bourbon," see Bellevue *Bossier Banner*, July 21, 1881.

Apostles of Bourbonism in Louisiana identified themselves with propertied interests and posed as upholders of the true Southern ideals. So did other conservative Democrats. Yet the Bourbons were visibly marked off from the patricians, because they rejected the *noblesse oblige* implications of the Old South code and unblushingly embraced the sort of Negrophobia which elsewhere was usually attributed to ignorant poor whites.

The Bourbon mentality was most prevalent in parishes where cotton ranked as the major crop and blacks outnumbered, or almost outnumbered, the white population. Plantation owners and middle class residents of the interior river towns seemed especially susceptible. But just as some moderates could be found anywhere, so also was Negrophobia not restricted to special regions or economic groups. The wealthier Bourbons politically concerned themselves with more than skin color; they, as a rule, inclined toward reaction on every public question. This was not true of the majority of Democrats. Even so, whenever other issues threatened to split the white vote, the Bourbons would see to it that race drifted into the political dialogue.

In lasting influence no Louisiana Bourbon rated above Henry J. Hearsey, who in the early 1870's had been one of the founders of the Shreveport *Times*. Major Hearsey was a man of many hates. But he displayed an ardent love for at least two things: the Lost Cause and whiskey.[35] Florid-faced and goateed, Hearsey perfectly played the role of a Dixie Don Quixote; with his circa 1830 nullification rhetoric, his pistol duels and mint juleps, he seemed like an out-of-date burlesque on Southern manners. Yet his ability to mold public opinion was no laughing matter. After helping inflame the

35 Bibulous though he was, it is unlikely that Major Hearsey really was intoxicated "every night of his adult life," as related in Edward La Rocque Tinker, *Creole City: Its Past and Its People* (New York, 1953), 192.

Shreveport area during Reconstruction, Hearsey moved to New Orleans and for a time wrote for a new Bourbon journal, the *Democrat.* Then in 1880 he became an editor-publisher, founding the New Orleans *Daily States.*[36] The *Daily States* shortly emerged as Louisiana's leading afternoon newspaper. During the remainder of the nineteenth century, Hearsey's perfervid attacks upon the North, Negroes, Southern white reformers, and public education were absorbedly read by subscribers throughout the lower Mississippi River valley. Many weeklies in remote villages spiced their pages with excerpts from the *Daily States,* often with approving commentaries attached.[37] Major Hearsey never held nor sought elective office, but after Reconstruction his political prestige climbed with his readership. By 1900 the *Daily States* came to be called "the recognized newspaper head of the Democracy in Louisiana." [38] Party chieftains frequently deferred to its editor, fearing his venomous pen. They were less afraid of being challenged by him to fight a duel, since Hearsey was a notoriously poor shot.[39]

The passing years merely hardened Hearsey's opinions, epecially about Northerners and the "malodorous nigger." [40] He considered it one of his special missions to teach the new generation to hate; he was keenly determined that men too young to remember the Civil War and Reconstruction should learn to revere the "old war whoops and cries." If they did not, he wrote, it would be "better that such boys should have

[36] Henry Rightor, *Standard History of New Orleans, Louisiana* (Chicago, 1900) , 279–84.

[37] This observation is based on the writer's examination of over three dozen Democratic weekly newspapers in the rural parishes for the 1880–1900 period.

[38] Rightor, *Standard History of New Orleans,* 280. See also *National Cyclopaedia of American Biography,* IX, 499.

[39] Bastrop *Morehouse Clarion,* February 6, 1880.

[40] New Orleans *Daily States,* quoted in Plaquemine *Iberville South,* February 1, 1896.

died in their infancy." [41] Hearsey was equally firm in his opposition to Negro schools because "the very worst nigger for
a voter is an educated nigger." [42] He did, nonetheless, once
make a facetious proposal that black people might elevate
themselves by purchasing monkeys, thereby to "enjoy the
novelty of slave holding." [43]

While Hearsey and other Bourbons carried the White
League tradition into the post-Reconstruction years, another
faction in the state Democratic Party perpetuated a carpetbagger legacy. But the men of the Louisiana Lottery Company
disliked reminders of their operation's Republican genesis.
Created by a gambling syndicate from New York, the Lottery
in 1868 had bribed Governor Warmoth's legislature into grant-
ing a monopolistic charter of twenty-five years duration. In
return the state obtained $40,000 per annum. By 1877 the
company was on its way to becoming the most lucrative ven-
ture of its kind in American history. Out of its headquarters
in New Orleans, utilizing the mails in defiance of federal law,
the Lottery sold millions of dollars in tickets each year. The
bulk of its revenue came from beyond the borders of Louisiana.[44] Yet the survival of the Lottery necessitated a compliant host state.

Charles T. Howard, the Lottery's chief spokesman, looked
after the company's political interests and public image. When
Republican power began to wane in Louisiana, Howard trans-
ferred his attentions to the party of white supremacy. In seeking respectability for the Lottery, he purchased the services

41 New Orleans *Daily States,* quoted in Baton Rouge *Daily Advocate,* December 5, 1897.

42 *Ibid.,* January 4, 1898.

43 New Orleans *Daily States,* quoted in Alexandria *Louisiana Democrat,*
March 2, 1887.

44 John T. White, "The History of the Louisiana Lottery" (M.A. thesis,
Tulane University, 1939), 20–27; Alwes, *Louisiana Historical Quarterly,*
XXVII, 972–94, 1003–29.

of two former Confederate generals of "unblemished records and pure fame": P. G. T. Beauregard and Jubal A. Early. Beginning in 1877 these worthies earned impressive salaries by clothing themselves in symbolically gray suits and showing up at Lottery drawings; they were there, so the advertisements said, "really as representatives of the people" to insure that everything was conducted honestly.[45] The two also worked as legislative lobbyists for the company.

It was hardly a coincidence that Beauregard and Early were hired during the same year that the Lottery, as previously mentioned, placed the Democratic Party under fealty by helping finance the restoration of "home rule." The first of many installments on this debt was soon paid. At the legislative session of 1877 the Democratic leaders quietly tabled a bill which aimed at repealing the company's old carpetbagger-granted charter. The same thing happened at the next session in 1878.[46]

Edward A. Burke became the Lottery's key man inside the state government. Burke, who had managed Nicholls' gubernatorial campaign and then played a vital part in the national compromise of 1877, actually outdistanced all of his contemporaries—even the carpetbagger Warmoth—in audacity. Thirty-five years old at the end of Reconstruction, Burke had lived in Louisiana only since 1870. His origins remain a mystery. He claimed Kentucky as his birthplace but he was probably from Ohio or Illinois. Enemies sometimes described him as "the Carpetbag Boss." Burke kept discreetly silent about his war record, or lack of one, but friends always referred to him as "Major" Burke and insisted that he earned that rank in the service of the Confederacy. On the other hand, one of several

<hr />

45 Lottery advertisement in New Orleans *Daily Picayune,* December 11, 1878.

46 John Samuel Ezell, *Fortune's Merry Wheel: The Lottery in America* (Cambridge, Mass., 1960) , 245–46.

rumors was that in 1864 young Burke had acted as a Union spy who, at Mobile, had furnished Admiral Farragut "with a great deal of valuable information." [47]

Whatever his background, Burke settled in New Orleans during the heyday of Reconstruction. Penniless at first, he found work as a common laborer at one dollar per day, but he shortly talked his way into an office position with a local railroad. By the mid 1870's the Major's activities had expanded in all directions; he became involved with the Lottery, joined the city Democratic machine and attached himself to the rising star of banker-politician Louis Wiltz. Burke instinctively fitted into the rowdy spirit of the times. One October afternoon in 1874, at a downtown streetcorner in New Orleans, he fired his pistol at Governor Kellogg when that dignitary leaned out of a carriage and reportedly made an insulting gesture at Burke "with his finger." [48] The Governor, also armed with a pistol, shot back; but neither man was injured, nor prosecuted. Later, Burke's success as the state Democratic campaign manager in 1876 and his role in the great compromise which followed earned him a reputation as Louisiana's shrewdest political tactician.

Ability had its reward. In 1878 Burke obtained the Democratic nomination for state treasurer and, pledging to be "a safe custodian of the public funds" as well as "a safe adviser to State officers," easily won election.[49] For the next ten years he occupied that post, but he fell rather short on his promises. In the meantime, managing the public finances for

[47] New York *Times,* November 19, 1879; New Orleans *Democrat,* December 13, 1879; Philadelphia *Sunday Times,* quoted in New Orleans *Daily Picayune,* May 11, 1881. See also Woodward, *Reunion and Reaction,* 192.

[48] New Orleans *People's Exponent,* quoted in Natchitoches *People's Vindicator,* August 17, 1878; Shreveport *Times,* quoted in Winnfield *Southern Sentinel,* July 23, 1886. For one account of Burke's ugly encounter with Governor Kellogg, see New Orleans *Daily Picayune,* October 30, 1874.

[49] New Orleans *Daily Picayune,* November 1, 9, 1878.

good or ill would take up only a portion of this busy man's time. In 1879 the Lottery bought the New Orleans *Democrat* and the state treasurer became its managing editor. Two years later Burke merged that paper with the *Times* to form the powerful *Times-Democrat*.[50] By then few men dared cross him. The Lottery's epicenter was New Orleans. From there it could shake every corner of the state. In the city, during Reconstruction, the old Tammany-model Democratic organization had fallen into the hands of Wiltz, Burke, Howard and other persons of Lottery or associated interests. The Ring, as it was simply called, wrested City Hall from the Republicans in 1872, but this change in administration did not noticeably uplift the conduct of municipal affairs. Wiltz served as mayor from 1872 to 1874. Subsequently, with Burke's assistance, he controlled most of the large Orleans Parish Democratic delegation in the state legislature. Then in 1876 Wiltz was elected to the lieutenant-governorship on Nicholls' ticket. He had been placed there, apparently, as a concession to the Ring. Although holding the second most important post in the Nicholls administration, he was no friend of Nicholls.[51]

The New Departure era, immediately after Reconstruction, presented new challenges as well as opportunities to the Ring. Partly because the Lottery needed the votes of rural legislators to protect its monopolistic charter, and also to achieve personal political goals, the men of the Ring set to work building a statewide machine which would merge the Lottery interests with the forces of Bourbon reaction. Few Bourbons were at first pro-Lottery. Quite the contrary;

50 Richard H. Wiggins, "The Louisiana Press and the Lottery," *Louisiana Historical Quarterly*, XXXI (1948), 781–85.

51 Natchitoches *People's Vindicator*, August 17, 31, 1878; Alcée Fortier (ed.), *Louisiana: Comprising Sketches of Counties, Towns, Events, Institutions, and Persons, Arranged in Cyclopedic Form* (Atlanta, 1909), II, 654; New York *Times*, November 19, 1879.

their more articulate spokesmen, including Mayor Jastremski of Baton Rouge, J. H. Cosgrove of the Natchitoches *People's Vindicator,* and Henry J. Hearsey, loudly berated the gambling company during the early post-Reconstruction days. Cosgrove particularly wanted to crush "this hideous, infamous monster." [52] Hearsey quit the *Democrat* in a rage when it passed into Burke's control and then founded the *Daily States* in order to curse the "filthy swine" of the Lottery along with Negro "buzzards." Hearsey and Burke subsequently fought a duel. [53] Nevertheless, in a matter of time these and other prominent men of the Bourbon temperament would make peace with the Lottery and support the Ring's candidates for state office. By 1879 Cosgrove, for example, became accommodating. It took Hearsey somewhat longer. But ultimately even he bestowed elaborate praise on the Lottery, saying that it "came forward in the hour of need . . . to establish home rule in Lousiana and to throw off the yoke of negro domination." The story that the company had carpetbagger origins, Hearsey decided, was "vile and false." [54]

Perhaps a Lottery-Bourbon alliance was inevitable. Both the gambling syndicate and the reactionaries had their separate reasons for wanting Governor Nicholls out of the way once he had served his purpose as a façade of respectability in the critical time of 1876–77. The Lottery correctly perceived that the Governor could not be depended upon to protect company interests, while the Bourbons feared that he

52 Natchitoches *People's Vindicator,* June 1, 1878.

53 New Orleans *Daily States,* quoted in Baton Rouge *Daily Capitolian-Advocate,* May 25, 31, 1882; Bastrop *Morehouse Clarion,* January 30, February 6, 1880. Hearsey and Burke came through their pistol duel unscathed. However, in 1882, Burke exchanged shots with the editor of the *Daily Picayune* and was hit in both legs. The latter duel took place below the New Orleans Slaughterhouse. See Baton Rouge *Daily Capitolian-Advocate,* June 8, 1882.

54 Natchitoches *People's Vindicator,* May 31, August 16, 1879, March 27, 1880; New Orleans *Daily States,* May 3, 11, 22, 27, 1890.

really meant to honor his and the legislature's civil rights pledges. From April of 1877 on, Lieutenant Governor Wiltz appears to have worked with Burke and others to undermine the Nicholls administration.[55] The foremost Negro publication in Louisiana concluded that Nicholls desired "to be just and impartial, but was thwarted at every turn." [56]

Nicholls' New Departure was most vulnerable in promising local Republicans that they would not be prosecuted for their "past political conduct." Desire for revenge ran strong among white Louisianians, notably among the larger property holders; not forgiven were the innumerable raids on public funds, the high taxes and the labor upsets associated with Reconstruction. As usual, Negroes bore the brunt of Democratic wrath. Within a month after the military withdrawal in 1877, at least three leading black Radicals were assassinated and many others threatened with death.[57] The more moderate Democrats deplored these acts of terror, but at the same time most of them believed that corrupt Republicans, black or white, should now be tried before courts of law, Nicholls' pledges notwithstanding. Among the first to be jailed for theft were two Negro members of the "compromise" legislature of 1877, Senator David Young of Concordia and Representative P. J. Watson of Madison Parish.[58]

The malodorous old returning board provided the choicest target for revenge-minded conservatives. On July 5, 1877, the Superior Criminal Court of Orleans Parish ordered the arrest of all four members of the board, charging them with falsifying and forging returns in the previous year's election. "We don't care anything about the two niggers," wrote one

55 Letter from "Democrat," in New Orleans *Daily Picayune*, November 14, 1879; New York *Times*, November 19, 1879.

56 New Orleans *Weekly Louisianian*, January 17, 1879.

57 Natchitoches *People's Vindicator*, June 2, 9, 1877; New Orleans *Daily Picayune*, May 24, 1877.

58 New Orleans *Daily Picayune*, June 25, October 28, 1877.

prominent Democrat, but "Wells and Anderson are scoundrels who ought to be in the Penitentiary and we propose to convict them." Grimly he added: "We presume Nicholls will pardon [them]." [59] Others also assumed that the Governor believed himself morally obligated to free Wells and his associates if they were sentenced by a state court. The arrests appear to have been part of a skillful design by anti-Nicholls forces to embarrass the Governor and capitalize on the public discontent with his conciliatory attitude. Nicholls witnessed an indication of the popular mood when an unruly crowd of Baton Rouge whites hurled rocks in his direction. One stone struck him on the shoulder.[60]

The four Republicans were released on bail and their trials delayed until February of 1878, a time which, not without significance, coincided with the next session of the state legislature. A rumor spread that following the inevitable sentencing of Wells and the others, and Nicholls' anticipated pardons, the Governor would be impeached.[61] Actually, however, the plot was more subtle. Instead of impeachment, the Bourbon and Lottery forces planned to have the legislature call a constitutional convention—for the despised Reconstruction organic law of 1868 was still in effect—and the new constitution which they envisioned would cut Nicholls' term of office by requiring a sudden gubernatorial election.[62]

59 Letter from "a prominent Louisiana Democrat," in New York *Times,* July 17, 1877.

60 New Orleans *Democrat,* July 6–7, 1877; *Nation,* XXV (July 12, 1877), 17; New York *Times,* July 13, 1877.

61 New York *Times,* July 7, 9, 1877.

62 Winfield S. Hancock to William T. Sherman, February 15, 1878, in Hayes Papers. Hancock was sent to Louisiana in 1878 to appraise the situation for the Hayes administration, and his letters, addressed to General Sherman, were forwarded to the White House. Hancock obtained Nicholls' unqualified promise to pardon any member of the returning board who might be convicted, but the Governor said that he preferred to wait until the legislature had voted on the proposed constitutional convention. Hancock's role is ironic since he was destined to be the Democratic nominee in the next (1880) presidential election.

Anderson went on trial first. He was speedily found guilty and on February 25 was sentenced to two years hard labor. Wells's case came next on the docket. While he waited, the fierce old scalawag composed an unsurpassably malicious account of state affairs and telegraphed it to the New York *Times*. Among other things, Wells charged: that the presiding judge at Anderson's trial was "in a beastly state of intoxication" throughout the proceedings and, moreover, that this same judge had once embezzled $600,000; that the prosecuting attorney was a known murderer; that E. A. Burke's real name was "A. E. Burk" and that as a young man this "Burk" had fled from justice in Illinois to hide out in the South under a changed identity. Wells went on to accuse Democratic Congressman Randall L. Gibson of the gravest charge of all. Gibson's swarthy complexion, he averred, was traceable to Negro ancestors in Adams County, Mississippi.[63]

Before Wells's trial could begin, the Louisiana Supreme Court on March 18 astonished almost everyone by ordering the release of Anderson. In the court's opinion, the prosecution had failed to prove any specific violation of state law. The charges against Wells, Kenner, and Cassanave were subsequently dropped. Governor Nicholls was thereby spared the odium of pardoning the returning board men; and the 1878 legislative session, to his relief, adjourned without calling a constitutional convention.[64] Burke, Wiltz, and the Bourbons had been temporarily thwarted. But their day was coming.

---

[63] Letter from J. Madison Wells, in New York *Times*, February 19, 1878.
[64] William P. Kellogg to Rutherford B. Hayes, March 18, 1878, in Hayes Papers; New York *Times*, March 19, 1878; *Nation*, XXVI (March 21, 1878), 192.

III

Land and Labor After Reconstruction

THE CIVIL WAR and Reconstruction dislocated and severely depressed Louisiana's once-rich economy. In 1860 the state, with property valued at $602,118,568 ranked first in the South and second in the nation in per capita wealth. What followed was a generation of calamity. The first federal census after Reconstruction estimated the actual value of property at only $422,000,000, a plunge to thirty-seventh in wealth among all states and territories. And this decrease in wealth was unhappily compounded by an increase in population. Louisiana had 939,946 inhabitants in 1880, a rise of over 30 percent since the fateful year of Abraham Lincoln's election.[1]

One fact had not changed. Louisiana, as before the war, remained fundamentally rural. New Orleans, with 216,090 inhabitants in 1880, was the tenth largest community in the United States; but beyond this single great cosmopolitan center there was no place in the state worthy of being called a city. Shreveport ranked second in size, yet it had barely 8,000 inhabitants. Only four other towns reported more than 2,500 people in 1880.[2] Seventy-four percent of the population

[1] *Tenth Census, 1880,* VII, *Valuation, Taxation and Public Indebtedness,* 5, 12. Some writers have mistakenly assumed that Negroes, being slaves, were not reckoned into the per capita wealth estimate for 1860. But they were included, as a simple application of mathematics will show. For an example of this error, see Coulter, *The South During Reconstruction,* 192–93.

[2] *Tenth Census, 1880,* I, *Statistics of Population,* 196–99.

lived in the countryside. Excepting New Orleans and its immediate environs, the rural proportion of the state stood at an astonishing 97 percent.

The majority of Louisianians of both races had returned to agricultural pursuits at the close of the Civil War. A lack of economic opportunities in New Orleans and the lesser communities discouraged any massive migration from country to town.[3] To the Negro half of the population, 1865 brought sudden release from slavery, but their freedom began under an overcast, unfriendly sky. The fact of emancipation had not changed the dominant whites' low opinion of black capabilities; nor, for that matter, did release from legal bondage give the Negro much of a chance to improve his standard of living. The American traditions of self-help and laissez faire were too strong, in that age, for the sort of sweeping federal program which would have genuinely helped the freedman to make the great transition from slavery to propertied citizenship. By far the majority of Negroes remained in the rural bottomlands, the milieu of their previous degradation; their lack of training for anything but plantation work predestined most of them for a lifetime of agricultural peonage.

Rural whites, for the most part, were nearly as immobilized as the blacks. Many old planters had been ruined by the war, or by subsequent labor troubles and the extortionate credit rates of the Reconstruction era; but with cotton and sugar temporarily selling for twice and over the 1860 prices, the plantation system managed to survive in modified form.[4]

3 Although several thousand rural Negroes did migrate to New Orleans at the end of the Civil War, the shift was not as significant as is indicated by William Edward Highsmith's "Louisiana During Reconstruction" (Ph.D. dissertation, Louisiana State University, 1953), 160–61. New Orleans's Negro population did increase, but only by 25,000 between 1860 and 1870. The city remained predominately white. During the following twenty years (1870–90) the New Orleans black population rose by only 14,000; the white by 38,000. *Compendium of the Eleventh Census, 1890,* I, 489.

4 James E. Boyle, *Cotton and the New Orleans Cotton Exchange: A Cen-*

Owners might change, but the old way of life was, as much as possible, retained. Thirty-cent cotton provided a potent lure in the hill country, too. Small landowning whites of the northern and Florida parishes after 1865 began reducing their garden crops and came to pin their hopes for a better life on the soft white fiber.[5] Necessity also played a role in the yeoman and poor white's shift to cotton. Immediately after the war many lacked even the rude belongings they had in 1860; often they were on the verge of starvation. More than before, they needed store credit. And few merchants ever granted advances unless the prospective debtor could pledge a money crop.

Despite high prices for crops and some of the most fertile soil in the world, prosperity seemed to elude Louisiana agriculture. A comparative analysis of the statistics available in the federal census of 1860 and of 1880 provides some measure of the depths into which the rural economy had fallen.

The rural population had increased by 31 percent, and more people than ever were engaged in commercial agriculture, but the production of the two chief money crops, cotton and sugar, actually declined. The two most important subsistence crops, corn and sweet potatoes, shrank to almost half their former bushel totals. Among the cereals, only rice and oats showed any increase. The number of swine remained about equal to the antebellum figure, but all other livestock had a collective decrease of approximately 10 percent. Yet, most alarming of all was the plummet of land values. The amount

tury of Commercial Evolution (Garden City, N.Y., 1934) , 155; J. Carlyle Sitterson, *Sugar Country: The Cane Sugar Industry in the South, 1753–1950* (Lexington, Ky., 1953) , 303.

5 Opelousas *Courier,* August 6, 1881; *Tenth Census, 1880,* V, *Report on Cotton Production in the United States,* Pt. 2, p. 67; Walter L. Fleming, "The Economic Conditions During the Reconstruction," in Julian A. C. Chandler and others (eds.) , *The South in the Building of the Nation* (Richmond, 1909) , VI, 9–10.

of tilled land and permanent pastures (improved acres) increased by almost thirty-three thousand acres, but the value of farm land and buildings declined over 70 percent. By 1880 all the improved land in the state was worth less than that tilled in just eighteen sugar parishes before the war. Livestock valuation was down 50 percent. A further indication of rural Louisiana's decrepitude can be seen by dividing the amount of improved acreage into the value of farm implements (machinery and tools) for both periods. The cash value of these essential assets averaged $6.88 per acre in 1860 and had shrunk to a trifling $1.98 per acre by 1880.[6]

Much of this financial loss was traceable to the shattered sugar plantations. Prior to the Civil War, Louisiana produced 95 per cent of the total sugar crop of the South.[7] During the 1820's the introduction of expensive steam machinery had eliminated most of the small producers; dominating the region by the 1840's were the great planters who owned refining mills and possessed scores of slaves. Planters who owned their mills—there were fewer than fifteen hundred of them in 1860—were as much industrialists as agriculturists.[8]

Recovery in the sugar parishes was painfully slow. In 1877, only 127,000 hogsheads of sugar were produced, this being less than one-third of the output of the peak antebellum years.[9] Reformers, led by agricultural columnist Daniel Dennett of the *Daily Picayune,* believed that a division of

[6] *Eighth Census, 1860,* II, *Agriculture,* 66–67; *Tenth Census, 1880,* III, *Report Upon the Statistics of Agriculture,* 3–9, 118–19. The distinction between "rural" and "urban" used in this study follows the rule first adopted by the Federal Bureau of the Census in 1910: incorporated towns of over 2,500 population plus densely settled fringe areas are considered urban; all else, rural.

[7] *Annual Report of the Commissioner of Agriculture for the Year 1878* (Washington, 1879), 275.

[8] Paul Wallace Gates, *The Farmer's Age: Agriculture, 1815–1860* (New York, 1960), 125–27, 284.

[9] William C. Stubbs, "Sugar Products in the South," in *The South in the Building of the Nation,* V, 193.

the great estates into small farms would solve the problems of the sugar country. Dennett did not suggest any sort of confiscation or forced sale; rather, he proposed that the planters bring in white labor from Northern and Western states and set up a progressive type of tenant farming. The thrifty among these white tenants, Dennett assumed, would eventually purchase the tracts of land they worked. Then the ex-landlords would engage solely in refining.[10] Few planters, however, seemed interested in such suggestions. Great estates continued to predominate, and as new refining mills were built, the men who owned the mills also possessed the land upon which a majority of the cane was grown. Thus during the latter part of the century, sugar factories and fields continued on in much the same way as they had in the antebellum period, with poorly paid Negro gang labor as a substitute for slavery.[11] In 1892 the traveler Fannie Barbour, eyeing the miserable hovels where the sugar workers lived, thought that they probably "long for the good old times" of absolute but more paternalistic bondage.[12]

Land ownership did undergo shifts in the sugar country after 1865, but by a process which kept most sugar plantations intact. The potential profits of the postwar years lured many Northerners with capital into buying up old estates from impoverished planters. One antebellum owner who was able to hang on in the new era estimated that nine-tenths of the Louisiana sugar estates changed hands between 1865 and 1877.[13]

Some of the new owners bought land for purely speculative reasons; over 30 percent of the former cane fields remained

10 New Orleans *Daily Picayune*, March 18, April 15, October 21, 1877.

11 Sitterson, *Sugar Country*, 240, 261–62.

12 Fannie C. W. Barbour, "Overland by the Southern Pacific," *Chautauquan*, XV (July, 1892), 392.

13 Letter from "Rusticus," in New Orleans *Daily Picayune*, September 23, 1877.

fallow and weed-choked throughout Reconstruction. At least half the newer proprietors were Northern men or men supported by Northern banks.[14] Prominent among them were Republican politicians. Former Governors Warmoth and Kellogg used their ill-gotten fortunes to become members of the sugar aristocracy. Warmoth was notably successful in achieving status among his neighbors.[15] Two years after Reconstruction several of Louisiana's most influential Democrats, whose conservative ideas harmonized with most of Warmoth's beliefs, visited the carpetbagger's plantation in Plaquemines Parish and wished him luck "in everything—except his infernal politics." [16]

Negroes made up most of the population of the eleven great sugar-producing parishes of southern Louisiana.[17] Few white laborers or tenants could be discovered at work in the cane plantations. As before the war, the French Catholic "Cajuns" who made up most of the white population in the parishes near the Gulf Coast tilled their small acres, tended livestock, or engaged in fishing or trapping. Some raised sugarcane on little plots and sold the stalks to the planter-refiners. Outsiders who passed through the region in the 1880's were astounded by the Cajuns' continuing lack of contact with, and indifference to, the rest of humanity. The author Charles Dudley Warner could not shake the impression that he and his

[14] Roger W. Shugg, *Origins of Class Struggle in Louisiana: A Social History of White Farmers and Laborers During Slavery and After, 1840–1875* (Baton Rouge, 1939; paperback, 1966) , 249.

[15] James E. Richardson to J. M. Currie, August 1, 1882, in William E. Chandler Papers, Division of Manuscripts, Library of Congress.

[16] Warmoth had enhanced the cheer of the occasion by greeting the Democrats on his dock "with a steady firing of champagne corks." New Orleans *Daily Picayune,* November 24, 1879.

[17] Plaquemines and St. Bernard (in the First Congressional District) ; Jefferson, St. Charles, St. James and St. John the Baptist (Second District) ; Ascension, St. Martin, St. Mary and Terrebonne (Third District) ; West Baton Rouge (Sixth District) .

traveling companions "had been in a country that is not of this world." [18]

King cotton, rather than sugar, retained first place among the money crops of the state. Cotton acreage in 1880 quadrupled the amount of land planted in cane. In twenty-nine parishes, half those of the state, cotton exceeded any other crop in number of acres planted. The Fourth and Fifth Congressional districts, situated north of the thirty-first degree of latitude, produced 78.5 percent of the state's major crop. Yet cotton was also important in much of the southeastern and southcentral sections. It ranked first in tilled acreage in the Sixth Congressional District, which sprawled westward from the Florida Parishes across the Mississippi River and into the prairies of St. Landry Parish. Farther southward, patches of cotton appeared at intervals among the cane fields of the Third District. The overall geographic predominance of cotton showed up in the fact that in 1880 only seven parishes in the state reported no bales ginned, whereas in twenty-five northern and hill parishes no sugar was refined. However, throughout the uplands some farmers planted cane for home use as molasses.[19]

In one respect cotton was akin to sugar. It, too, grew best in the dark alluvial soils along the rivers. Certain parishes which bordered the great waterways of the state continued, after the Civil War, to lead the state in number of bales ginned. The tier of six parishes adjoining the Mississippi River from the Arkansas border south to Baton Rouge contributed one-third of all Louisiana's cotton; one of them, East Carroll, topped every parish and every county in the South in productivity per acre.[20] During the antebellum era these same

18 Charles Dudley Warner, "The Acadian Land," *Harper's*, LXXIV (February, 1887), 354.

19 *Tenth Census, 1880*, V, Pt. 2, pp. 3–5; Monroe *Observer*, quoted in New Orleans *Daily Picayune*, October 29, 1877.

20 *Tenth Census, 1880*, V, Pt. 2, pp. 3–5.

six parishes had boasted some of the wealthiest and most extensive landholdings in America. A generation later, after Reconstruction, the plantations remained; but these estates had become patchworks of tenant farms where Negro occupants rented or worked on "shares" for the few white landowners. In this region in 1880 lived 77,116 Negroes and only 12,247 whites.

Alluvial cotton plantations were not confined to the land along the Mississippi. The same crop and way of life dominated fertile stretches adjacent to the Red, Black, and Ouachita rivers, tributaries of the mighty stream. But these rich bottomlands were narrower than the delta of the Mississippi. A few miles distant, in some places next to the rivers' banks, oak uplands or unfertile piney woods took command of the countryside. The hilly oak regions, spreading over most of ten parishes in the northwest and north central portions of the state, included many varieties of soils. Some of the oak uplands ranked close to the alluvial belt in fertility.

Far less esteemed were the longleaf pine hills and the pine flatlands which prevailed in the unaffluent parishes of Catahoula, Calcasieu, Grant, Vernon, and Winn in northern and western Louisiana; and in Livingston, St. Tammany, Tangipahoa, and Washington parishes of the southeast.[21] Along with these, because of similar economic handicaps, should be included the desolate coastal lands of Cameron and Vermilion. These eleven parishes, nine of them pine and two of them marsh, can be considered as the "backland" of post-Reconstruction Louisiana. Of the group—when an untypical alluvial portion of Catahoula is subtracted—Winn was relatively the most prosperous and St. Tammany by far the poorest.[22]

---

[21] Catahoula is here considered as primarily a pine hill region because at the time is included present-day LaSalle Parish. However, the eastern portion of Catahoula boasted black bottomland and had a plantation economy.

[22] *Tenth Census, 1880,* V, Pt. 2, pp. 3–5.

This vast backland region, making up over 30 percent of the total land area of the state, was also the most thinly populated and the most meagerly tilled. But here, in the years following the Civil War, numerous small farmers attempted to emulate the alluvial planters by commencing the raising of cotton. In all eleven parishes, even in coastal Cameron and Vermilion, cotton was the chief money crop in 1880. However, in four of them—Calcasieu, St. Tammany, Cameron, and Vermilion—either lumbering, livestock, trapping, or fishing surpassed cotton's economic significance in the primitive economy. The backlands' white population was double that of the Negro: 55,009 to 23,025.

Although many parishes fit neatly into classifications as "alluvial," "oak upland," "piney woods," or "coastal marsh," others defy a blanket description. Huge St. Landry Parish, for example, held practically every soil type known in the state.[23] Natchitoches, Ouachita, and Rapides offered other instances of great diversity of soil and economy inside parish borders. Along the western edge of the Florida Parishes, the Mississippi River bluffs gave much the same appearance as the oak uplands of northern Louisiana; yet the original fertility of the bluffs and special historical factors had promoted the growth of plantations and so gave this bluff region the same kind of population and economy as the black bottomlands.

Louisiana never did yield easily to generalization. But, in this regard, it requires notice that parishes which contained marked variations in topography and soil, such as Natchitoches and St. Landry, suffered some of the worst of the state's political difficulties during the nineteenth century. And racial conflict was frequently not the main issue. It was a well known fact of Louisiana politics that the hill and bottomland

23 St. Landry in 1880 also comprised the later-created parishes of Acadia (1886) and Evangeline (1910).

whites "do not get along harmoniously." [24] Naturally this was most true when abrupt changes in terrain threw them into juxtaposition, and into the same local units of government.

When the white small landowners of the backland and of the less prosperous pockets of other parishes entered into the cultivation of cotton after the Civil War, they often did so for reasons additional to the need for credit and the temporarily high prices commanded by the staple. The abysmal decline of land values everywhere in the South encouraged those who possessed even a few dollars to expand the size of their small farms. Probably many hoped to purchase sections of old bottomland plantations. But black alluvial soil, even at Reconstruction prices, could not be afforded by many ordinary whites. Thus men without ready cash for better land saw no way to obtain the necessary funds except by first raising cotton for sale on the less desirable acres they already held. It was the "only product upon which the farmer can depend for money." [25] Louisiana's commissioner of immigration expressed his astonishment in 1867 at the great number of poorer white farmers who were planting cotton. "In every part of the state," he wrote, "as soon as you leave the great plantations . . . we find not only white men, but boys and girls laboring all hours in the fields." [26]

Slowly, these small agriculturists would come to realize how unfounded had been their hopes. Part of the blame lay with themselves. Those who deliberately neglected their food crops and livestock for the sake of cotton thereby lost whatever economic independence they might have once en-

---

24 Trinity *Herald*, July 6, 1889. The name of the town of Trinity was later changed to Jonesville.

25 *Tenth Census, 1880*, V, Pt. 2, p. 67.

26 Quoted in James L. Watkins, *King Cotton: A Historical and Statistical Review, 1790 to 1908* (New York, 1908), 202.

joyed. Overproduction of cotton was serious enough in the antebellum South; after the war, small producers compounded the problem.[27] The great plantations, their output only temporarily restricted by the war and emancipation, were reviving, and during the 1870's cotton production began to climb back toward prewar levels. A steady drop in cotton prices was then inevitable.

All too frequently, the small farmer made his situation worse by carrying over into commercial farming the same sloppy, haphazard methods of earlier, less ambitious days. From his column in the *Daily Picayune,* Daniel Dennett lashed out at the "ignorant, rough, unattractive farming" so prevalent in the backcountry. He was most distressed by the brutalizing effects of such a life upon the farm children. Dennett wrote of the environment of a typical Louisiana rural boy: "He works all day in the field . . . with a half fed horse, a dull plow. . . . Often there are no books to read, no newspapers, and no schools, and the boy grows up in ignorance, his ignorant father his only teacher, and a poor old worn out farm his only school house." [28]

Worse, in a sense, than the careless and slovenly farmers were those who became too engrossed in the pursuit of cotton profits and attempted "to get rich too fast." [29] The Farmerville *Home Advocate* described a man of this type in Union Parish, who, "possessed with the insane idea that he must 'own all the land that joins him,' makes slaves of himself and family." Individuals of such a nature showed concern for their draft animals but worked their wives to death.[30] Other small landowners, aping the planters, tried to live in

27 Matthew Brown Hammond, "Cotton Production in the South," in *The South in the Building of the Nation,* VI, 88, 96.
28 New Orleans *Daily Picayune,* May 2, 1877.
29 *Ibid.,* December 23, 1877.
30 Farmerville *Home Advocate,* May 22, 1885.

leisure by hiring one or two Negro families and expecting from them prodigious feats of labor. A Richland Parish farmer crudely admitted: "Too many of us bait our hooks with a 'nigger' and set it [sic] out and expect to catch a crop." [31] When results proved disappointing, the black man was blamed. But not all farmers took this narrow attitude. One, in Grant Parish, believed that it was mistreatment, not congenital laziness, which caused Negro inefficiency. "Treat them as human beings," he pleaded. "Why should they not have justice and fair dealing?" [32]

Although the personal shortcomings of Louisiana farmers were doubtless numerous, it is nevertheless unlikely that general prosperity would have ensued had all been models of husbandry. Misfortune, like rainfall, fell upon the hardworking and honest as well as the lazy or avaricious. Circumstances largely beyond the farmer's control worked relentlessly against the rural producers of both races. The advantages of cheap land and high farm prices during Reconstruction were mostly illusory, being offset by unfriendly legislation, postwar depression, difficulties with transportation, and a lack of reasonable credit facilities. Then, by 1877, cotton had declined to its prewar price of about ten cents a pound, while many of the malign aspects of Reconstruction agriculture remained.[33] Least able to meet any new trouble was the rural Negro. He bore all the common ills, along with the added incubus of his color and background of slavery.

Thirty-cent cotton in the early days of Reconstruction had been as much a boon to federal tax collectors as to the state's farmers. The special levy which Congress placed on cotton at

[31] H. P. Wells, "Leaks in Farming," in *Proceedings of the Third Annual Session of the Louisiana State Agricultural Society* (Baton Rouge, 1889), 8–9.
[32] Letter from "Old Hoss," in Colfax *Chronicle,* May 1, 1886.
[33] A useful table of middling cotton prices at the New Orleans exchange from 1827 to 1934 is found in Boyle, *Cotton and the New Orleans Cotton Exchange,* 176–88.

the end of the war wrung $9,642,535 from the state's producers. This figure might be compared with the information that as late as 1878 the total capital stock of all state and national banks in Louisiana was only $6,968,000.[34] Wretched and costly transportation facilities had further undermined the margin of profit. Yet even as the price of cotton slipped back to its antebellum level—a return at which only large producers could make an adequate profit—the statewide crop in the late 1870's was still 22 percent below prewar production. The future held bigger crops and lower prices.

Few common whites were ever able to purchase good alluvial soil in either the cotton or sugar regions. Usually when plantations changed hands the land was sold as a unit to wealthy buyers, not in small parcels that the less fortunate might afford. It is true that a welcome of sorts awaited impecunious whites who might come into the bottomlands, but they were desired as laborers or tenants to replace what a planter near Lafayette scornfully called "the trifling negroes, who go reluctantly through the forms of scratching the earth for a living." [35] The owners of plantations might wish for white labor, but they obtained little. Particularly in northern Louisiana was there a lack of white migration to the lowlands. "It cannot be," declared a spokesman of the planters of Tensas Parish, "that these people will remain on those barren hillsides when in sight of them lie unlimited quantities of rich land." [36] Even so, few of the hill folk were willing to come and work on land they could not own.

Land in Louisiana was still plentiful. Only 8.6 percent of

34 Based on figures available in Watkins, *King Cotton*, 201–202; and Stephen A. Caldwell, *A Banking History of Louisiana* (Baton Rouge, 1935), 128–29.

35 Letter from "Acadian," in New Orleans *Daily Picayune*, May 1, 1877.

36 St. Joseph *North Louisiana Journal*, October 30, 1880. See also, Franklin *St. Mary Banner*, March 8, 1890.

the state's approximately thirty million acres was being tilled at the end of Reconstruction. Dennett maintained that about sixteen million acres were suitable for cultivation.[37] His optimism, however, left important questions unanswered. In addition to the problem of the dubious fertility of much of this unused soil, there was the fact that settlers would need additional money or credit for implements and other necessities before such land could be broken for cultivation. Accessibility to markets was another limiting factor; land too far from a railroad or navigable waterway would be unprofitable to farm, no matter how fertile.

In 1866, Congress had been told that 6,228,103 acres of surveyed but unsold federal land existed in Louisiana.[38] The Southern Homestead Act, passed that year, was supposedly designed to bestow this land "to all the poor people" of both races.[39] Heads of families could apply for 80 acres (later raised to 160) and pay nothing except nominal service fees. After "improving" the land and residing on it for five years, the settler would receive his final deed.

Homestead offices in Louisiana were located at New Orleans and Monroe. The federal lands open to settlement were scattered throughout the state. Most of the available acres, however, were located in the pine flatlands of Calcasieu, St. Landry, Livingston, Tangipahoa, and St. Tammany parishes.[40] By 1880, alleged homesteaders had applied for 958,627 of these acres. Yet, of this amount, final proof of ownership had been given for only a fraction over 200,000 acres.[41] Unfortu-

---

37 *Tenth Census, 1880*, III, 3; New Orleans *Daily Picayune*, March 22, 1877.
38 *Congressional Globe*, 39th Cong., 1st Sess., 715.
39 *Ibid.*, 717. Negroes and "loyal" whites were given first choice. Confederate veterans could apply after one year.
40 New Orleans *Daily Picayune*, May 4, 1877.
41 St. George Leakin Sioussant, "State and Federal Lands and Land Laws in the South," in *The South in the Building of the Nation*, VI, 28.

nately, most of the original applicants never intended to farm and had not even lived on the land. Northern lumber companies were in the habit of inducing their employees to take advantage of the Southern Homestead Act. A tiny shanty would be set up as proof of "improvement," and the land was then stripped of its timber and abandoned to weeds. Vacant homesteads of this character dotted portions of the state. Worse, any bona fide farmers who desired these denuded acres could not apply because of the difficulty of proving that the first homestead was fraudulent. Some lumber firms actually did not bother to take out dummy homesteads, but boldly cut timber wherever they found it. When the Department of the Interior tried to crack down on timber thieves in southwestern Louisiana in 1877, Congressman Joseph H. Acklen of the Third District zealously defended the prosecuted "Calcasieu sufferers." [42]

The monopolization of Louisiana land by lumber and other nonfarming interests accelerated in the years after 1876, when Congress opened public acreage in the South to cash buyers as well as homesteaders. The outcome did not serve the state's best interests. Between 1880 and 1888 the great majority of Louisiana land sold went to just fifty individuals or firms who purchased over 5,000 acres each. Of these, forty-one were Northerners who obtained a total of 1,370,332 acres. Six were natives of the state. These latter purchased 99,278 acres.[43] Many local people resented this absorption of land by outside capitalists, especially since the new owners tended to be reluctant to pay even the microscopic taxes assessed; but other Louisianians welcomed the trend. The Shreveport *Daily Standard,* an uncritical admirer of any entrepreneur, looked forward to the day when "all the vast body of unculti-

<hr>

42 New York *Times,* October 3, 1878, May 30, 1879.
43 Compiled from figures in Paul Wallace Gate, "Federal Land Policy in the South, 1866–1888," *Journal of Southern History,* VI (1940)) , 318–20.

vated . . . lands" would be taken up by Northern business-men.[44]

All the while the state government owned great stretches of land which remained virtually untouched. Ten years prior to the Civil War, Congress gave Louisiana possession of all swamp lands and coastal marshes previously unsold. Most of it was, of course, inaccessible or covered with water. In 1888 over five million of these acres were still in the hands of the state land office.[45]

Without doubt, the greatest deterrent to homesteading was that prospective settlers lacked the initial capital required. Particularly were Negroes handicapped in this respect. A homestead claim itself was of no value unless the settler had adequate tools, plow animals, fencing, and other essentials. In St. Landry Parish, to cite a typical example, a homesteader had to spend an estimated $655 before the first crop was raised. This figure included fencing for no more than ten acres. But it was a rare sharecropper or cane field laborer who cleared, after expenses, more than twenty dollars per year.[46] In theory, then, an average family of agricultural workers would have to scrimp for thirty-three years or more before accumulating the wherewithal to set up debt-free homesteading.

In northern and central Louisiana the problems of potential homesteaders were entangled with the infamous "Backbone Railroad" land grant. Congress in 1871 had authorized the New Orleans, Baton Rouge, and Vicksburg Railway Company to build a line diagonally across the state from New Orleans to Shreveport, and over to Marshall, Texas. The company was to receive ten sections of land for each mile of track it

44 Winnfield *Southern Sentinel,* March 20, June 5, July 3, 1885; Shreveport *Daily Standard,* quoted in New Orleans *Daily Picayune,* November 21, 1880.

45 Baton Rouge *Daily Capitolian-Advocate,* April 15, 1888.

46 Estimated from figures in the following: *Tenth Census, 1880,* V, Pt. 2, pp. 83–84; New Orleans *Daily Picayune,* April 27, 1877, April 2, 1881; Baton Rouge *Weekly Truth,* May 28, 1886.

laid; if the line were completed, this would amount to a princely domain of over two million acres. The railroad could select its land from a swath of territory eighty miles wide, although it could not disturb any prior, legal landholdings. The managers of the Backbone Railroad were given five years, until 1876, to complete the line.[47] One disgusted commentator wrote that the government evidently assumed "this railroad company had been since 1803 a joint owner . . . of the lands of Louisiana." [48] The Backbone project, in the nature of other carpetbagger-inspired projects, issued copious stocks and bonds but laid not one foot of track. Its land grant was thereby forfeited in 1876.

Settlers, assuming the Backbone claim was beyond hope of resurrection, began moving into the territory. They were mistaken. In 1881 officials of the defunct company sold their "rights" to the New Orleans Pacific-Texas Pacific combine of Jay Gould, Russell Sage, and others. The price paid was one dollar.[49] At the time of the transfer the New Orleans Pacific was actually constructing a road from New Orleans to Shreveport; it would eventually join the Texas Pacific and link Louisiana with California. The Gould-Sage interests made progress along another line as well, for the entire Louisiana delegations to Congress between 1877 and 1881 signed pledges "to maintain the integrity of the grant and secure it for the [New Orleans Pacific] company." [50] For several years the Federal authorities refused to act, holding the old Backbone grant "in reservation." Suddenly, in 1885, the Secretary of the Interior approved patents for 679,287 acres of the controversial grant

47 *Congressional Globe,* 41st Cong., 3rd Sess., 392–93.

48 Opelousas *St. Landry Clarion,* November 8, 1890.

49 Colfax *Chronicle,* January 27, 1883; Henry V. Poor, *Manual of the Railroads of the United States for 1881* (New York, 1881), 782–85; Lewis Henry Haney, *A Congressional History of Railways in the United States: 1850–1887* (Madison, Wis., 1910), 132.

50 Letter from Congressman Newton C. Blanchard, in Colfax *Chronicle,* February 17, 1883.

to the Gould-Sage group.[51] The whole thing was, in the considered opinion of the Colfax *Chronicle*, "a fraud of the first magnitude"; and the hill farmers were furious.[52]

But while the Backbone grant worked an injustice on the hill country whites, the vast majority of Negroes in the plantation parishes had other and more pervasive worries. Very few Louisiana Negroes owned the land they tilled, or had any hope of owning it. Reports from the alluvial belt and from the better upland regions indicate that only 2 to 5 percent of the Negro farm families possessed any land. Black proprietors were most numerous in the less productive regions; almost half the freedmen of St. Landry, Tangipahoa, and Winn parishes held their farms in fee simple ownership. These three parishes were the only exceptions in an otherwise bleak picture.[53]

Nearly all blacks in the cotton parishes labored in exchange for a share of the crop, usually one-third; or they paid rent in the form of a stipulated amount of cotton per acre, which, although called tenantry, usually amounted to the same thing as sharecropping. And more often than not, the cropper and renter's portion was placed under a crop-lien mortgage to the landlord or a local merchant as security for credit purchases of food and other supplies. The rate of interest, figured into the "credit price" of the articles bought, varied anywhere from 15 to 200 percent. One white legislator in 1886 even spoke of interest rates in some parts of Louisiana running as high as 500 percent.[54]

Frequently black laborers discovered, at the end of the year,

[51] *House Executive Documents*, 49th Cong., 1st Sess., No. 1, pp. 43–44; Winnfield *Southern Sentinel*, March 27, June 5, 1885.

[52] Colfax *Chronicle*, January 27, 1883.

[53] *Tenth Census, 1880*, V, Pt. 2, p. 84; Baton Rouge *Daily Capitolian-Advocate*, March 28, 1882.

[54] New Orleans *Weekly Louisianian*, April 5, 1879; Fred A. Shannon, *The Farmer's Last Frontier: Agriculture, 1860–1897* (New York, 1945), 91; Baton Rouge *Weekly Truth*, May 28, 1886.

that their store purchases equaled or exceeded the value of their crop share. About the best they could hope for was a few dollars to spend. But Negroes were not alone in the lien system's trap. White farmers, the majority of whom did own some land, increasingly became enmeshed in what the Catholic Bishop of Natchitoches termed "the new form of slavery for both white and colored people." [55]

Defenders of this system of virtual peonage, and they were men of power, agreed with the *Weekly Advocate* that the "principle" of the crop-lien "is high prices in order to cover great risks." According to that source, "the negro is willing to pay the high prices, because he don't expect to have anything beyond money for a Christmas revel anyway." [56] There were indeed risks facing those who extended credit. Not the least of these was that some black debtors, aware that their share of the crop would, after deductions, provide them with little or no cash in hand, might abandon their cotton fields on the eve of picking time and hastily depart for another locality. Other croppers and renters furtively stowed away part of the cotton and later, in the dark of night, exchanged it for liquor at so-called "deadfall" stores: unlicensed shanty saloons hidden along backwoods lanes. Yet families who deserted their unpicked crop were likely to be taken back and forced to work while the brash capitalists who operated "deadfalls" met with stern and sometimes lethal disapproval from the planter class.[57]

Sharecropping and the crop-lien had emerged across the cotton-growing South after the Civil War as makeshift arrangements for reviving agricultural production. Former

[55] Pastoral letter from Bishop Anthony Durier, in Natchitoches *Enterprise,* March 2, 1899.

[56] Baton Rouge *Weekly Advocate,* June 17, 1881.

[57] New Orleans *Daily Picayune,* March 20, 1877; Colfax *Chronicle,* September 1, 1880, March 3, 1883.

slaves thus returned to the land to work on shares and the lien laws provided for a crude form of credit in a region where money was scarce. These methods, despite some drawbacks for all concerned, became self-perpetuating and in time were looked upon as not only necessary but, from the standpoint of the large landholders, desirable.[58] The plantation system was at least able to survive in modified form and ultimately to expand. By 1900, Louisiana would contain more plantations and fewer small farms than in 1860.[59]

Some of the largest planters, such as the Bosley family of Red River Parish, bought supplies for their laborers from New Orleans commission merchants.[60] Other big landlords operated stores located on their plantation. But this still left storekeepers at the small towns and crossroads with two broad classes of crop-lien customers: white proprietors of limited acres whose need for equipment and provisions drove them to seek credit; and Negro sharecroppers whose landlord did not distribute supplies or set up a plantation store. By the late 1880's, about 70 percent of the hill farmers were in debt to local merchants and the percentage for Negro agriculturists was, of course, higher still.[61]

Yet there appeared to be little alternative to the crop-lien system. New Orleans bankers would not usually advance mon-

[58] Oscar Zeichner, "The Transition from Slave to Free Agricultural Labor in the Southern States," *Agricultural History*, XIII (1939), 22–32; Monroe *Ouachita Telegraph*, March 19, 1875; "Address of Gen. J. L. Brent," in *Proceedings of the Second Annual Session of the Louisiana State Agricultural Society* (Baton Rouge, 1888), 14–25; "Address of W. L. Foster," in *Proceedings of the Sixth Annual Session of the Louisiana State Agricultural Socsiety* (Baton Rouge, 1892), 21–27.

[59] Roger W. Shugg, "Survival of the Plantation System in Louisiana," *Journal of Southern History*, III (1937), 311–25.

[60] Business statements from Chaffee and Powell, Cotton Factors and Commission Merchants of New Orleans, to H. G. Bosley, December 18, 20, 1886, in Bosley Family Papers, Department of Archives, Louisiana State University.

[61] Will H. Tunnard, "Louisiana Union Moving," *National Economist*, I (June 15, 1889), 196.

ey for mortgages on rural land, and so the farmer had no collateral except the growing crop. Rural banks simply did not exist. As late as 1886 there were no state or national banks to be found outside of Orleans Parish. Even when small private banking institutions in a few of the river towns were counted, the great majority of parishes had no banking facilities whatsoever.[62]

Credit merchants who kept books on an ignorant clientele had abundant chances to practice dishonesty. The system was scarcely fair under the most honest of storekeepers. But the cruelty of the arrangement was in large part due to circumstances over which the merchant had no control. For he had creditors too. As Professor C. Vann Woodward has observed, the Southern merchant became not "the villain in the piece," but rather "only a bucket on an endless chain by which the agricultural well of a tributary region was drained of its flow." [63]

Sharecropping and its twin, the crop-lien, held the cotton regions in a double vise. But the sugar parishes escaped their grip. There another form of economic organization had evolved. During and immediately after the war the "share" system had been tried by numerous planters, but it was soon dropped. The sugar planters found they disliked any method that failed to afford opportunities for close supervision. Thus by the 1880's most planters relied upon Negro gang laborers who were paid a stipulated wage.[64] Neither did the crop-lien have the same importance in the sugar country. Many of the smaller growers were entangled in it, but not so the workers or the large planters.

[62] New Orleans *City Item*, quoted in Colfax *Chronicle*, March 17, 1888; *Official Journal of the Constitutional Convention of the State of Louisiana*, 1898, p. 207.

[63] Woodward, *Origins of the New South*, 184–85.

[64] New Orleans *Daily Picayune*, June 23, 1877; J. Carlyle Sitterson, "The Transition from Slave to Free Economy on the William J. Minor Plantation," *Agricultural History*, XVII (1943), 223.

Most sugar plantations paid wages by the month. A few paid by the week or day. Wages were naturally higher when laborers purchased their own rations and were lower when the employer supplied food. Planters, who feared that Negroes might wander off before the backbreaking harvest work commenced, resorted to the device of withdrawing one-third of each month's wages and holding this money until the end of the year. With all its drawbacks, Negroes seemed to prefer the wage system to sharecropping. As evidence of this, thousands migrated from the cotton fields to the sugar lands during Reconstruction.[65]

Nevertheless, labor unrest did come to the cane fields. Wages, which just after the war ran as high as forty-five dollars per month with rations, crept downward during the late 1860's. Rates paid for labor took a swifter plunge with the beginning of the great nationwide depression in 1873.[66] The drop in wages was compounded by an oversupply of labor in some areas, caused by blacks who had arrived from the upriver parishes. Planters such as Donelson Caffery, Sr., hoped to lower wage rates as far as possible, reasoning that "if labor is plentiful labor is cheap." [67] In October of 1877 Caffery organized the cane growers of St. Mary, the leading sugar parish, for the purpose of ending competition for labor. Wages in St. Mary for the January-October growing season were thereupon fixed at fifteen dollars per month with rations, and eighteen without. Only able-bodied men were to be paid the specified rates. Women and children were used only during the grinding season, and they were paid fifty cents or less per day. "Infamous laborers or those engaged in strikes" were to be blacklisted.[68] Sugar planters near the Mississippi River followed the example of the St. Mary landowners; by late No-

---

65 New Orleans *Daily Picayune*, April 28, December 21, 1877, June 15, 1879.
66 Sitterson, *Sugar Country*, 245.
67 New Orleans *Daily Picayune*, October 3, 1877.
68 *Ibid.*, December 21, 1877.

vember of 1877 a statewide organization of large producers, the Louisiana Sugar Planters' Association, was taking shape under the leadership of Duncan F. Kenner.[69]

Though the majority of Louisianians remained close to the soil, many state officials and journalists were urging that the Pelican State join in the procession toward an industrialized "New South." But the advocates of industry had to tread carefully. While the welcome mat was being extended to Northern capitalists, it was deemed essential to somehow adjust this economic New Departure to the Procrustean bed of Southern tradition. Consequently, emotional as well as practical arguments were used on behalf of industrialization; it was pictured as a sort of non-violent continuation of the Civil War. The idea was advanced that, although "we have lost the victory on the field of fight, we can win it back in the workshop, in the factory." [70]

More to the point, it was argued that new factories and railroads would reduce unemployment and raise living standards. The benefits of industry could extend to the countryside as well as the city. Sawmills set up in the pine parishes would hire local men and thereby bring the jingle of money and the hum of civilization to the backland. One textile mill was already in operation in rural Claiborne Parish. More mills, it was believed, would locate in the countryside if proper inducements were offered. But of all lures to Northern business, the facts most stressed were the low rate of taxation and the abundance of cheap labor.[71]

Promoters of the New South idea could pridefully note that with the exception of the sugar refineries, Louisiana's infant

---

[69] New Orleans *Times*, December 7, 1877; Sitterson, *Sugar Country*, 253.

[70] Columbus (Ga.) *Register*, quoted in New Orleans *Daily Picayune*, March 24, 1881. See also, Baton Rouge *Weekly Advocate*, March 25, 1881.

[71] *Biographical and Historical Memoirs of Louisiana* (Chicago, 1892), I, 17, 135.

industries by the end of Reconstruction had shown considerable vitality in recovering from the ravages of war. Though the number of manufacturing establishments decreased from 1,774 to 1,553 between 1860 and 1880, the actual value of products rose from $15,587,473 to $24,205,183. The amount of invested capital showed similar growth. Fifteen hundred industrial plants, most of them small, were producing 56 percent as much wealth as all the commercial crops raised throughout the state. Only 12,167 men, women, and children labored to create the value of these manufactured items. Yet the hundreds of thousands of Louisianians who toiled in the hot sun of the fields could not double that amount.[72]

The moral to many was obvious. Since machinery tended to produce more in value than agriculture, it followed that industry would regain for Louisiana her lost riches. Capital investment could "make the Pelican State more powerful than Holland . . . build cities more beautiful than Venice."[73] Textile mills were particularly desired. New Orleans was the world's chief port for cotton export; by the late 1870's one-third of all the nation's cotton passed through the city, and yet the number of bales remaining in the state to be fashioned into textiles was pitifully small. Why, it must have been asked, did Louisiana grow so much but create so little?

Trade in fiber and produce was the life blood of New Orleans. But despite the fact that her commerce relied upon goods from plantations and farms, the Crescent City was the only place in Louisiana not saturated with an agricultural environment. In 1880 two-thirds of all manufacturing plants in the state were inside the city. Yet the 9,504 industrial workers (7,666 of them adult males) made up only a fraction of the city's labor force. One year after Reconstruction's end it was

[72] *Compendium of the Tenth Census, 1880,* II, 928, 975.
[73] Edward King, "Old and New Louisiana," *Scribner's Monthly,* VII (December, 1873), 156.

estimated that New Orleans contained at least 45,000 men who worked for wages.[74] Occupations were as varied as the life of the city itself. Skilled workers—typographers, screwmen, mechanics—these had formed benevolent and protective labor societies long before secession, and after the war their societies or unions were clearly the strongest among the labor associations of New Orleans.[75] Somewhat lower on the economic ladder, but still organized, were laborers in the tobacco manufacturing plants and cottonseed oil mills. But most urban workers had no real skills and toiled for thirty-five cents or less an hour. From this unskilled majority, there occasionally emerged ineffective labor associations. Longshoremen and the levee roustabouts formed a Laborers' Union Society in 1877 and attempted to resist the hiring of degraded, poverty-stricken newcomers to the city who were willing to work for ten cents an hour.[76]

Wage earners in New Orleans, even those with skills, had tended to sink into despair during the latter years of Reconstruction. For during the time that Louisiana's cauldron of political troubles boiled over, between 1874 and 1877, depressed economic conditions were at their worst. Racial animosity among the working class was meanwhile on the rise. Bitter competition for jobs combined with political issues to divide Negro and white laborers into hostile camps.[77] Charitable associations seemed unable to provide sufficient food for the unemployed and helpless. Landlords and business leaders blamed the hard times on the carpetbaggers, and few whites but the carpetbaggers disagreed.

[74] *Compendium of the Tenth Census, 1880*, II, 928, 975, 1068–71; New Orleans *Daily Picayune*, November 10, 1878.
[75] Arthur Raymond Pearce, "The Rise and Decline of Labor in New Orleans" (M.A. thesis, Tulane University, 1938) , 4, 17.
[76] New Orleans *Daily Picayune*, November 4, 1877.
[77] Shugg, *Origins of Class Struggle*, 303.

"Death is staring us in the face," a laborer wrote during the last depression days of Reconstruction. "How long! Oh, how long! will these poor men and women and children . . . be kept in bondage and misery in our distracted city and state?" [78] Under the circumstances, it is not surprising that white labor in New Orleans and the small farmers of the up-country willingly marched in the ranks behind the politico-economic Democratic elite in the gloomy days of 1876–77.

Underprivileged whites generally accepted the conservative verdict that Republican Radicalism and its social turmoil had caused the hard times and halted any chance for economic recovery. In 1876 the white population, rich and poor, had united in a "common sympathy" of race and regional pride to fight for home rule under the Democratic banner.[79] The victory was won, but white unity would one day be tested in the fire of class conflict.

[78] Letter from "J. W. J.," in New Orleans *Daily Picayune*, April 15, 1877.
[79] New Orleans *Issue*, June 4, 1892. The *Issue* was an organ of the laborite-Populist coalition in New Orleans during the 1890's.

IV

A Slight Discord

"N o w t h a t the State Government is happily once more in the hands of our own people," wrote one reform-minded gentleman in 1877, "we have a right to expect a great deal from it." Within a year he would register sharp disappointment.[1] Many who welcomed the overthrow of Packard and Kellogg's carpetbagger crowd believed, at first, that Louisiana was being redeemed not only from Radicalism but also from her malign political habits which predated Reconstruction. This prospect dimmed with the first months of "home rule," then faded out of sight in 1878.

The legislative sessions of 1877–78 accomplished fiscal retrenchment but not genuine reform. Governmental expenditures were slashed by over $2,700,000; all state services and institutions suffered thereby, Negro schools most of all.[2] Large planters and businessmen were favored with tax reductions, but even so, many continued to avoid payment. The wealthy families' resistance to any taxation, explained the city attorney of Shreveport, was something "they got into the habit of" during Reconstruction.[3] Governor Nicholls complained that

1 Vermilionville *Cotton Bowl,* September 5, 1877, March 8, 1878. The town of Vermilionville was later renamed Lafayette.

2 Margaret M. Williams, "An Outline of Public School Politics in Louisiana Since the Civil War" (M.A. thesis, Tulane University, 1938), 21–29; Fortier (ed.), *Louisiana,* I, 427.

3 Shreveport *Daily Standard,* quoted in Natchitoches *People's Vindicator,* June 18, 1881.

people of little property usually paid their assessments but "men of large means" deliberately abstained and nothing was done. The legislature, however, failed to act upon the Governor's suggestions for correcting the abuses.[4]

Using carpetbagger methods as a guide, the Democratic solons devised election laws which were marvels of ingenuity but did not point in the direction of honesty. Police jurors in each parish, appointed by the governor, received the authority to select polling places and name the election commissioners. In turn, the commissioners supervised all elections, counted the ballots, and signed the official tally sheets. This procedure was contrived at the bidding of whites in the heavily Negro plantation parishes. Ominously, the new laws did not declare the falsification of returns to be a crime.[5] The Bourbon legislator-editor J. H. Cosgrove blithely told his fellow Democrats to "pile up your majority. The returning board is on our side now."[6]

Murmurs of discontent began to rise from elements within the white population. The legislature's fiscal conservatism and queer election laws were almost immediately challenged by the more astute farmers and laborers. A Grant Parish politician in 1878, meeting this, uneasily noted that "a slight discord has manifested itself among the Democrats of our [region]."[7] According to one grumbler, "the rulers" seemed to look on Louisiana's earth and the people who toiled in it as part of "the same mass, and beneath . . . respect and relief."[8]

[4] *House Journal*, 1879, pp. 7–19; New Orleans *Daily Picayune*, January 8, 1879.

[5] New Orleans *Daily Picayune*, January 8, 1879; New York *Times*, November 24, 1879; *Congressional Record*, 47th Cong., Special Sess., 120.

[6] Natchitoches *People's Vindicator*, October 26, 1878. Actually, after 1877 there was no longer a returning board with powers to revise returns at the state capitol. With Democratic commissioners everywhere at the precinct level, a state returning board would have been superfluous.

[7] Colfax *Chronicle*, August 31, 1878.

[8] Letter from "B. J. S.," in New Orleans *Daily Picayune*, January 1, 1878.

The fact that public schools had deteriorated since Reconstruction—indeed had sunk below the standards of the late antebellum years—angered many who could not afford to send their children to private academies. By 1880 several parishes, including relatively populous Ouachita, did not have a single public school for whites or Negroes.[9] As to politics, many who had approved of the gross frauds used against Republicans during Reconstruction now thought that a halt to vote stealing should be called; fears were expressed that Democratic managers might become colorblind and, as subsequently happened, commence "bulldozing" white men.[10]

The autumn elections of 1878 revealed the paucity of the New Departure spirit in both state and nation. Across America the congressional races that year, being the first since the end of Reconstruction, held more than ordinary significance. In the North some Republican candidates approved of Hayes's pacific policies but others unfurled that proven vote-getter, the "bloody shirt." Southern Democrats likewise differed in their approaches to sectional issues; those of the Bourbon mentality harped upon the ugly past. Almost everywhere, however, a new and complicating factor was thrust into the campaign because of a sudden swell of agrarian, inflationist sentiment. Debtor farmers in many sections, responding to the appeal of cheap money, were calling for Congress to increase silver coinage and repeal the Resumption Act of 1875 which, if allowed to remain a law, would place the "greenback" paper money on par with gold by 1879. The nation had not yet fully emerged from the recent depression, and small

9 Letter from C. Doubleyou, in Covington *St. Tammany Farmer*, June 28, 1881; Williams, "An Outline of Public School Politics," 28; Frederick W. Williamson and George T. Goodman (eds.), *Eastern Louisiana: A History of the Watershed of the Ouachita River and Florida Parishes* (Louisville, 1939), I, 281.

10 *Senate Reports*, 45th Cong., 3rd Sess., No. 855, p. 221; Rayville *Richland Beacon*, July 2, 1881.

agriculturists looked to inflation as a panacea for their economic troubles.[11]

President Hayes, a gold standard conservative, stood with major banking interests in opposition to silver and paper. Many Southern Democrats privately sympathized with the President and Eastern capitalism. Yet almost to a man the Southerners, taking note of the popularity of cheap money and fearful of an inflationist third party movement in their region, temporarily backed away from financial orthodoxy and announced in favor of the debtor demands. This seemingly leftward turn in Dixie politics in 1878 evoked wrathful outcries from Whiggish Northern Republicans, and "bloody shirt" wavers from Maine to Kansas began equating patriotism with gold, claiming that the ex-rebels were involved in a socialistic machination to damage the economy of the section which had won the war.[12]

For Louisiana the 1878 election brought out local as well as congressional candidates. A state treasurer, most of the legislature and all of the municipal officials of New Orleans were to be chosen on November 5, along with the state's six members of the United States House of Representatives. The campaign lacked little of the usual invective and violence even though it took place in the midst of a calamitous distraction: the worst yellow fever epidemic of the late nineteenth century. From June until the first cold weather in November, grisly corpse wagons rumbled through the streets of New Orleans; about four thousand persons in the city and hundreds more in the countryside died of "yellow jack." Towns free of the fever posted quarantines against all travelers, freight, and packages from infected districts. Ordinary means of communication

11 New York *Times,* May 2, August 7–9, 1878; Irwin Unger, *The Greenback Era: A Social and Political History of American Finance, 1865–1879* (Princeton, N.J., 1964) , 382–85.

12 *Nation,* XXVII (August 15, 1878) , 89–90; Woodward, *Origins of the South,* 47–49.

broke down. Some parishes north of the Red River did without mail service or outside newspapers for nearly four months.[13] In the interval, Democrats and their opposition held conventions and, where conditions permitted, campaigned.

When the state Democratic convention assembled in August, the Bourbon and Lottery forces, acting together, outmatched the Nicholls faction. Major Burke obtained the nomination for state treasurer.[14] The party platform, drawn up by the coalition, called for a new constitution to replace the one which an Opelousas paper indelicately described as the "miserable abortion" of 1868.[15] To appease Nicholls' friends, or perhaps to lull their suspicions, a disclaimer was hastily added to the platform: "It is not proposed to displace or interfere with the incumbent officials of the State government." [16]

Commentators beyond Louisiana were primarily interested in, and astonished by, the money plank in the state Democratic platform of 1878. For the August convention at Baton Rouge, although dominated by men known to be among the most reactionary in the South, had nevertheless issued what amounted to a liberal agrarian manifesto. The platform asked Congress to repeal the Resumption Act, abolish the national banking system, and return to the printing of inflationary greenbacks. It expressed "warmest sympathy" for all laboring people and accused the Republicans of grinding down the working class.[17] True, at the time, nearly all Southern Democratic leaders were making similar efforts to placate debtor farmers. But only the Democrats of Louisiana—"more reckless than the rest" according to the New York *Times*—came out for inflation in such unequivocal language. Their money

---

13 New Orleans *Daily Picayune,* October 29, November 3, 1878; Coushatta *Citizen,* quoted in *ibid.,* November 29, 1878; McGinty, *Louisiana Redeemed,* 238.
14 New Orleans *Democrat,* August 7, 1878.
15 Opelousas *Courier,* September 28, 1877.
16 Colfax *Chronicle,* October 19, 1878.
17 New Orleans *Democrat,* August 7, 1878.

plank, fumed the *Times*, "contains about as mischievous a se-
ries of demands as the most rabid of the Labor-Greenback
Conventions have yet formulated." [18]

"Vicious and unprincipled," exclaimed E. L. Godkin's
Nation, in berating the authors of the Baton Rouge platform.
But the genteelly conservative *Nation*, which was then earning a reputation as the best weekly magazine "not only in
America but in the world," [19] possessed insight into why the
Pelican State's Democrats had appeared to embrace Greenbackism. "The fine gentlemen" of Louisiana, wrote Godkin,
merely wished to pacify "the mob," and were "hoping that the
platform will pass for buncombe outside their own State, and
that no mischief will result in Congress." [20] As if to bear out
Godkin's analysis the *Daily Picayune*, with consummate be-
fuddlement, praised the platform but also stated that the
anticipated colossal Democratic majority in the forthcoming
election should not be misunderstood by outsiders as an endorsement of inflationist heresies.[21]

Bona fide Greenback sentiment assuredly existed in Louisiana although the extent of it became obscured by Democratic duplicity. After the Baton Rouge convention, Burke and
most local nominees of the dominant party shunned any discussion of the monetary question; one candidate, typical of
others, thought it sufficed to say that "the Democratic platform is as good a document as any Greenback man could
wish," and then immediately proceed to another subject.[22]
Generally this subterfuge appeared to work. Yet not all inflationists were so easily misled. A number of farmers in the hill
parishes, including many hitherto docile Democrats, turned

18 New York *Times*, August 7–8, 1878.
19 Ari Hoogenboom, "Civil Service Reform and Public Morality," in H.
Wayne Morgan (ed.), *The Gilded Age: A Reappraisal* (Syracuse, N.Y., 1963),
72.
20 *Nation*, XXVII (August 15, 1878), 89.
21 New Orleans *Daily Picayune*, November 1, 1878.
22 Colfax *Chronicle*, October 12, 1878.

toward a new political organization which styled itself the National Party.

From New England to California the National Party (designated as "Greenback-Labor" in some areas) entered candidates in various congressional and local contests of 1878.[23] Their platform, written at a Toledo, Ohio convention in May, emphasized the cheap money ideas of rural debtors but also made appeals to urban labor. Aglow with idealism, the Nationals presumed to be able to bury North-South enmity with a broad program for economic reform; instead of the sectional-conscious "bloody shirt" they hoisted the class-conscious "ragged shirt." [24] The new party loomed strongest in farming regions of the North and West, but its spokesmen expressed optimism over three states of the Deep South: Texas, Mississippi, and Louisiana. According to one of the National movement's founders, Negro voters of the latter state would unite with disgruntled white Democrats and carry the inflationist party to victory.[25]

Southern Greenbackism traced its spiritual ancestry, if not all its monetary views, back to the era of Jacksonian Democracy. Since that time, despite the passions of Civil War and the pressures for white solidarity during Reconstruction, thousands of yeoman farmers still retained something of the older, equalitarian attitudes. And when Reconstruction ended, many Southern Jacksonians awoke to find themselves wandering in a political no man's land. Whiggishness and Bourbonism ruled

23 The National Party of 1878 was an outgrowth of the smaller Independent (or Greenback) Party which had nominated the eccentric Peter Cooper for President in 1876. Only 80,000 votes were recorded for Cooper in the entire nation but in 1878 the National Party managed to elect eleven congressmen and claimed over one million total votes for its candidates in various states. Unger, *The Greenback Era*, 376–83; Fred E. Haynes, *Third Party Movements Since the Civil War, with Special Reference to Iowa: A Study in Social Politics* (Iowa City, 1916) , 124.

24 St. Louis *Evening Post,* September 26, 1878.

25 New York *Sun,* quoted in *ibid.* See also, Theodore Saloutos, *Farmer Movements in the South, 1865–1933* (Los Angeles, 1960) , 52–53.

the Democratic Party, and most of Dixie's Republicans were either Whiggish, thievish, or Negro. Consequently, in nearly all Southern states the restoration of "home rule" was shortly followed by the birth of local "independent" parties—mostly white, but with some Negro support—which provided a measure of opposition to the conservative Democrats.[26] The National Party planned to coalesce these scattered independents.

In Louisiana as in other states the most immediate forebear of this post-Reconstruction agrarianism was the Patrons of Husbandry, better known as the Grange. A social and economic fraternity of American farmers, officially nonpolitical, the Grange had reached its peak nationally in the early 1870's. But the upsets of Reconstruction sorely handicapped the Grange in the Pelican State; there was no statewide organization until 1874, and it never had over ten thousand members.[27] In neighboring states the Grange was bigger and stronger.

Membership in the Louisiana Grange during Reconstruction appears to have been mostly recruited from medium-sized and small landowners who raised cotton, corn, or livestock. The uplands of North Louisiana and the Florida Parishes became the heartland of the Grange. The great landlords, especially the sugar barons, shunned it. The Grange's general-deputy for Louisiana later commented that the large planters in the southern portion of the state "have never taken any interest in our organization." [28]

Like Grangers elsewhere, the Louisiana membership in

26 Woodward, *Origins of the New South,* 76–77; De Santis, *Republicans Face the Southern Question,* 96.

27 Thomas C. Atkeson, *Semi-Centennial History of the Patrons of Husbandry* (New York, 1916) , 45–46; Solon Justus Buck, *The Granger Movement: A Study of Agricultural Organization and its Political, Economic and Social Manifestations, 1870–1880* (Cambridge, Mass., 1913) , 58ff.

28 Curley Daniel Willis, "The Grange Movement in Louisiana" (M.A. thesis, Louisiana State University, 1935) , 16–18, 20–23; New Orleans *Daily Picayune,* March 23, May 30, 1877; *Journal of Proceedings, Fifteenth Session of the National Grange of the Patrons of Husbandry* (Philadelphia, 1881) , 59, quoted in Saloutos, *Farmer Movements in the South,* 33.

some localities had set up cooperative store enterprises. A state wholesale agency, headquartered in New Orleans, served the local outlets.[29] But poor management, not to mention the depressed economic conditions of the mid 1870's, caused the demise of the state agency in 1877. The local stores soon met the same fate. The only survivor was the Grange store at Winnfield, which was still doing business in 1885 under the management of George P. Long, an older brother of Huey P. Long, Sr.[30]

Economic troubles combined with the political turmoil of 1876–77 to kill virtually all Grange activity in the state. Indeed it was reported that upcountry white farmers even neglected the planting of their crops as they waited for news from Washington and New Orleans during the tense spring of 1877.[31] Attendance at the lodge halls dropped off, most members failed to pay their dues, and subsequent efforts to revive the Grange proved unsuccessful.[32]

Yet for all its failures the Grange had at least introduced the concept of united agrarian action; it had promoted the idea that farmers must to some degree put aside their traditional atomistic individualism and, like other special interest groups, join hands for the purposes of economic advantage and political pressure. It had at the same time attempted to instill in rural folk a sense of the importance of their labor. "Agriculture was the first calling of man," Grangers were told. "No order or association can rank with the tillers of the soil." [33] Moreover, for a flickering moment some members of

29 New Orleans *Son of the Soil,* quoted in Monroe *Ouachita Telegraph,* April 23, 1875.
30 New Orleans *Our Home Journal,* quoted in Opelousas *Courier,* March 31, 1877; Winnfield *Southern Sentinel,* August 28, September 25, December 11, 1885.
31 Natchitoches *People's Vindicator,* March 17, 1877.
32 New Orleans *Daily Picayune,* November 23, 1877, February 18–19, 1881.
33 *Manual of Subordinate Granges of the Patrons of Husbandry* (Philadelphia, 1873)) , 48.

the Louisiana Grange had attempted to bridge the chasm between the races; in the first lodge organized in the state, whites and blacks assembled together "on a basis of mutual interest and common defense." [34] Not many lodges appear to have been biracial, but the few that were set an example which would be followed by local reformers later in the century.

As the agricultural writer Daniel Dennett remarked a decade later, the Grange was "the great pioneer" of agrarian reform in Louisiana.[35] The Farmers' Union and the Alliance of the 1880's and the Populist Party of the 1890's would list among their leaders men who once had been active in the Grange.

The National Party organization of 1878 was, however, undertaken without the participation of those who headed the moribund state Grange. The Grange as such played no political role that year. Indications are that officials of the Louisiana Grange had always tended to be more conservative than the average member; many of the more radical farmers had quit the order for precisely that reason.[36] But from the Granger rank and file came the local, self-delegated leadership for the new inflationist third party. Not surprisingly, the first stirrings of National activity in Louisiana were observed where the Grange had been strongest, among the dirt farmers of the hill parishes.

Upon first hearing of the Louisiana Nationals in May of 1878, the Shreveport *Evening Standard* suddenly lost confidence in its recent prediction that the South "is forever safe from communistic disturbances." That Bourbon organ was thunderstruck by the news that some white men who had

34 Willis, "The Grange Movement in Louisiana," 16.

35 Daniel Dennett quoted in Leesville *People's Friend*, March 21, 1889.

36 New Orleans *Times*, August 5, 1875, quoted in Willis, "The Grange Movement in Louisiana," 25.

borne arms in the Reconstruction disturbances at Colfax and Coushatta were now breaking away from Democratic conservatism.[37] Three Confederate veterans, Robert P. Webb, Jesse M. Tilly and the Reverend Benjamin Brian, became the leading apostles of Greenbackism in the uplands. Webb owned a moderately large plantation in Claiborne Parish. Tilly and Brian were small farmers; Brian, who was also a Baptist preacher, had been involved during Reconstruction in an "independent" political movement in Winn and Grant parishes.[38] One feeble newspaper, the Haynesville *Greenback Dollar*, carried the new party's message to a limited number of rustic subscribers.[39]

Lack of funds, the semi-paralysis in communications resulting from yellow fever quarantines, as well as political amateurism on the part of its leadership, hampered the National movement in the Pelican State. But these were not necessarily the severest of its handicaps. Its major platform plank, inflation, had been stolen by the Democrats. Presently the Republicans confused the picture even more by capturing the National name. When the Greenbacker state convention met in September, a heavy influx of Republican delegates gained control of the assemblage and composed a strange platform which absolutely avoided the vital monetary question. Dr. John S. Gardner, a Baton Rouge physician, was named as Major Burke's opponent in the state treasurer's race. The convention endorsed a slate of congressional aspirants who were variously listed under a "National," "Greenback-Republican," "Independent" or some other opaque designation.

[37] Shreveport *Evening Standard,* May 8, 10, 1878.

[38] *Biographical and Historical Memoirs of Northwest Louisiana* (Nashville, 1890), 204–205, 457–58, 662; Colfax *Chronicle,* September 30, 1876, October 5, 19, 1878. See also, Benjamin Brian's obituary in Natchitoches *Louisiana Populist,* November 6, 1896.

[39] *Biographical and Historical Memoirs of Louisiana,* II, 169; Colfax *Chronicle,* November 15, 1879.

The nominee for Congress in the Fourth District was that indefatigable old scalawag, J. Madison Wells.[40]

Not all Republicans and not all Greenbackers went along with the fusion campaign. Many of the latter were doubtlessly bewildered by what had transpired and so, perhaps, were some of the former. Although cooperation between hill country liberals and the G.O.P. was not entirely unprecedented, their presumed merger in 1878 was not only politically addled, but morally bankrupt. E. North Cullom, one of the ranking Republicans involved, admitted privately that his party simply hoped to split the white vote by any device at hand. In a letter to President Hayes, Cullom explained that in Louisiana there was "nothing to be gained by taking the field under a square Republican banner" and that the National movement provided a convenient mask. "It was the only alternative," he added, "outside of entire inaction." [41]

Nevertheless, one of the self-righteous statements of the fusionist platform made curious reading in light of the previous activities of Cullom, Wells, and several other "National" candidates: it denounced Burke and the Bourbon Democrats as "a flock of comorants" and compared them, accurately but hypocritically, to the Radical Republicans "who wallowed in the corruptions of the Warmoth and Kellogg administrations." [42] Notably in the case of Wells was it late in the day to condemn Reconstruction's rascality.

The National Party, having fallen into Republican hands, still more or less identified itself with Greenbackism in North Louisiana. But in the New Orleans area its candidates sought to capitalize on anti-foreign emotions and ignored the

40 Uzee, "Republican Politics in Louisiana," 45–46; New Orleans *Democrat,* September 20–21, 27, 1878.

41 E. North Cullom to Rutherford B. Hayes, February 6, 1879, in Hayes Papers.

42 New Orleans *Daily Picayune,* November 3, 1878.

pros and cons of inflation. The urban Nationals instead wooed remnants of the earlier American (Know Nothing) Party, along with native-born white and Negro laborers, with the argument that European immigrants debased politics and lowered wages. And in certain Protestant parishes the party reputedly dabbled in anti-Catholicism. Democratic spokesmen, probably jealous of any competition in the use of prejudice, chided the Nationals for their intolerance and "fanaticism." [43] Major Burke and the New Orleans *Democrat* announced the discovery of a vicious band of Nationals called the "Red Warriors" who were said to be plotting to drive naturalized citizens away from the polls on election day.[44] When that date came, however, no "Red Warriors" turned up, but Democratic terrorists were conspicuously present.

In certain parishes, independent movements flared up during the campaign which held little or no association with any statewide party. Tensas furnished the most singular example. A "Country People's Ticket," representing a combination of white farmers—most of whom were Confederate veterans—and Negroes, strove to take the parish offices from under the sway of Democratic boss Charles C. Cordill. The population of Tensas was 90 percent black, and Cordill, a large planter, once headed the local Republican organization; but by 1878, with Reconstruction over, he and his subordinates had shifted parties and continued to dominate political affairs under the emblem of white supremacy. Negro leaders, disgusted with Cordill's new posture, approached the yeoman whites of the parish and effected a shaky coalition. Most of the wealthy resident landowners sided with the Cordill Republican-turned-

---

[43] Shreveport *Evening Standard*, October 22, 1878; New Orleans *Daily Picayune*, November 1, 1878.

[44] Covington *St. Tammany Farmer*, October 26, 1878; Natchitoches *People's Vindicator*, October 26, 1878.

Democratic machine. The oddity of the Tensas situation drew notice, especially after it erupted into bloodshed.[45]

Another newly born political fragment which came in for some attention in 1878 was the leftist Workingman's Party of New Orleans. John C. Fleming, describing himself as "an humble mechanic," headed its ticket in the municipal contests. Fleming's laborites, desiring to rally a biracial proletarian movement of the sort envisioned by Union General Benjamin F. Butler in 1862,[46] issued a blistering manifesto which urged poor whites and Negroes to cast away both the major parties; black voters were reminded that Hayes's Republicans had abandoned them to the "bulldozers," while the "so-called Democracy refuses to recognize the manhood of their race." The city and state Democratic administrations were pilloried as "imbecile" and as "the vilest government that ever disgraced a civilized community." [47]

The Workingman's platform, for added measure, raised the ghosts of the victims of the 1878 yellow fever epidemic: those thousands of dead who "are crying aloud for retributive justice upon those who by their neglect forced them into untimely graves." But mayorality candidate Fleming hastened to say that although the patience of the "oppressed and neglected" was wearing thin, his party stood for nonviolence. "God knows," he stated, "we have misfortune enough . . . without bringing about others by . . . conflict." [48] Neither did Fleming

45 New Orleans *Daily Picayune,* November 1, 1878, January 8, 1879; New York *Times,* January 8–9, 1879. Ex-Governor Henry Clay Warmoth commented upon the political transformation of "my old friend Charlie Cordill" in his autobiographical *War, Politics and Reconstruction: Stormy Days in Louisiana* (New York, 1930) , 253–54.

46 There is no direct evidence, however, to indicate that General Butler's program and statements, when he headed the Union occupation forces in New Orleans in 1862, inspired the Workingman's Party of 1878.

47 New Orleans *Daily Picayune,* October 30, 1878.

48 *Ibid.,* November 2, 1878.

make proposals of an overtly socialistic nature. Still the *Daily Picayune*, which guessed the labor ticket's strength at two thousand votes, sneered at it as "a half-hearted communism." [49]

Louisiana, after Reconstruction, demonstrably contained a number of local liberal and quasi-liberal movements. Their true cumulative strength can only be conjectured since the "official" election returns from many parishes were anything but trustworthy gauges of public opinion. Clear, however, is the fact that the various rural and urban reformers failed to combine forces. Indeed they showed little effort in that direction; upland Greenbackers and the city Workingmen's ticket, for instance, apparently never communicated with each other in 1878. The pseudo-National Party pretended to be a state-wide vehicle of protest, but it was a sham. Even when the yellow fever epidemic is taken into account, local reformers themselves were probably much to blame for their lack of unity. On the other hand, it would have required something near the talents of a Machiavelli to set up an effective threat to the adroit politicians of the state's Democratic and Republican parties.

Protest activities in other Southern states faced immense difficulties too, but none so overwhelming as in Louisiana. For there the general regional problem of political alienation between poor whites and blacks was compounded by unique ethnic divisions within the white race. Protestant hill farmers did not even speak the same language as the Catholic Latins of the coastal lowlands. Nor did either of these rural people have much meaningful contact with the wage earners of New Orleans, many of whom were born in Ireland, Germany, or Italy. Sicilian-Italian immigrants arrived in increasing numbers during the latter decades of the nineteenth century; some

49 *Ibid.*, November 1–2, 1878.

of them fanned out from the city to find work in agriculture.[50] Passing judgment on their value, the editor of the official journal of the state government decided that Sicilians were "superior to the negro" as laborers but, regrettably, proved not nearly so "docile [or] manageable." [51]

From among each ethnic group of whites as well as from the Negroes there were many resentful voices raised against the powerful white elite. But Democratic leaders, with mounting self-confidence in the years following Reconstruction, treated these fragmented protests oftener with derision than conciliation. V. O. Key's statement that "the ruling oligarchy of Louisiana" took advantage of the special situation and "really pressed down harder than did the governing groups of other states" is a warranted conclusion.[52] And when, in 1882, a conservative New Iberia paper referred to "the masses" as "them asses" there was reason to suspect more than an innocent typographical error.[53]

A time was approaching when Louisiana's politico-economic elite would presume itself invulnerable to disturbances from below. Eventually the common whites were to be widely scorned as "hayseeds" or "the nondescript mass" and publicly derided by some members of the leadership class as being no better, as one put it, than the Negro "black cattle." [54] In 1878, however, the pattern of Democratic mastery over the state was not yet complete, and that sort of talk might have

50 Vermilionville *Cotton Bowl,* April 2, 1873; "Report of Louisiana," *National Economist,* I (May 25, 1889), 155–56; Trinity *Herald,* June 6, 1889; "The Mafia in New Orleans," *Harper's Weekly* XXXIV (November 8, 1890), 874; Julian Ralph, *Dixie: Or Southern Scenes and Sketches* (New York, 1896), 117–20.

51 Baton Rouge *Daily Advocate,* May 11, 1894.

52 V. O. Key, Jr., *Southern Politics in State and Nation* (New York, 1949) , 160.

53 New Iberia *Star,* quoted in New Orleans *Daily Picayune,* January 5, 1882.

54 For specimen examples of this later frankness, see Plaquemine *Iberville South,* February 1, 22, 1896; Baton Rouge *Daily Advocate,* January 31, April 19, 1896; New Orleans *Daily Picayune,* March 3, 1896; Shreveport *Evening Journal,* March 4, 13, 1898; Natchitoches *Enterprise,* March 2, 1899.

been dangerous. The party's inflationist plank that year, although deceitful, at least indicated a certain respect for the potential strength of agrarianism. Furthermore, a sizable minority of seats in the legislature and one congressional district were still in Republican hands.[55] Despite some purging of the registration rolls, Negro voters yet held a slim statewide majority over the whites, and memories of military Reconstruction were too fresh to risk an arousal of Northern hostility by a premature disfranchisement of the whole black race.[56] There were other reasons, too, for allowing Negroes to remain on the voting rolls; not the least of which was the prospect that their ballots, if properly manipulated or falsified, could overwhelm any agrarian or laborite white opposition to conservative rule.[57]

White supremacy, rather than the superiority of which whites, still seemed the primary concern of Democratic orators in this first post-Reconstruction election. The more delicate latter question they held, for the most part, in abeyance. Temporarily the spirit of the Reconstruction era's White League, an emphasis on Caucasian solidarity, was retained. Major Burke and other Democrats insisted, as they continued to do as late as 1880, that the heroic task of redeeming Louisiana from Republicanism was unfinished as long as the hated Radicals remained lurking in the background.[58] The state's

[55] Otis A. Singletary, "The Election of 1878 in Louisiana," *Louisiana Historical Quarterly*, XL (1957) , 47.

[56] In 1878 there were 78,123 Negroes and 77,341 whites on the state's voter registration rolls. This does not include Bossier Parish, which had a Negro majority but made no official report. Two years later Bossier listed 2,000 colored and 800 white voters on its rolls. *Report of the Secretary of State*, 1902, pp. 546–48.

[57] E. North Cullom to William E. Chandler, July 14, 1882, in Chandler Papers; New Orleans *Weekly Louisianian*, December 6, 1879; Baton Rouge *Weekly Truth*, May 28, 1886; Homer *Louisiana Journal*, November 24, 1886.

[58] Shreveport *Evening Standard*, October 15, 1878; "Speech of E. A. Burke," in New Orleans *Daily Picayune*, November 3, 1878; St. Joseph *North Louisiana Journal*, October 30, 1880.

most influential Bourbon weekly suggested that if "patriotic white men stand solid now" then perhaps in the future "the discontented can talk." [59]

The tone taken with black voters was more candid. Democratic candidates did seek support from the colored majority. But threats were apparently as frequent as pleadings. Edward Hunter, for example, speaking before a Negro gathering in North Louisiana, informed his hushed audience that white men possessed "all the intelligence" and the blacks "are ignorant." Warming to the subject, he observed that "intelligence is bound to rule." Hunter said he was doing them a favor by telling them to vote Democratic since "we are going to carry the election anyhow. . . . We can get along without you." [60] Apropos of this, the Shreveport *Evening Standard* cautioned that if "the negroes . . . do not appreciate these efforts and still join the enemies of the State . . . they must take the consequences." [61] A nasty taste of "the consequences" was already being administered during the campaign, particularly in Caddo, Natchitoches, and Tensas parishes.

Harsh treatment, or threats of it, similarly befell many whites who were active in Greenbacker or independent movements among the northern parishes. The entire slate of reform candidates in Morehouse had been compelled to flee to a healthier climate by election day.[62] Benjamin Brian stood his ground in Grant Parish, although told by a Democratic opponent that he was "a good dog gone astray. He was in the company of sheep-killing dogs and he had to be killed." [63] In stormy Natchitoches not even politically inactive whites could

[59] Natchitoches *People's Vindicator*, October 12, 1878.

[60] Colfax *Chronicle*, October 12, 1878.

[61] Shreveport *Evening Standard*, October 15, 1878.

[62] New York *Times*, November 4, 1878.

[63] Colfax *Chronicle*, October 5, 1878. Brian ran for the state senate as a liberal independent (with Republican backing) in 1876, 1878 and 1879. He was successful only in the third attempt.

avoid trouble, since the *People's Vindicator* collected and threatened to publish the names of all Caucasians who were failing to register to vote. That Democratic journal added: "We regard and will treat all who do not aid us as negroes, whether their skins be white or black." [64]

As if by mutual consent neither the Democrats nor the pseudo-National Party, once the campaign began, said much on the subject of currency inflation. Yet economic issues were not ignored everywhere. In Caddo Parish, to cite one instance, a Republican-Independent coalition lashed out at the crop-lien system; Negro voters were told that planters and merchants encouraged the spread of the crop-lien because it kept most blacks, as well as many rural whites, in a condition of peonage. Local Democrats were outraged by these charges, which they assailed as "incendiary" and as "efforts to incite labor against capital." [65] A Caddo judge warned that if the agrarian malcontents won offices, then "Grant and the troops" would soon march through the streets of Shreveport, and "the place would be made so desolate the bats and owls would roost on our wharves." [66]

Every major Louisiana election between the Civil War and the twentieth century drew a measure of human blood, and that of 1878 was no exception. Across the state about fifty persons died that year as a result of political disturbances.[67] By far the most dramatic were events in Tensas; there, Judge

[64] Natchitoches *People's Vindicator,* October 19, 1878.
[65] New York *Times,* January 20, 1879.
[66] New Orleans *Daily Picayune,* January 11, 1879.
[67] Allie Bayne Windham Webb, "A History of Negro Voting in Louisiana, 1876–1906" (Ph.D. dissertation, Louisiana State University, 1962) , 37–56. The Republicans claimed a much higher figure of dead. Albert H. Leonard, the ex-White Leaguer who once co-edited the Shreveport *Times* with Major Hearsey but who subsequently became a Republican district attorney, said that in Caddo Parish alone seventy-five Negroes were murdered during the 1878 campaign. *Nation,* XXVII (December 12, 1878) , 358.

Cordill precipitated violence by calling for outside armed help against the "Country People's Ticket," whom he said were "trying to excite the negroes." [68] The assistance Cordill requested arrived from Franklin and Concordia parishes. And nearby Mississippians, hearing that "property" and the "honor of women and children were involved," reacted instinctively and came across the river in numbers, hauling a small cannon with them. But after someone explained that it was "not a niggers' war," the Mississippi volunteers lost interest and returned to Natchez. The New York *Times* archly speculated that their intrusion posed a violation of states' rights.[69] At any rate they were not needed; the reinforcements from the adjoining parishes allowed the Tensas planters to crush the local protest effort before election day. Alfred Fairfax, the "Country People's" Negro leader and their candidate for Congress, was indicted for murder after he shot one of a group of whites that barged into his home.[70]

Violence simultaneously broke out in South Louisiana, but on a lesser scale. The vote count in November, however, indicated a general pattern of fraud across the state. Only in the sugar regions where the white Republicans enjoyed economic power, in a few hill parishes such as Grant and Winn, and in the community of Baton Rouge did the Democrats' opposition make a showing commensurate with their probable true strength. Certain wards in New Orleans seemed relatively free of chicanery, but the Workingman's Party was denied rep-

68 C. C. Cordill to F. T. Nicholls, October 13, 1878, in *Senate Reports,* 45th Cong., 3rd Sess., No. 855, p. xv.

69 New York *Times,* October 18, November 4, 1878. See also, Natchez *Democrat,* quoted in Natchitoches *People's Vindicator,* October 26, 1878. It was reported that the Negroes of Tensas were "much relieved" to hear that this armed band of whites was made up of Mississippians instead of Louisianians.

70 Webb, "A History of Negro Voting in Louisiana," 56–61; St. Joseph *North Louisiana Journal,* April 26, 1879.

resentation at the polls and obtained only one-tenth of its estimated strength. Overall, twenty-six seats in the legislature—less than one-fourth the total—went to assorted "Nationals," Republicans or independents.[71] Among them was a new solon from Plaquemines Parish, Henry Clay Warmoth.

Regular Democrats took all but one congressional seat. It was the Third District, along the Gulf Coast, which prevented a total sweep. Incumbent Representative Joseph H. Acklen, being repudiated by the Democratic hierarchy, ran and won under a vaguely independent label. But Acklen's situation was unusual and had nothing whatever to do with agrarian discontent. A youthful *bon vivant* bachelor, he was accused of having seduced a fifteen-year-old girl connected with the prominent Palfrey family; the girl bore a child and later died. Acklen had gained further notoriety because of a tawdry scene involving a female in a Washington restaurant.[72] Despite everything, the voters of the Third District returned him to Congress.

The largest Democratic majorities in 1878 were reported from several of the primarily Negro northern parishes. Remarking on this, the *Carroll Conservative* insisted that "the colored vote . . . for the Democracy" was cast "with such zealous enthusiasm that the excitement became intense." [73] In Natchitoches, where it was claimed that "election day was spent joyously by white and black," the alleged harmony produced an official vote count of 2,811 to 0 in favor of the Democrats; and J. H. Cosgrove, brimful of bathos, could write that he was "deeply effected [*sic*]" by the scene. Actually, he said,

[71] Uzee, "Republican Politics in Louisiana," 205–207; New Orleans *Daily Picayune*, November 1, 6, 9, 1878; *Report of the Secretary of State*, 1902, pp. 570–72.

[72] New York *Times*, September 29, October 1, 5, 1878.

[73] Lake Providence *Carroll Conservative*, November 23, 1878.

it transported him back to antebellum times; "back to those happy days when we coon hunted with Ike and Steve . . . or were snugly seated in our old loving 'mammy's' lap." [74] This was the kind of "New Departure" which he and other Bourbons could accept; but the Republican variety, said Cosgrove's newspaper, was "clap-trap." [75]

As the awesome returns from previously Republican strongholds poured in, the New Orleans *Democrat* commented that its party's "immense majorities . . . are confusing—almost incomprehensible." [76] Musing over the reported totals, the *Daily Picayune* writer was less perplexed. Since "frauds in Louisiana elections . . . are things of the . . . past," the latter paper solemnly stated, the only logical explanation was that most Negroes had voluntarily abandoned their false friends in the Radical ship. Therefore the 1878 election gave "ample evidence that race antagonism was dying out." [77]

But the bulk of evidence really pointed in another direction. So did common sense. Abundant testimony exists that the great majority of blacks would have supported anything besides the Democratic ticket if allowed the opportunity.[78] Many endured severe hardships, and even death, in attempting to vote against the dominant party. Governor Nicholls, to his credit, expressed dismay at the acts of intimidation and pointedly condemned the white violence in Tensas, saying it was "utterly wrong . . . utterly without justification." [79] Of course some Negroes likely did mark a Democratic ballot of

[74] Natchitoches *People's Vindicator,* November 9, 1878.
[75] *Ibid.,* November 23, 1878.
[76] New Orleans *Democrat,* quoted in Uzee, "Republican Politics in Louisiana," 48.
[77] New Orleans *Daily Picayune,* November 9–10, 1878.
[78] See the mass of testimony concerning the 1878 election in Louisiana in *Senate Reports,* 45th Cong., 3rd Sess., No. 855, *passim.*
[79] New York *Times,* January 8, 1879.

their own free will. As the *North American Review* observed, probably also in Ireland there were a few Catholic peasants who loved their English landlords and cheered for the Tory Party.[80]

[80] Robert Smalls, "Election Methods in the South," *North American Review*, CLI (November, 1890) , 594.

· V

Kansas Fever

A M O N G T H E Negroes of Louisiana, unhappiness with Democratic rule reached an acute phase early in 1879. Simultaneously, an emotional movement known as "the Exodus," or "Kansas Fever," gained hold of the imagination of the black population throughout the lower Mississippi River valley. Some observers even saw in it a modern parallel to the hegira of the Hebrew peoples from ancient Egypt.[1] More than ten thousand Negroes left the state that year and probably five times as many tried, futilely, to depart.[2] Those who did manage to flee were joined by thousands of others from neighboring states.

Talk of some kind of black migration had flickered back and forth for several years. In 1874 Benjamin "Pap" Singleton, a Tennessee Negro, began sending circulars into the Deep South advertising a freedman's colony he envisioned in Kansas. More distant was the journey planned by a group of Shreveport Negroes in 1877, who tried and failed to start a

[1] F. R. Guernsey, "The Negro Exodus," *International Review*, VII (October, 1879) , 379.
[2] This estimate represents an evaluation of Exodus reports from various sources, but particularly from the following newspapers: New Orleans *Daily Picayune*, March 1–December 30, 1879; New Orleans *Weekly Louisianian*, March 15–December 15, 1879; St. Joseph *North Louisiana Journal,* January 18–May 24, 1879; Natchitoches *People's Vindicator*, March 15, 1879–January 31, 1880; Shreveport *Daily Standard*, April 22, 1879–January 4, 1880.

mass emigration to Liberia.[3] There were stories also that local territory might be violently taken over by the race. From Pointe Coupee Parish in 1878 there came disquieting reports of a Negro plot to "kill the leading white men of the region and establish a nation of their own"; as it turned out, however, no whites died and five blacks were lynched.[4] But across Louisiana the rumors of an impending great migration, or some other kind of drastic action, persisted.

The Exodus of 1879 was born of profound despair. Why it burst out at that particular time, and began in Louisiana, is clear enough. Two years had gone by since the final collapse of Reconstruction, and in the interval economic as well as political oppression had become more severe. With "home rule" restored many landlords and merchants—although not all—were avariciously squeezing black sharecroppers and renters with greater impunity, while the intimidation and killing associated with the 1878 election made a ghastly mockery of the previous civil rights pledges by the Nicholls legislature. And countless Negroes believed, as one of their leaders told them, that 1878 was just a foretaste of "the wrongs to come." [5]

By chance the United States Senate played a role in precipitating the Exodus. In January of 1879, members of Senator Henry M. Teller's (R.-Colo.) subcommittee arrived in New Orleans for the purpose of investigating first-hand Louisiana's most recent political misbehavior. The Teller subcommittee set about summoning witnesses from the "bulldozed" parishes; yet probably none of the senators present, most of whom were Republicans, looked upon their work as anything more than a wearisome repeat of similar hearings dur-

---

[3] John G. Van Deusen, "The Exodus of 1879," *Journal of Negro History*, XXI (1936), 119; New York *Times*, June 9, 1877; Shreveport *Herald*, quoted in New Orleans *Daily Picayune*, January 5, 1878.

[4] New Orleans *Democrat*, June 7, 1878.

[5] "Address of G. T. Ruby," in New Orleans *Daily Picayune*, April 22, 1879.

ing Reconstruction. As in the past, scores of rural blacks flocked into the city to unburden their troubles into Northern ears. But this time, knowing the total absence of federal military protection within the state, the Negroes feared that once they testified their trip home might abruptly terminate in the Great Beyond. Already two had been killed on the way down.[6] These disconsolate, uprooted people provided some of the tinder for a flashfire movement which soon swept across the Gulf South and ultimately made itself felt in the Carolinas.

While Teller's investigation commenced in New Orleans another Republican senator, William Windom of Minnesota, spoke in Congress on the possibility of "promoting and encouraging" a migration of maltreated freedmen to western states and territories where they might obtain homestead privileges.[7] Word of Windom's resolution, and exaggerations about it, quickly reached the South where Negroes did not seem to share in the verdict of prominent local whites that the idea was "stupid and idiotic." [8] Thousands of excited plantation laborers in Louisiana and Mississippi, thinking that federal land and supplies awaited their arrival, began selling their meagre belongings for steamboat passage to the North and West. The first band left Madison Parish in February. Days later they debarked at the icy river docks of St. Louis, Missouri, shivering, "dead broke and hungry." [9]

Most of the later throngs of "Exodusters," as they were described, followed the route of the Madison vanguard: northward by boat to St. Louis and from there, if funds allowed, by

6 New Orleans *Times,* January 20, 1879; New Orleans *Daily Picayune,* quoted in New York *Times,* December 22, 1878.

7 *Congressional Record,* 45th Cong., 3rd Sess., 483.

8 New Orleans *Weekly Louisianian,* March 15, 1879; New Orleans *Daily Picayune,* March 17, 1879. See also, *Nation,* XXVIII (April 10, 1879) , 240.

9 St. Louis *Post-Dispatch,* March 18–19, 1879. See also, Vidalia *Concordia Eagle,* March 27, 1879; Opelousas *Courier,* May 31, 1879.

rail to the plains.[10] The majority pictured Kansas as their new home. This choice of destination may have been partly inspired by "Pap" Singleton's earlier activities, but more important was the special connotation which the Sunflower State held for Southern Negroes. "Kansas," said one Exodus promoter, "with her freedom and broad prairies, with the memories of John Brown and his heroic struggle, seems naturally the State to seek." [11] By the end of March, cotton planters along the river were estimating, with rising alarm, that "at least 5,000" of their workers had fled and more were making preparations to leave.[12]

Of all the interwoven causes of "Kansas Fever" probably economic frustration was the most basic. The great mass of rural blacks found their lives little improved, materially, from the bleak conditions of 1865. As one succinctly put it: "We've been working for fourteen long years, and we ain't no better off than we was when we commenced." [13] In parishes where their numbers were greatest, not one Negro family out of twenty owned land—in Madison, not one out of fifty.[14]

The presumption that Negroes were unambitiously content with sharecropping and chronic debt was firmly denied by their spokesmen. According to P. B. S. Pinchback, "the most potent cause" of the 1879 Exodus was frustration of the blacks' hopes to own land. "They are unwilling to be peons." [15] He and others likewise believed that planters and merchants were reaping wealth from a systematic cheating of defense-

10 *Nation*, XXVIII (April 10, 1879) , 242.
11 "The Great Negro Exodus," *Harper's Weekly*, XXIII (May 17, 1879) , 386; New Orleans *Daily Picayune*, April 22, 1879.
12 New Orleans *Daily Picayune*, March 27, 1879; St. Joseph *North Louisiana Journal*, April 12, 26, 1879.
13 Quoted in Earl Howard Aiken, "Kansas Fever" (M.A. thesis, Louisiana State University, 1939) , 5.
14 Letter from "Nota Bena," in New Orleans *Daily Picayune*, July 17, 1881; Baton Rouge *Daily Capitolian-Advocate*, March 28, 1882.
15 New Orleans *Weekly Louisianian*, June 21, 1879.

less clients. Assuredly, those who did greatly prosper were apt, in the words of one white farmer, to demonstrate a personality somewhere "between a fox and a hog." [16] Yet the majority of planters and merchants were not as wealthy, and probably not as venal, as some critics assumed. For they in turn paid staggering interest rates and charges to New Orleans wholesale houses and factors. And from there much of the profit went to New York or other Northern banking centers.

Nevertheless, there is no denying the fact that landless Negroes bore the heaviest burden of economic injustice and were in many instances swindled or otherwise mistreated by their creditors and employers. The onset of Kansas Fever prompted an admission to this effect from one planter newspaper. The *Carroll Conservative* declared that local landowners had been guilty of "worse than folly" in abusing their laborers, and were now paying the penalty.[17] Certain purblind Bourbons, however, continued to insist that the croppers were "well and humanely treated" and had no just cause for departure. With special rancor did the *People's Vindicator* dismiss Negro protests as "miserable twaddle" and call for "the rope and the nearest lamp post" for any agitators who promoted the Exodus.[18] The *Daily Picayune,* searching as it did on most occasions for forces outside the state to blame, saw the migration as nothing more than a Radical plot to lure the blacks North in order to augment Republican voting strength.[19]

Concerned sugar planters in South Louisiana kept a watchful eye for signs of Kansas Fever among their workers. Dur-

[16] Letter from Hiram Hawkins, in Baton Rouge *Daily Advocate,* April 9, 1893.

[17] Lake Providence *Carroll Conservative,* February 1, 1879.

[18] Natchitoches *People's Vindicator,* April 5, June 7, 1879.

[19] New Orleans *Daily Picayune,* April 17, 1879. Since Kansas was already a solidly Republican state, the *Picayune's* suspicions were groundless.

ing the summer of 1879 it came, although not with the same impact as in the cotton parishes. Living conditions for Negroes in the cane fields were scarcely idyllic, but as wage earners rather than sharecroppers they appeared "more satisfied." [20] Mounting unrest, on the other hand, was reported among the many sugar workers whose "wages" were paid in script redeemable only in outrageously priced goods at plantation stores. A Negro in St. John the Baptist Parish complained, as did laborers in the cotton fields upriver, that "I begin de year wid nothin' and end wid nothin.' " [21]

The sugar parishes at least enjoyed a relative freedom from political intimidation. Many plantations there had fallen into white Republican hands during Reconstruction; moreover, those sugar growers who were nominally Democrats, being equally desirous of federal protection against foreign sugar, were at odds with their party's traditional low tariff position. Frequently then did Negro field hands in South Louisiana discover themselves to be in political accord with their employers. And the local prestige of the Republican planters gave blacks in the sugar districts a measure of protection from Democratic "bulldozing." But economic issues were another matter. Republican growers ordinarily paid the same low wages as did Democrats; the mighty Sugar Planters' Association looked after the interests of landowners of both parties, and almost no planter, regardless of how he voted, would tolerate unionism or strike activity among his workers.[22]

20 Opelousas *Courier,* June 14, 1879; New Orleans *Daily Picayune,* April 28, 1877, June 15, 1879.

21 Covington Hall, "Labor Struggles in the Deep South" (MS, undated, in Tulane University Library), 30–31. The Negro laborer of St. John quoted in New Orleans *Daily Picayune,* March 29, 1880.

22 Uzee, "Republican Politics in Louisiana," 147–49; Thibodaux *Sentinel,* November 26, 1887; Jeanerette *Teche Pilot,* May 5, 1888.

An action by the government of Louisiana early in 1879 unwittingly served to intensify Negro unrest in every portion of the state. The legislature, bending to the will of Bourbon and Lottery interests, scheduled a constitutional convention for the month of April. Influential whites had long demanded an overturn, or at least a modification, of the Radical organic law of 1868. Many conservatives who were neither outright Bourbons nor Lottery men joined in the clamor. The *Daily Picayune's* editor, for example, wrote of the burning need for a new constitution which, unlike the old one, would be written by "the real people." [23]

Immediately, Negro leaders voiced apprehensions that "the real people" were planning to further eviscerate Negro civil rights. Meanwhile among the illiterate rural blacks, there swept rumors that the upcoming convention would reduce them to the level of antebellum slavery.[24] These new fears, piling on top of economic frustration and the latest political violence, produced the desperation known as Kansas Fever.

On April 18, 1879, while the newly-elected delegates to the state constitutional convention—98 of 134 of them were Democrats—were arriving in New Orleans, a less formal assembly crowded through the doors of the Free Mission Baptist Church on Common Street. This self-styled "Exodus Convention" had been organized by George T. Ruby, T. Morris Chester, the Reverend Emperor Williams and other black activists. Many in attendance were frightened country blacks who had recently testified before the Teller subcommittee. Ruby, who edited the militant New Orleans *Observer*, dominated the gathering. He insisted that the Exodus was not to any

23 New Orleans *Daily Picayune,* November 9, 1877.

24 New Orleans *Observer,* quoted in New York *Times,* March 11, 1879; New Orleans *Weekly Louisianian,* March 15, 1879; New Orleans *Daily Picayune,* March 27, 1879.

degree controlled by Republican politicians; on the contrary, he attributed the growth and potency of the movement to the fact that party leaders had nothing to do with it.[25]

According to Ruby the roots of the Exodus could be traced back to the activities of a Negro from Caddo Parish named Henry Adams. Adams had been a wandering apostle of black migration since about 1870. An ex-slave, but a Union veteran, he was considered the founder of the "Committee"—at first it possessed no other name—which in 1874 was redesignated as the "Colonization Council" and three years later tried unsuccessfully to initiate an exodus to Liberia. Adams' organization, working in secret out of Shreveport, was said to have sent agents into the plantation districts of various states and now, if the claims of Adams and Ruby were to be believed, this association had swollen to a membership of 92,800—two-thirds of which lived in Louisiana, the rest in Mississippi, Texas, Arkansas and Alabama.[26]

Adams, giving testimony later to a United States Senate committee, said that his real efforts began with the establishment of the Colonization Council in 1874. "After the White League sprung up," Adams related, "we then organized." But their supplications to the President and Congress for a separate Negro "territory in the United States" and then for "an appropriation of money to ship us all to Liberia" went unanswered and very possibly unread. The attempted migration to Kansas represented a last desperate hope. Adams indicated that from the beginning his Council deliberately shunned all local Republican leaders, black or white. "No politicianers didn't belong to it," he stated, nor were they allowed to "know nothing about it . . . we didn't trust any of

25 New York *Times,* April 20, 1879; New Orleans *Daily Picayune,* April 19, 22, 1879.
26 *Senate Reports,* 46th Cong., 2nd Sess., No. 693, Pt. 2, p. 39.

them." [27] Yet, apparently the Windom Resolution, weakly worded though it was, had rekindled Southern Negroes' faith in the national government. Many believed that the power which had once emancipated them would provide land and necessary equipment in Kansas. The dream of "forty acres and a mule" died hard.

Certainly Adams and Ruby exaggerated the number of blacks who were formally enrolled in the Colonization Council. It served their purpose to do so. Kansas Fever, when it happened, looked more spontaneous than planned. But proof that such an association did exist, and had for several years, was at hand; neither is there reason to question a modern opinion that the Exodus of 1879 deserves recognition as one of the most genuine grass-roots upheavals in American history. [28]

That the movement originated among Negroes in the Shreveport area is not surprising. Few if any places held a sorrier record in race relations. "White supremacy, first, last and all the time, has always been the motto of the white people . . . of Caddo," a city journal once proudly remarked; "and they prove their faith by their works." [29] There, during and after Reconstruction, the terroristic spirit displayed itself in ways both great and small. In the year of the Exodus a white baseball team unashamedly adopted the name of "Caddo Bulldozers." [30]

The Exodus lacked proper organization. This much was admitted by the *Observer's* editor at the April convention in New Orleans. Ruby suggested that future emigrant parties should send out advance men to Kansas to search for the best

[27] *Ibid.*, 101–11.
[28] Leslie H. Fischel, Jr. and Benjamin Quarles (eds.) , *The Negro American: A Documentary History* (Glenview, Ill., 1967) , 289.
[29] Shreveport *Evening Judge,* February 24, 1896.
[30] New Orleans *Daily Picayune,* May 29, 1879.

possible homestead locations. "Meanwhile," he said, "we advise an abandonment by the colored people of all the turbulent bulldozed [cotton] parishes of this State." He quickly added that in the sugar lands of South Louisiana "life and personal property are comparatively secure," and that the wage system which prevailed there would give Negroes a better opportunity to accumulate funds for the long Western journey.[31] His proposals had obvious merit. But there was a trace of suspicion that Ruby and some of his associates were in the pay of sugar planters who wished to amass a bigger labor surplus in their region. A convention of cotton growers, meeting at Vicksburg in May, evidently thought the sugar barons had something to do with the Exodus excitement.[32]

Negro politicians almost to a man opposed the Exodus, and several attempted to break up the convention at the Free Mission Church on Common Street. State Senator David Young's negative speech to the assembly almost caused a riot. He was hooted down as a "bloated capitalist." [33] P. B. S. Pinchback and James Kennedy of the *Weekly Louisianian* insisted that Negro grievances, however great, did not warrant a mass migration. Pinchback's newspaper scorned Kansas Fever as "a wild goose chase" and blamed it on "the influence of an illiterate and misguided clergy." [34] Even Alfred Fairfax, who approved of the movement and who presided over the state Negro Baptist Association, conceded that there were too many unworthy black preachers involved in the Exodus. Fairfax noted that a single publishing shop in Iberville Parish had within the last month printed and sold over five hundred "licenses" to preach.[35]

---

31 *Ibid.*, April 22, 1879.
32 *Ibid.*, May 3, 1879.
33 New York *Times*, April 20, 1879.
34 New Orleans *Weekly Louisianian*, March 29, April 26, 1879.
35 New Orleans *Daily Picayune*, April 19, 1879.

Frederick Douglass, one of America's most respected black men, sent from the North words of caution to New Orleans. His message, read by Senator Young, asked that the Exodus agitation cease "because it is an untimely concession to the idea that colored people and white people cannot live together in peace and prosperity." But the gathering at Free Mission Church was less than impressed. Someone in the crowd perspicaciously inquired "why Fred Douglass had left the South, where he now advises his race to stay?" [36] If any attempt was made to answer that question, it was not recorded.

The New Orleans Exodus gathering served to publicize the movement but accomplished little else. Money was supposed to have been raised for organizational purposes but the finance committee reported a pitiful total collection of $11.05. On the last day the assembly dutifully heard an address by one Mr. Turcke, a German-born agent for something called the Honduras Immigration Society. Presumably Turcke praised the virtues of sunny Honduras over the shortcomings of snowy Kansas, but his speech was delivered in such a confused mixture of Teutonic and Spanish accents that his listeners were unable to ascertain what it was all about.[37]

Kansas Fever reached its peak in North Louisiana and in Mississippi during April. Muddy river roads in the cotton parishes were then crowded with rickety sharecropper wagons. Observers reported about three thousand Negroes standing or sitting on the levee between the towns of Vidalia and St. Joseph, awaiting transportation North. Those unable to pay for steamboat tickets were said to be striking out on foot for "somewhar." [38] Some Mississippi River boats summarily

36 New Orleans *Weekly Louisianian,* May 10, 1879; New Orleans *Daily Picayune,* April 19, 1879.

37 New Orleans *Daily Picayune,* April 22, 1879.

38 Aiken, "Kansas Fever," 10; New Orleans *Daily Picayune,* April 27, 1879; St. Joseph *North Louisiana Journal,* April 26, 1879.

raised their passenger fares and a few captains, under pressure from the planters, declined accommodations to all Negroes.[39] Black laborers had also gathered in smaller numbers along Red River landings, but leading ship companies there publicly announced that any emigrants "must walk, as [we] don't intend to transport a single one of them." [40]

Since the Civil War many Louisiana planters had incessantly complained about the general worthlessness of Negro labor. This topic seemed to rank alongside politics and the weather as a favorite subject of genteel conversation. Nonetheless, the landowners' conduct during the crisis of Kansas Fever indicated that black agriculturists were not so despised after all. The day of mechanized agriculture was still in the future, and until that distant time the cotton and sugar fields would need labor in abundance. Only those whites whose prosperity did not directly depend upon the Negro could agree with the Opelousas *Courier* that the state should willingly "let them go." [41] Even so extreme a Negrophobe as J. H. Cosgrove, who looked forward to the eventual migration of the black race from Louisiana, strongly objected to the Exodus of 1879 because it was too "sudden." [42]

A few whites proposed that Chinese coolies might fill any vacuum created by departing Negroes; the *North Louisiana Journal* believed that yellow people would be more "patient and reliable" laborers than the blacks and were less apt to become excited over politics.[43] Others hoped for and actively sought cheap European workers although there was considerable sentiment against adding new complexities into Lou-

39 *Harper's Weekly*, XXIII (May 17, 1879), 386; Guernsey, *International Review*, VII, 378.

40 Natchitoches *People's Vindicator*, quoted in New Orleans *Daily Picayune*, April 15, 1879.

41 Opelousas *Courier*, June 14, 1879.

42 Natchitoches *People's Vindicator*, August 23, 1879.

43 St. Joseph *North Louisiana Journal*, April 12, 1879.

isiana's ethnic *potpourri*. As a Baton Rouge writer quaintly understated it: "Already we have a heterogeneous mass that makes it difficult to work all of the material into one beauteous, harmonious structure." [44] The Chinese idea was almost unanimously rejected. In 1880 the state legislature resolved "that the needs of . . . Louisiana don't require Mongolian immigration at this time." [45]

Most planters in 1879 were wholly absorbed in discouraging their black labor from going, rather than in inducing foreigners to come. "What are our lands worth without labor?" wrote anguished T. L. Van Fossen of East Carroll Parish. "Would we not be senseless idiots to drive away our sole dependence?" [46] A St. Joseph publisher asked his readers to "let no means remain untried" in halting the flight of Negro workers.[47] In Bastrop these means included a determination to pour "a coat of tar and feathers" on anyone advising the blacks to emigrate.[48] At least one planter-merchant, Abe Cohen of Hard Times community in Tensas Parish, followed his "old hands" all the way to Kansas and importuned some of them to return. Cohen, in a not original remark, expressed confidence that the Negroes would begin "to see that their old masters are their best friends." [49]

Horror stories born of fertile minds were sent circulating among the Negroes. Planters unable to dream up their own rumors could quote the columns of local newspapers: St. Louis was a pesthole of smallpox and pneumonia; evil Kansas Yankees threatened to shoot arriving "Exodusters"; even

44 Baton Rouge *Weekly Advocate,* April 15, 1881.

45 New Orleans *Daily Picayune,* March 18, 1880.

46 Letter from T. L. Van Fossen, in St. Louis *Republican,* quoted in New Orleans *Daily Picayune,* April 12, 1879.

47 St. Joseph *North Louisiana Journal,* April 12, 1879.

48 Bastrop *Morehouse Clarion,* quoted in New Orleans *Daily Picayune,* May 2, 1879.

49 New Orleans *Daily Picayune,* May 16, 1879.

the less murderous towns in the Sunflower State refused to permit "any more of Uncle Abe's misguided children" inside corporation limits.[50] Alaska's frigid climate, it seemed, held no worse terrors than the "wailing winds and drifted snowbanks" of the "barren wastes of Kansas." [51] Of all canards, however, doubtless the most imaginative was that Jefferson Davis, with ten thousand armed Confederate veterans and four gunboats, had seized control of the Mississippi at Memphis for the purpose of compelling "back into slavery every darkey who tried to go upriver." [52]

In May of 1879, Kansas Fever began to subside in North Louisiana. The turning point came in Concordia. Virtually the entire black population of that parish—numbering 13,500 as compared with only 1,200 whites—had been reported as preparing to leave.[53] The man chiefly responsible for dissuading them was a Negro, Senator David Young. Among his own constituents he showed greater influence than at the recent Exodus assembly in New Orleans. Young, unlike many officeseekers of his race in the cotton parishes, enjoyed an immunity from Democratic frauds at election time. He also represented the parish at the constitutional convention then meeting in the capital. For no white Bourbon could have been as effective an instrument of planter interests, and at this critical moment his services were particularly in demand.

Young, praised by the *Ouachita Telegraph* as a sterling example of the obsequious "old-time darkey the white people

---

[50] Opelousas *Courier,* May 31, 1879; St. Joseph *North Louisiana Journal,* March 22, April 12, 1879; Lake Providence *Carroll Conservative,* quoted in *ibid.,* May 10, 1879.

[51] Shreveport *Daily Standard,* January 4, 1880; Natchitoches *People's Vindicator,* April 5, 1879.

[52] Aiken, "Kansas Fever," 25.

[53] New Orleans *Daily Picayune,* April 27, 1879; New Orleans *Weekly Louisianian,* May 24, 1879.

all loved," [54] had stolen several thousand dollars of public school funds during Reconstruction.[55] Admiration for him was not universal. But in 1879 the *Daily Picayune* ceased calling him hard names and used the appellation "Mr. Young." [56] Leaving his seat at the constitutional convention, Young hastened upriver to the levee near Vidalia and, by all available accounts, stemmed the Exodus tide with his oratory. On returning to New Orleans he exclaimed: "I never felt prouder in my life!" [57] Later, after the Negro Senator's usefulness had ended, the Democratic legislature expelled him and after his reelection, expelled him again.[58]

Not all the measures which cotton planters used to slow the Exodus were disgraceful. Some had always endeavored to treat their workers fairly, and now others, prodded by events, grudgingly followed suit. Many Negro sharecroppers and renters who agreed to remain were offered an equitable adjustment of their contracts; in Concordia and elsewhere all previous debts at plantation stores were wiped off the ledgers. And a political concession of a sort was forthcoming. In July the Democratic majority in the constitutional convention, with Republican help, defeated an ultra-Bourbon attempt to impose poll tax restrictions on manhood suffrage.[59] Of that, more is to be said presently.

Kansas Fever no longer assumed epidemic proportions anywhere in the state. Nevertheless, even as it faded in the

54 Monroe *Ouachita Telegraph,* quoted in Williamson and Goodman (eds.) , *Eastern Louisiana,* I, 172.

55 *Annual Report of the State Superintendent of Public Education,* 1875, p. 366; New Orleans *Daily Picayune,* October 28, 1877.

56 New Orleans *Daily Picayune,* May 3, 1879.

57 New Orleans *Weekly Louisianian,* May 24, 1879.

58 *House Journal,* 1880, pp. 77–79, 88–89; Baton Rouge *Daily Capitolian-Advocate,* May 10, June 15, 1882.

59 New Orleans *Daily Picayune,* May 3, 1879; New Orleans *Times,* July 16, 1879; New Orleans *Weekly Louisianian,* July 26, 1879.

northern parishes, it spread in weakened form southward toward the sugar fields.[60] By now Texas, Alabama and the South Atlantic states were to some degree affected. The majority of ragged migrants, however, came out of Louisiana and Mississippi. Estimates vary, but in the South as a whole perhaps 200,000 Negroes made an effort to depart for Kansas or, as an alternative, Iowa or Minnesota. For one reason or another most did not succeed in leaving. How many actually reached the Sunflower State is uncertain, because some did not stay long enough to be counted. Forty thousand were reported there at the end of 1879.[61]

Although better than the howling Siberia depicted by Louisiana's press, Kansas did not prove to be the Negroes' promised land. Free federal homesteads were, as in the South, available in the less desirable areas. But the great obstacle, as elsewhere, lay in the fact that a minimum of about $700 worth of supplies and equipment would be essential to begin homesteading.[62] Most "Exodusters" arrived on the plains penniless. The anticipated government aid never came and paying jobs were scarce.

Blacks who had made the journey from the Deep South encountered, at the end, little overt brutality but also little sympathy. Comments from whites in the plains region were often revealing; notably, the Le Mars (Iowa) *Sentinel* stated that "if there was only an ounce of [grit] to a ton of nigger, he would remain right in Louisiana or old Mississippi, and maintain those rights with which the Republican party invested him, or die in his tracks." [63] On reading the above, a Loui-

---

[60] Opelousas *Courier*, June 14, 21, 1879; New Orleans *Democrat*, July 15, 1879.

[61] Francis Butler Simkins, *A History of the South* (New York, 1956), 515; Fortier (ed.), *Louisiana*, I, 400–401.

[62] New York *Sun*, quoted in Covington *St. Tammany Farmer*, July 26, 1879.

[63] Le Mars (Iowa) *Sentinel*, quoted in New Orleans *Weekly Louisianian*, August 2, 1879.

siana Negro could not help but observe that Northern whites had been willing to shed copious tears over the wrongs done freedmen in the South, but "when we dare to leave this section . . . we are then only 'niggers'—and nothing more." [64]

Amid the Exodus disturbance a new state constitution was written and, on the date of its ratification, a new governor elected. The Constitution of 1868 gave way to that of 1879, while the office held by Francis T. Nicholls was won by Louis A. Wiltz. Thus simultaneously vanished from state government both Radical law and patrician conservatism.

Together, Bourbon reactionaries and Lottery men wrote the Constitution of 1879. Yet events at the convention revealed some differences within the coalition and indicated also that the opinions of rank-and-file whites could not at present be altogether ignored. The more extreme Bourbons' proposal to limit manhood suffrage was voted down. A grim warning may have influenced that decision. To the Shreveport delegate who wished to disfranchise all the "blind, ignorant" masses, a more cautious conservative replied that such an action might intensify Kansas Fever and—far worse—engender an alliance "between the poor white and colored people, which would inaugurate a reign of communism and secret societies, attended by labor strikes." [65] None of the delegates spoke openly of the uses which conservatives had made and might make of a large manipulated Negro vote. But some present may have pondered the matter.

Conservative bondholders were thwarted in their attempt to have the new constitution retain the high 7 per cent interest rate on state debts. Most of the bonded debt, a legacy of Reconstruction, was considered either fraudulent or, at best, questionable. Nonetheless, some delegates argued that the dubious origin of the bonds was irrelevant; it was the credit

64 New Orleans *Weekly Louisianian,* August 2, 1879..
65 New Orleans *Daily Picayune,* July 10–11, 1879.

and honor of Louisiana—her "fair fame and name" said Donelson Caffery—which should be considered.[66] Wealthy resident Democrats as well as foreign capitalists now possessed these bonds; New Orleans businessmen joined English investors in fervid appeals to the constitutional convention. Popular opposition to the previously high interest was so great, however, that the rate was scaled down to 4 percent.[67]

Democratic delegates from the poorer rural areas were no less disappointed than the bondholders over the state's revised indebtedness, but for quite another reason; many white farmers had hoped to see a repudiation of most of the principal. The chief spokesman of this agrarian faction, Captain E. E. Kidd of Jackson Parish, threw a momentary fright into urban businessmen with his sarcastic comments on the nature of the bonded debt.[68] But conservative Democrats, with the unanimous support of the minority of Republican delegates, managed to defeat Kidd's move for sweeping repudiation. Instead, the principal was slightly lowered.[69] What the New Orleans *Times* had described as "the communistic spirit" of the pine hills thus won only a partial victory.[70]

Except for the suffrage and bond questions the Constitution of 1879, as a recent analysis by the State Law Institute pointed out, "fully . . . reflected the demands of diverse, powerful, and articulate pressure groups." [71] Louisiana's property tax was reduced to a paltry six mills on the dollar. Parish and

[66] New Orleans *Catholic Messenger,* quoted in Opelousas *Courier,* June 21, 1879.

[67] London *Times,* June 10, 1879; New Orleans *Times,* July 11, 27, 1879; *Constitution of 1879,* Art. 233; McGinty, *Louisiana Redeemed,* 164.

[68] New Orleans *Daily Picayune,* June 6, 9, July 4, 1879; *Congressional Record,* 47th Cong., Special Sess., 145.

[69] Uzee, "Republican Politics in Louisiana," 63; New Orleans *Weekly Louisianian,* August 2, 1879; New Orleans *Daily Picayune* July 2, 1879.

[70] New Orleans *Times,* quoted in Woodward, *Origins of the New South,* 91.

[71] *Project of a Constitution for the State of Louisiana: With Notes and Studies* (Baton Rouge, 1954), I, 418.

local taxes could not exceed ten mills unless resident prop-
ertyholders voted for a higher amount; but the list of projects
for which such an increase might be considered was limited.[72]
All but the tiniest manufacturing establishments were to be
absolutely exempt from taxation for a period of ten years,
and this immunity, as it turned out, would be extended by a
constitutional amendment for another full decade.[73]

Another article in the new constitution, building on a device of carpetbagger inspiration, strengthened the already considerable powers of the office of governor. In a related move,
so many new restrictions were placed upon the legislature's
scope of action that its functions became, as one contemporary
writer stated it, "almost mechanical." [74] Symbolically perhaps, and certainly for geographic reasons, the seat of state
government was moved from New Orleans back to its antebellum location in Baton Rouge. This transfer was completed
in 1882. Whereupon Negro legislators who had previously
been served in the white saloons and restaurants of New Orleans would discover, to their dismay, that upriver in Baton
Rouge the custom of segregation made no exceptions.[75]

The increase in gubernatorial power and the corresponding diminution of legislative and local authority was politically the most significant work of the 1879 constitutional convention. Bourbon and Lottery interests became the prime
beneficiaries. Their task was now simpler: they might never
be able to control all minor officeholders, but domination
over the state as a whole would be assured if the proper sort

---

[72] *Constitution of 1879*, Art. 209.

[73] *Ibid.*, Art. 207; Baton Rouge *Daily Capitolian-Advocate*, May 12, 1888.

[74] *Constitution of 1879*, Arts. 68–75; *Project of a Constitution*, I, 400; *Bio-graphical and Historical Memoirs of Louisiana*, I, 46.

[75] Fortier, *Louisiana*, I, 158–59. On the rigid segregation practiced in Baton Rouge in the 1880's, as contrasted with the more lenient situation in New Orleans, see the complaint of Negro legislator T. T. Allain as reported in Baton Rouge *Daily Capitolian-Advocate*, May 19, 1882.

of man obtained the Democratic nomination for the governorship. Henceforward that nomination, arranged at state party conventions, meant a virtually certain victory over any Republican or agrarian opponent.

Clearly, Governor Nicholls was not the man desired by either the Bourbons or the Lottery. Through some adroit work on the part of Burke and Wiltz during the closing days of the convention, provision was made for a new state election in December of 1879, coinciding with the date on which voters were to ratify or reject the constitution.[76] Nicholls' term of office was thereby shortened by one year. The governor might legally succeed himself, but in this instance he stood no chance of becoming his party's nominee. Nicholls, weary and claiming ill health, left for an extended vacation in Virginia.[77] His followers in the country parishes reacted with anger at the turn of events, particularly when one of the men responsible for it all, Wiltz, sought and won the Democratic gubernatorial nomination in September.[78]

Also cut short were the terms of all other state officials and legislators, with one exception. State Treasurer Burke, the constitution provided, was to remain at that post "as if elected . . . in December, 1879." [79] Instead of being abbreviated his term was actually lengthened; he would not have to face the voters again until 1884. Burke's friend J. H. Cosgrove, who had been awarded the printing contract for the constitutional convention, brazenly explained that "it was done for the good and sufficient reason that Major Burke had been so loyal and true to Louisiana's interests and people as to beggar himself," and presumably Burke could not afford the cost of another

76 *Constitution of 1879*, Art. 262.

77 New Orleans *Times*, July 24, 1879; Natchitoches *People's Vindicator*, August 16, 1879.

78 Plaquemine *Iberville South*, August 2, 1879; Colfax *Chronicle*, August 2, 1879; Natchitoches *People's Vindicator*, September 13, 27, October 25, 1879.

79 *Constitution of 1879*, Art. 264.

campaign.[80] Moreover, said Cosgrove, it is "to him, more than to any single man," that "we owe our present happy condition." [81] Yet even a few Bourbons were repulsed by the egregiousness of the Burke-Wiltz arrangement. "Shall the people submit to this?" the *Ouachita Telegraph* wanted to know. "If so," it opined, "Louisiana should bear, without a murmur, the evils of every vial of wrath that may be emptied upon her!" [82]

Prior to the constitutional convention the state legislature, in a rare moment of reform, had voted to repeal the charter of the mighty Louisiana Lottery Company. Governor Nicholls at first vacillated but signed the repeal bill in March of 1879.[83] The Lottery, with which State Treasurer Burke was closely associated, then looked for its salvation to the upcoming convention. It could count on the support of all the Republican delegates even though it had helped finance the conservative restoration to power in 1877.[84] More vital to the Lottery's future was the backing of those among the majority of Democratic delegates who were allied with Burke and Wiltz.

The Lottery question consumed eight bitter days of debate at the convention. Delegate William Robertson of St. Landry Parish, the pro-Lottery Democrats' floor leader, drew up a proposed article designed to give the gambling company a constitutional charter of twenty-five years duration; one which would not expire until January of 1894. In return the Lottery, as it had in the past, was to pay the state $40,000 per year. As a sop to public opinion its friends did not seek to restore its

80 Natchitoches *People's Vindicator,* September 13, 1879.

81 *Ibid.,* August 16, 1879.

82 Monroe *Ouachita Telegraph,* quoted in *ibid.,* September 13, 1879. See also, Colfax *Chronicle,* August 2, 1879.

83 New Orleans *Democrat,* March 28, 1879; McGinty, *Louisiana Redeemed,* 190.

84 Alwes, *Louisiana Historical Quarterly,* XXVII, 996–98; New Orleans *Daily Picayune,* July 9, 1879.

previous monopoly status. Theoretically, under Robertson's proposal, future legislative sessions might charter all the lotteries they pleased. But the Louisiana Lottery Company would be the only one specifically named in the constitution.[85]

Most vehemently against the Lottery were those Democratic delegates from upland Baptist constituencies. The Catholic parishes as a rule demonstrated a more permissive attitude toward gambling; but even there this particular company had numerous critics. Both sides in the dispute seemed to agree that there was considerable public opposition to the Lottery. Robertson, however, ingeniously suggested that the hostility had been directed mainly against its old monopoly privileges.[86] In the end a majority of delegates voted for the company and, in Article 167, it obtained the desired constitutional recognition. Absurdly, a subsequent article read: "Gambling is declared to be a vice, and the General Assembly shall enact laws for its suppression." [87]

On December 3, 1879, election-satiated Louisianians went to the polls for the third time in thirteen months. Ratification of the new constitution was a foregone conclusion, and interest in the state and local races appeared at a low ebb. Nor did the Democratic or the Republican candidate for the governorship give either the white or black public much cause for enthusiasm. "Never," wrote one Democrat, "has there been such a coldness and apathy among the people; an utter indifference. . . . The people do not know where to look for relief." [88]

Wiltz was a New Orleans banker and a Catholic. These

85 White, "The History of the Louisiana Lottery," 38–41; New Orleans *Daily Picayune,* July 3–10, 1879.

86 New Orleans *Daily Picayune,* July 3, 1879.

87 *Constitution of 1879,* Arts. 167, 172.

88 Letter from "Democrat," in New Orleans *Daily Picayune,* November 14, 1879.

things counted against him in North Louisiana, while Nicholls men everywhere were in an unhappy mood. And Wiltz's pompous Republican opponent offered little contrast. One Custom House official was quoted as saying that "our party is billed for a funeral; and we thought it well to provide as respectable a corpse as possible." [89] The political cadaver referred to was Judge Taylor Beattie. A large and quite conservative sugar planter, Beattie happened to be an ex-slaveholder, an ex-Confederate, and an ex-member of the Knights of the White Camelia. His plantation in Lafourche Parish was named "Dixie." [90] Negro voters were said to be "disgusted" at Beattie's campaign and some reportedly preferred Wiltz.[91]

The returns gave Wiltz a 74,098 to 42,555 victory over Beattie, and the constitution was ratified by a similarly wide margin. Although it had not been vital to the outcome, Democratic commissioners in several plantation parishes sent in grossly inflated returns.[92] The Negro *Weekly Louisianian* suggested that as far as state politics was concerned, black people might as well be living in Russia and trying to vote against the Czar. Pinchback's newspaper, which earlier fought the Exodus movement, reversed its opinion after the 1879 election and announced that "there is no longer room to hope" that the White League spirit might fade away. It now advised "bulldozed" Negroes to adopt the slogan: "On to Kansas or any-

89 New Orleans *Evening Item,* quoted in Natchitoches *People's Vindicator,* November 1, 1879.

90 *Nation,* XXIX (October 30, 1879) , 284; New York *Times,* November 17, 1879; New Orleans *Daily Picayune,* November 29, 1879; Rightor, *Standard History of New Orleans,* 697.

91 W. E. Horne to Rutherford B. Hayes, November 10, 1879, in Hayes Papers; J. R. G. Pitkin to John Tyler, Jr., August 15, 1879, *ibid.*

92 Uzee, "Republican Politics in Louisiana," 72; *Report of the Secretary of State,* 1902, p. 561; New Orleans *Leader,* quoted in Bastrop *Morehouse Clarion,* January 16, 1880.

where else." [93] And migration fever, thought never quite as serious as in 1879, would flare up again in 1880 and continue sporadically during the next decade.[94]

[93] New Orleans *Weekly Louisianian,* December 6, 1879. See also, Aiken, "Kansas Fever," 37.

[94] Shreveport *Daily Standard,* January 4, 1880; Bastrop *Morehouse Clarion,* January 22, 1881; New Orleans *Weekly Pelican,* November 26, 1887.

VI

Bourbon Democracy

T H E C O U R T L Y old Creole historian Charles Gayarré told a Northern reporter in 1873 that Reconstruction had engendered such misery, and fear of "negro government" was so widespread, that Louisiana's white population stood ready to embrace any change in authority and submit, Gayarré said, to "any other species of despotism." [1] So it was that Bourbon misrule followed, after a short interval, Radical misrule. With Wiltz's inauguration in 1880 the road led rapidly downward and into measurably darkening shadows.

Forged by the Bourbon-Lottery alliance, the Constitution of 1879 served as the anchor of a regime remarkably powerful, backward, and corrupt. Throughout the 1880's and 1890's the state's political elite proclaimed the social stagnation around them to be the only alternative to turbulence, and raised storm warnings against every gentle wind of change.[2] Only in respect to industrialization did they show anything resembling a progressive spirit, but even then they appeared more solicitous about the prosperity of investors than about the welfare of Louisiana.

[1] Edward King, "Louisiana," *Scribner's Monthly*, VII (November, 1873), 13.

[2] For the last two decades of the nineteenth century, the files of the Baton Rouge *Daily Capitolian-Advocate* (shortened to *Daily Advocate* in 1890) provide abundant examples of the thinking of Louisiana's ruling class. As the official journal of the state government, it consistently mirrored the views of those in power.

The state's reputation was already such that one nationally esteemed writer in 1880 insinuated that Louisiana formed a moral cancer within the Union. Godkin of the *Nation* believed that the wild unscrupulousness of politics in Louisiana had directly inspired similar evils in other parts of the country.[3] Nevertheless, and perhaps fortunately for all concerned, America during the 1880's began to pay less attention than previously to unseemly happenings in the Pelican State. If Godkin's analysis were correct, then the diminution of publicity on the subject was to the national good. But inside the state there would be little concomitant easing of trouble.

It was Major Burke, the state treasurer, who emerged as Louisiana's strong man during the 1880's. Governor Wiltz suffered from acute tuberculosis. He failed to respond to treatment and died less than two years after his inauguration. Henceforth, Burke's new partner, the state's chief executive, was the man who had served Wiltz as lieutenant governor, Samuel D. McEnery of Monroe.

From October of 1881 until May of 1888 McEnery occupied the Governor's chair. He served out Wiltz's term and in 1884 was elected to a full four-year term. He came from a politically active family; his brother John McEnery had claimed to be the governor of Louisiana, in opposition to Kellogg, during the hectic latter years of Reconstruction. By all evidence, McEnery seems to have been an affable but weak man, possessing most of the faults common to American politicans of that era. Unfortunately, he was called upon to preside over an extraordinarily corrupted and demoralized segment of the nation.

McEnery settled readily into the status quo he found upon coming to the state's highest office; he appears not to have

3 "The Analogy Between Maine and Louisiana," *Nation*, XXX (January 1, 1880) , 5–6.

disputed Burke's mastery over the state government. Indeed, the state treasurer's power increased during the McEnery years. Congressman E. John Ellis probably exaggerated only slightly when he wrote a relative that McEnery "sold himself body and breeches to Burke." [4] Even in public, speaking in defense of McEnery, Major Burke could not refrain from relishing the fact that Louisianians understood who really ran the State House. "I hear it stated from one end of the state to the other," Burke remarked, "that this poor weakling of a governor . . . is under the control and domination of Burke and some others." [5] The "some others" included three powerful businessmen: Charles T. Howard and John A. Morris of the Louisiana Lottery Company, and S. L. James who, as chief lessee of the state penitentiary, was in effect the largest slaveholder of post-bellum Louisiana.

As titular head of the state and its Democratic Party, Mc-Enery received the greatest share of fulsome praise from those who benefitted from, or preferred, this sort of Bourbon regime. He was described as "the levee Governor," "the farmer's friend," and even "the executive Greatheart." [6] But his foes, wishing to direct attention to his apparent subservience to Burke and the Lottery, referred to him as "McLottery." [7] And the mounting evidence of fraud and favoritism in the McEnery administration provoked snide comments from some of the most firmly Democratic newspapers; when someone suggested a raise in salary for the Governor, because the state's first family could scarcely live decently on the miserable pittance of $4,000 per year, the *Daily Picayune* snapped that the "quality of the article paid for" should take primary

[4] E. John Ellis to Tom Ellis, February 6, 1882, in Ellis Family Papers, Department of Archives, Louisiana State University.

[5] New Orleans *Times-Democrat*, October 15, 1887.

[6] *Ibid.*, August 6, 1882; Baton Rouge *Daily Capitolian-Advocate*, December 7, 1887; *Biographical and Historical Memoirs of Louisiana*, II, 62.

[7] Bayou Sara *True Democrat*, February 21, 1892.

consideration. Viewed this way, Louisiana's $4,000 governor was "the most expensive in existence." [8]

Vulpine individuals of the Burke sort were not McEnery's only confidants. Men of personal courage and presumed integrity also stood near him. Here, in fact, lay the supreme tragedy of McEnery Bourbonism: that men who must have possessed the intelligence and capacity to give Louisiana enlightened government were so blinded by the memories of Civil War and Reconstruction, and race hatred, as to give unthinking allegiance to whoever trumpeted loudest the shibboleths of states' rights and white supremacy.

A case in point was Leon Jastremski. A close personal friend of McEnery's, Jastremski was mayor of Baton Rouge, editor of the official journal of the state government, and a leader in Confederate veterans' organizations. Jastremski, for a time at least, fought the Lottery and tried to pull McEnery away from its tentacles. The mayor-editor urged a cleansing of the corruption which had crept into the party of white supremacy. But, he insisted, "all reform has to be within the Democratic party. Where else do you have to go?" And if the party were not purified, if the venal elements still dominated, Jastremski nevertheless saw no course but to stay with the party. To do otherwise would be, he said, "like burning down the house to destroy the bedbugs." [9]

If Jastremski did not have a typical Southern name, neither was Louisiana a typical state. He seems to have been the classic spokesman for the upper and upper-middle class, without whose support the McEnery-style Democracy could never have flourished. In his social philosophy, nostalgia for the plantation Old South paradoxically mingled with the booster spirit of business opportunism. Jastremski gloried in the

8 New Orleans *Daily Picayune,* April 19, 1886.

9 Baton Rouge *Daily Capitolian-Advocate,* March 7, 23, 30, June 15, November 7, 1882.

epithet "Bourbon." Yet he suggested that "Stuart" was perhaps a more appropriate description; that McEnery's administration should be likened to the restoration of that jolly monarch, Charles II. He deplored the "great outcry in certain quarters about the reactionary tendencies of the Democratic party," and he insisted that the state's continuing backwardness was all due to the North's "mischevious interference in our social . . . organization." The "injustice" of the Civil War and Reconstruction was still to him the supreme fact of life.[10]

The penetration of the South by Northern business was, however, another matter entirely. Jastremski's newspaper expressed annoyance at bills introduced in the legislature by solons from the "big woods" who wanted to regulate railroad and riverboat companies; for common sense dictated that "capital shall always have in Louisiana all the remuneration it can earn." [11] He and all leading Bourbons praised the Constitution of 1879 for its wisdom in this regard. As the *Carroll Democrat* reiterated: "All manufacturers in Lousiana are exempt from . . . taxation until 1899. Come to Louisiana!" [12]

Hardly anything excited the business Bourbons more than a visit from a Northern millionaire. When Jay Gould, an object of loathing throughout much of America, visited the state in 1887, the leading citizens of Shreveport prepared an elaborate reception and were anxious to make his stay in their town a pleasant one. They wanted Gould to build another railroad in the area. But the wily old financier disappointed his Shreveport admirers by insisting upon a $50,000 subsidy, free depot grounds and a free right-of-way through the city

10 *Ibid.*, March 30, April 8, 1882.
11 *Ibid.*, May 20, 1882.
12 Lake Providence *Carroll Democrat*, August 11, 1888.

for a small branch line he proposed.[13] Gould meanwhile was adding thousands of acres to his sprawling timber empire in North Louisiana. The enthusiasm over him was not visible in Grant, Vernon, or Winn parishes where he was the largest landowner, but a most reluctant taxpayer.[14]

For some reason, outside businessmen—except those interested in timber and land—seemed reluctant to invest in Louisiana, despite its allures of low taxes and low wages. Certainly the state's failure to improve its political and social climate had much to do with their disinclination. The Pelican State by the 1880's had become a byword for political corruption and general lawlessness; and the Bourbon regime of that decade did virtually nothing to improve this sad reputation. Indeed, in the state's one great city, disrespect for life and property grew worse during the years after Reconstruction.

In 1881, for example, a high percentage of lawbreaking in New Orleans was done by policemen and minor city officials. During one week, two urban officeholders were arrested for highway robbery, two others became involved in shootings, two more allegedly committed murder, and another was charged with rape. Then a few days later the deputy coroner for Orleans Parish was indicted for picking the pockets of a corpse. Later in the year an investigation by the city council revealed that numerous policemen were drunkards, panderers or thugs. Alarmed citizens formed a "Committee of Public Safety" to protect themselves from officials, the police and other criminals. The *Daily Picayune* reluctantly admitted that the city had been a safer place during Reconstruction, when patrolled by Kellogg's force of metropolitans.[15] Nor did the state government reveal any significant improvement in char-

13 Galveston *Daily News,* January 24, 26, 1887.

14 Winnfield *Southern Sentinel,* March 20, July 3, 1885; Colfax *Chronicle,* April 2, 1887.

15 New York *Times,* July 13, 1881; New Orleans *Daily Picayune,* July 1, 18, October 27, 1881.

acter over that of the Reconstruction era. "How much are we better off now than when under Radical rule?" asked the *Sugar Planter*. "None but the officeholders see it; the masses do not." [16]

The plantation parishes reported nowhere near the crime rate of Louisiana's city, but they had their own peculiar forms of lawlessness during the 1880's. And here the Bourbon regime and its mentality were directly to blame. Because the Democratic organization in portions of the countryside continued, long after Reconstruction, to more or less openly practice fraud at the ballot box. Actually, the entire political structure of the state came to rest upon a rotten pedestal—the manipulated thousands of Negro votes.

According to the registration rolls Louisiana still comprised more black than white voters. In 1880 there were 88,-024 Negroes listed, a majority of 2,573 over the whites. Instead of decreasing, their numbers rose under Bourbon rule; by 1888 there were 128,150 Negroes on the rolls, and their number over the whites had increased to 3,743. Yet as Negro registration went upward, Republican voting strength mysteriously declined. In the heavily Negro parishes of the Fifth Congressional District, Republicanism for all practical purposes disappeared. Only in the sugar-growing regions of South Louisiana, where some influential Republican planters lived, were black men free to vote for more than one party; but even there occasional repression took place.[17]

Bourbon leaders made little effort to conceal their wrongdoing at the ballot box. Occasionally it was said that vote theft was necessary for the well-being of the state. The elections of 1876–79 had only "strangled, and not killed" the

[16] West Baton Rouge *Sugar Planter*, quoted in New Orleans *Daily Picayune*, July 19, 1881.

[17] *Report of the Secretary of State*, 1902, pp. 548–53; Webb, "A History of Negro Voting in Louisiana," 124, 140–41.

"monster" of Negro domination; to permit a free ballot would admit "a mongrel government made up of the worst elements of both races." [18] Governor McEnery thoroughly agreed. "It is time," His Excellency was quoted on one occasion, "that the law shall be silent and [we shall] uphold our liberty at all hazards." [19] Huge Democratic majorities in the black belt parishes were equated to the chastity of white women, the memory of the Confederate dead, and the Divine Wisdom of Heaven. "What recreant," thundered Major Hearsey's *Daily States,* could possibly, remembering Reconstruction, "stand up before almighty God and accuse the wisdom or integrity or beneficence of the Democratic party . . . ?" [20] In one sense, the fact that election frauds were undisguised only added to the enormity of the crime. Men who gloried in vote stealing unqestionably did great harm to their private standards of moral conduct, while the effect upon young people who were taught to believe that such cheating was patriotic and right can only be imagined.[21]

But the Bourbon rationale for vote fraud against Republican opponents in state and congressional elections scarcely told the whole story. Why, it can be asked, if Negro majorities were so menacing, were Democratic registrars so liberal in adding black men to the voting lists? The statewide totals showed white registration as decently under the actual number of males over the age of twenty-one; however, there were 8,335 more blacks on the rolls in 1888 than showed up for the census taker two years later. Many who departed with the Kansas Exodus remained on the voting lists a decade or more

18 St. Joseph *North Louisiana Journal,* October 30, 1880; Lake Providence *Carroll Democrat,* October 20, 1888.

19 Uzee, "Republican Politics in Louisiana," 84.

20 New Orleans *Daily States,* quoted in Lake Providence *Banner Democrat,* January 25, 1896.

21 Joseph P. Bishop, "The Secret Ballot in Thirty-Three States," *Forum,* XII (January, 1892) , 597.

afterward, and black cemeteries proved to be bastions of strength for the party of white supremacy. The remark that "a dead darkey always makes a good Democrat and never ceases to vote" became a truism of state politics.[22] Yet the supreme irony could be found in the census returns of 1890, which showed that the hue and cry over the supposed "black majority" was in fact a sham. Louisiana's white males of voting age outnumbered Negroes by 10,933. Thus a real white majority had been transformed into an alleged black majority of almost 4,000, through the counting of thousands of fictitious Negroes, and the failure of about 5,000 whites to be registered.

Most of the doctoring of registration rolls and election returns with fraudulent Negro names and votes was accomplished in the cotton plantation parishes of northern and central Louisiana. Behind it all, however, was something more complex than merely insuring the election of Democratic officials. For that matter, compliant Negro Republicans were sometimes permitted to win minor posts in such parishes as East Carroll and Concordia. And at any rate, most local officials were either appointed or could be removed by the governor. What was really involved was control of the Democratic party nominating conventions for state and congressional positions.

Under the convention system of Louisiana, each parish sent a delegation whose size depended upon the number of Democratic votes reported there at the previous election. Although each locale might choose its own method of selecting convention delegates, the size of the parish delegation was strictly based upon the prior Democratic vote allegedly cast. Swollen, false returns from the black belt, based on inflated Negro

22 Natchitoches *Louisiana Populist,* October 22, 1897. During the post-Reconstruction years, parish assessors acted as registrars of voters. Assessors were appointed by the governor. Hence, all registrars were Democrats.

registration, allowed delegates from the plantation parishes to throng into Democratic nominating conventions in commanding numbers. Moreover, since after 1877 Republican chances in the general elections were virtually nil, it was at these Democratic conventions that the real selection of officeholders took place.

The Bourbons who erected this device were actually perpetuating a Louisiana tradition. Prior to the Civil War the planter class had similarly used the presence of the Negro to politically overpower the primarily white, less affluent, sections of the state. The Constitution of 1852 had apportioned seats in both houses of the state legislature on the basis of total, including Negro, population. Thus all slaves, otherwise regarded by law as things of property, were to be counted as equal with whites for the special purpose of allotting the plantation parishes a controlling share of Louisiana's government. No other state had given slaveowners quite as much power.[23] Nor is there any indication that the post-Reconstruction Bourbons of any other state were able to so effectively use the helpless Negro as a means of political domination. True, there were oligarchies elsewhere in the South after 1877, and they sometimes used similar methods; but the Louisiana Bourbons differed from the others in the extent and degree of their control.[24]

Ballot box stuffing, and the packing of party conventions, reached its outermost limits in the Fifth Congressional District of northeastern Louisiana; no other part of the South seemed so egregiously undemocratic.[25] The four parishes

[23] *Constitution of 1852*, Art. 8; Shugg, *Origins of Class Struggle*, 136–38. Maryland was the only other slave state to base representation in both houses of the legislature upon total population. However, in Maryland, slaves made up less than one-seventh the population; whereas in Louisiana there were almost as many slaves as whites.

[24] This conclusion is based upon the writer's examination of the major books and articles dealing with the politics of the post-Reconstruction South.

[25] New York *Times*, November 2, 1880.

THE PARISHES OF
LOUISIANA 1877–1900

(1) Acadia Parish detached from
    St. Landry, 1888
(2) Part of St. Martin Parish

THE CONGRESSIONAL DISTRICTS
OF LOUISIANA,
1877–1900

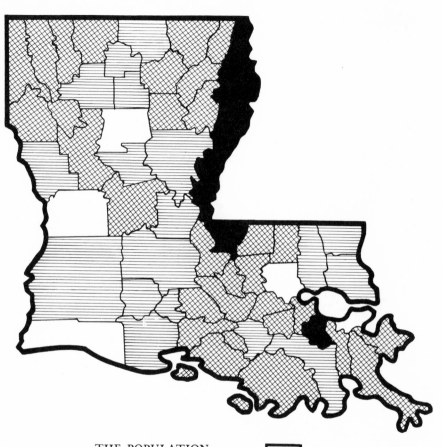

THE POPULATION
OF LOUISIANA,
1880

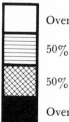

Over 80% white

50% to 80% white

50% to 80% Negro

Over 80% Negro

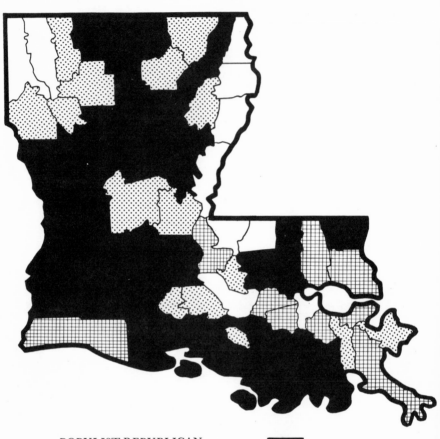

POPULIST-REPUBLICAN
"FUSION" VOTE IN THE
GUBERNATORIAL ELECTION
OF APRIL 21, 1896

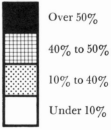

Over 50%

40% to 50%

10% to 40%

Under 10%

along the Mississippi River, where lived only 11.3 percent of the adult white males of the district were able, for example, to go into the congressional nominating convention of 1888 with seventy-five delegates. The other eleven parishes of the district, with 88.7 percent of the whites of voting age, were allowed seventy-nine delegates.[26] Much the same story was evident in northwestern Louisiana's Fourth District. There, Caddo, Bossier and Rapides parishes manipulated Negro majorities so as to dominate the other nine parishes, where most of the whites of the district lived. In the Sixth District the situation was not as extreme; even so, East and West Feliciana, Pointe Coupee and West Baton Rouge parishes carried much greater weight in Democratic conventions than their white population (i.e., actual, free voters) justified. The First, Second and Third districts of the southern part of the state were comparatively free of the sort of political fraud and injustice practiced elsewhere, although in New Orleans— half of which lay in the First and half in the Second District—voting irregularities were not uncommon on election day. Of course, the inflated strength of the cotton plantation areas made itself regularly felt in statewide contests and elections; all Louisiana was affected by the political power of a handful of whites in a dozen heavily Negro parishes.

Local politics more often than not reflected the malign aspects of the state and congressional campaigns. Few parishes, even where Democrats and Republicans were closely matched, used the primary system ballot in selecting party nominees. More common was the "mass rally" technique. When time came for making nominations for parish office, or

26 Lake Providence *Carroll Democrat,* August 4, 1888; Ruston *Caligraph,* quoted in *ibid.,* October 20, 1888; *Compendium of the Eleventh Census, 1890,* I, 782–83. Some of the disadvantaged parishes had significant pockets of planter strength—for example Ouachita Parish in the Fifth District, and when this influence was added into party conventions, the plantation interests as a whole enjoyed an absolute majority in district Democratic politics.

the selection of convention delegates, the local Democratic organization would call for the party faithful to assemble and make their wishes known. In theory this might be fair, but, grumbled the Crowley *Signal,* frequently the call was poorly advertised or held in an obscure place; the result then was "a sort of confidential limited mass meeting." [27] McEnery's associates were said to have a special trademark. They perpetuated themselves in certain North Louisiana courthouses by proclaiming open-air, free-for-all parish nominating rallies, but farmers up in the hills were given "a notice as short as that which the hawk gives the chicken." [28]

Republican leaders sometimes packed their "mass meetings" also, but the evil was most pronounced in the Democratic Party, and most harmful since the vast majority of state and parochial officials were selected at meetings of the latter. Drunken rowdies were often on hand at these rallies, so as to discourage timid folk from attending; and anyone who raised his voice in protest at the high-handed proceedings would likely be denounced as "a crank, and . . . howled down accordingly." [29] Once the nominees were chosen and the party label applied, a voter had this alternative: support the Democratic ticket or suffer obloquy as a traitor to the white race. Even worse, white men who were presumed to have cast a Republican ballot were sometimes described as "sleeping with the hogs." [30]

Local self-expression was also stifled by the executive appointment of police jurors, positions equivalent to that of county commissioners in other states. Begun on a partial basis under Nicholls, it was made total during the Wiltz-McEnery administrations. Beginning in 1880 every police juror in the

[27] Crowley *Signal,* quoted in Baton Rouge *Daily Capitolian-Advocate,* March 6, 1888.

[28] Shreveport *Democrat,* quoted in Baton Rouge *Daily Capitolian-Advocate,* November 10, 1887.

[29] Arabi *St. Bernard Voice,* quoted in Colfax *Chronicle,* October 22, 1887.

[30] *National Economist,* III (July 19, 1890), 279.

state received appointment from the governor.[31] The class of men appointed were almost certain to squelch any proposal to raise local taxes; a fact which, to wealthy planters and merchants, proved "the wisdom of this mode of selection." [32]

One student of Southern politics has suggested that the condition of public education can be the surest criterion by which to judge a governing oligarchy.[33] It is a reasonable assumption. Here, then, was further evidence that the people of Louisiana suffered under the South's least enlightened Bourbon regime. For no other state during the late nineteenth century permitted its public institutions to fall so low, or allowed its children to undergo a worse degree of educational neglect. And "heavier wrong" than this, admitted one of the wiser conservatives, "is not done under the sun. . . . Men made in the image of God continue as two-legged beasts." [34]

The oligarchy used certain arguments to explain its niggardly school appropriations. Louisiana was poor. Taxpayers needed a breathing spell after the excessive rates of Reconstruction. The state must encourage manufacturing, railroads, and capital investment; these would not come without the freedom from taxation provided for in the Constitution of 1879. Bourbon Democrats were fond of calling their rulership "a taxpayer's government." But apparently what they strove for was quite the opposite: a government of should-be taxpayers who paid little or nothing.

The plea of poverty was purposely exaggerated. Most Louisianians were poor, but by no means all. Individuals of great wealth could be found within the borders of the state, and these privileged few were able to use the poverty of the ma-

[31] *Police Jury Code of the Parish of East Feliciana: Containing a Digest of the State Laws Relative to Police Juries* (Clinton, La., 1883), 8–9.

[32] H. Thompson Brown, *Ascension Parish Louisiana, Her Resources, Advantages and Attractions: A Description of the Parish and the Inducements Offered to Those Seeking New Homes* (Donaldsonville, La. 1888), 11.

[33] Key, *Southern Politics in State and Nation,* 160.

[34] Homer *Louisiana Journal,* March 10, 1886.

jority as a specious excuse for avoiding taxation upon themselves. By 1892, according to the *Times-Democrat*, thirty-five millionaires lived in New Orleans alone.[35] Other immensely wealthy persons could be found in the plantation parishes. Governor Nicholls, who at least believed in some public services by the state, criticized those who made persistent efforts "to present Louisiana as a pauper, unable to . . . carry out the duties of her statehood." Such claims, he said, were "utterly without foundation."[36] For some, however, mendacity knew no limits; even the opulent Louisiana Lottery Company pretended to be "almost entirely profitless."[37]

A look at state institutional reports and related sources during the 1880–1900 period reveals a melancholy pattern of social neglect. Part of the trouble lay in the constitutional ceiling on state and local taxes. And the chief sufferer was public education. Only 1.25 mills of the state tax went into the current school fund, whereas 2.75 mills went to pay interest on the state debt; and the latter did not include interest on educational bonds, which had to be paid out of the 1.25 mill school fund.[38] This was all bad enough, but continuing indifference in high places made the picture even darker.

Antebellum Louisiana had once shown a genuine interest in public education; in the early 1850's about half the white children of educable age managed to obtain rudimentary instruction, and in 1860 only 10 percent of the adult whites were classified as illiterate.[39] After the war, Louisiana's school system was revived by the carpetbaggers and for the first time

---

[35] New Orleans *Times-Democrat*, May 11, 1892, quoted in Shugg, *Origins of Class Struggle*, 291.

[36] *Official Journal of the Proceedings of the Senate of the State of Louisiana*, 1890, p. 414 (hereinafter referred to as *Senate Journal*).

[37] Lottery advertisement in New Orleans *Daily Picayune*, January 1, 1877.

[38] *Constitution of 1879*, Art. 209.

[39] Fortier (ed.), *Louisiana*, II, 428–29; *Eighth Census, 1860*, I, *Population*, 188–89, and IV, *Statistics of the United States*, 508.

Negro children were eligible for public education. Reconstruction schools were by law racially integrated, although in practice few biracial schools existed outside of New Orleans. Unfortunately, as the Negro state superintendent of public education reported in 1875, in "too many instances" the Reconstruction school money was "squandered or misappropriated." [40] Expenses had quickly outrun revenue and teachers were forced to hawk pay warrants at a fraction of their face value. But even the *Daily Picayune* was forced to agree with the Republicans that New Orleans "brokers and money lenders were the real recipients for the greater part of the money appropriated for . . . education in Louisiana for many years." [41]

If judged alone by the results of their handiwork it would appear that the Democratic Party, after it came to power in 1877, held Negro and poor white children personally responsible for the failings of the Reconstruction school system. Funds for education were pruned immediately. The Constitution of 1879 encouraged further emasculation. A Bourbon Democratic program of fiscal retrenchment took place in other Southern states as well, but what happened to education in Louisiana after Reconstruction was without parallel elsewhere. The following figures reveal part of the outline of a social disaster of frightful magnitude:[42]

[40] *Annual Report of the State Superintendent of Public Education,* 1875, p. 95.

[41] New Orleans *Daily Picayune,* April 23, 1877.

[42] *Abstract of the Eleventh Census, 1890,* pp. 205, 228–29; *Compendium of the Eleventh Census, 1890,* I, 748. The educable child-teacher ratio is found by dividing the number of public school teachers into the number of inhabitants of the five-through-twenty-year age group, which the Bureau of the Census considered "educable." It is true that Louisiana had more parochial school teachers than the other states listed, but even when they are added, Louisiana still retained the bottom ranking in all categories. Especially was this true of Negro education. Counting public, parochial, and private schools in 1890, there were only 828 teachers for over 200,000 blacks of school age. *Compendium of the Eleventh Census, 1890,* II, 221, 223.

Louisiana Public Schools in 1890 Compared with
Education in the Four Poorer Southern States

	True Value of Property	State and Local Taxes for Schools
LOUISIANA	$459,301,000	$388,000
Arkansas	455,147,000	786,000
Mississippi	454,242,000	613,000
South Carolina	400,911,000	428,000
Florida	389,489,000	531,000

	Educable White Children Per Teacher	Educable Colored Children Per Teacher
LOUISIANA	115	309
Arkansas	91	107
Mississippi	53	103
South Carolina	71	191
Florida	45	104

States with Illiteracy Rate
Above Forty Percent
(age ten and over)

1880: (Seven States)

	Percentage of Native white Illiterates	Percentage of Colored Illiterates	Average Percentage All Races
(1) South Carolina	22.39	78.55	55.41
(2) Alabama	25.05	80.61	50.89
(3) Georgia	23.18	81.58	49.86
(4) Mississippi	16.57	75.17	49.52
(5) LOUISIANA	*19.83*	*79.06*	*49.05*
(6) North Carolina	31.71	77.44	48.33
(7) Florida	20.73	70.66	43.42
(national average)	(8.75)	(70.00)	(16.97)
1890: (Three States)			
(1) LOUISIANA	*20.33*	*72.14*	*45.83*
(2) South Carolina	18.11	64.07	44.95
(3) Alabama	18.44	69.08	41.00
(national average)	(6.23)	(56.76)	(13.34)

Louisiana, as the latter set of figures demonstrates, climbed from fifth to first place in ignorance between 1880 and 1890. She was the only state, South or North, to show an absolute rise in the percentage of native whites who could not read or write, and the sole state where black illiteracy continued above 70 percent. At the end of Reconstruction, Louisiana's rulers had vowed to promote and encourage education for black and white; but Governor Nicholls paid scant attention to public schools for either race and Wiltz and McEnery, even less. And those who shouted loudly for white supremacy might well have pondered the following statistics: in 1890 Louisiana's white children of native parentage, in the ten to fourteen year age group, were 27.74 percent illiterate. By contrast, black children of the same age group were better off in some of the former slave states; notably, the rate of illiteracy for Negro youths was only 19.69 percent in Missouri, 26.18 percent in Texas and 26.18 percent in Florida.[43]

The young of post-Reconstruction Louisiana came dangerously close to having no school system at all. "When the intelligent classes . . . secured possession of the government," one official remarked, "there were many who said of the public school, 'cut it away. Why cumbereth it the ground?'"[44] At the constitutional convention of 1879 a serious attempt was made to abolish the office of state superintendent of public education. This backward step failed to win approval, but other hurtful provisions did go into the constitution. For instance, parish superintendents were limited to a salary of $200 per year.[45]

Many prominent Democrats scorned the possibility of federal aid to education. The proposed Blair Bill, debated off

43 *Compendium of the Eleventh Census, 1890*, III, 314.

44 *Proceedings and Papers of the Second Annual Convention of the Louisiana State Public School Teachers' Association* (Baton Rouge, 1894), 18.

45 New Orleans *Daily Picayune*, May 28–29, 1879; *Constitution of 1879*, Art. 224.

and on in Congress from 1883 to 1888, would have poured an estimated $4 million into Louisiana's schools; petitions for its support were passed in the legislature and both the state's United States senators backed the measure.[46] No state needed the money more. But some of the same Louisianians who perpetually clamored for national help to the state's levees were horrified at the Blair Bill and, though that may not have been their real objection, castigated it as an infringement on states' rights. Many newspapers agreed with the Shreveport *Times* that federal assistance to education would be "humiliating" and "squinting too much in the direction of centralization." [47] Major Hearsey of the *Daily States*, as might have been expected, fought the Blair Bill because he descried in it a plot to teach Southern children with textbooks that gave a Yankeeized version of the War Between the States.[48] Hearsey need not have feared; the bill never passed Congress.

The Louisiana political leaders willing to accept federal money for education were, however, more numerous than those of that class who were agreeable to increasing the miserly state and local school appropriations. So utter was their neglect that there was probably some truth to the charge, made by Populist reformers in the 1890's, that the Bourbon Democracy deliberately sabotaged Louisiana's school system; and sabotaged it not so much for the sake of economy, but in order to hold public intelligence down to the lowest common denominator and so keep rural people of both races docile.[49]

[46] Monroe *Bulletin,* quoted in Baton Rouge *Weekly Truth,* April 16, 1886; Allen J. Going, "The South and the Blair Education Bill," *Mississippi Valley Historical Review,* XLIV (1957) , 267–68, 276–78.

[47] Shreveport *Times,* quoted in New Iberia *Enterprise,* September 23, 1885.

[48] New Orleans *Daily States,* quoted in Homer *Louisiana Journal,* May 5, 1886.

[49] Montgomery (La.) *Mail,* quoted in Colfax *Chronicle,* September 9, 1893; Natchitoches *Louisiana Populist,* June 5, 1896.

If so, there was one wretched Louisiana school which epito-mized the system. Its classes met inside a sheep barn.[50]

But the Bourbon fist fell hardest upon Negro education. By 1890 only 51,000 of the state's 137,000 Negro children (from nine to nineteen years of age) were able to read or write. Even in Mississippi the blacks of this age group ranked 20 per-cent higher in literacy.[51] Black poverty along with Bourbon penuriousness depressed education for the race. School books and materials cost more than most Negro parents were able to afford. Yet governmental attitudes hurt the most. Lo-cal officials were allowed to decide how the state school money should be divided between white and Negro schools and the result, in some cases, was no division at all. The superinten-dent of public education in St. Mary Parish baldly stated that all school funds in his district went for white children only; the blacks, he said, "must work out their own salvation." [52] Such indifference— and that is the kindest word that can be applied to it—would persist for decades. Far into the twenti-eth century, in 1938, State Superintendent T. H. Harris was quoted as saying that "there is no serious intention in most parishes to provide school facilities for Negro children." [53]

A gesture was made by the state toward higher education for Negroes. Southern University, by allowance of the Consti-tution of 1879, was established "for the education of persons of color." The legislature appropriated a small fund but failed to provide for one detail—construction. Subsequently, the

---

[50] C. B. Caldwell, "Our Public Schools," in *Proceedings of the Ninth Annual Session of the Louisiana State Agricultural Society* (Baton Rouge, 1895) , 28.

[51] *Compendium of the Eleventh Census, 1890,* III, 314–15.

[52] Quoted in Betty Porter, "The History of Negro Education in Louisiana," *Louisiana Historical Quarterly,* XXV (1942) , 805.

[53] T. H. Harris interview in New Orleans *Item,* July 5, 1938, quoted in Williams, "An Outline of Public School Politics in Louisiana," 66.

board of trustees managed to pay for a single building by reducing faculty salaries and by putting up future salaries as collateral for a loan. The faculties' money was still being used in 1902 to pay off this mortgage. Neglected, the university did not turn out a single graduate until 1887, and as late as 1898 it had only ten students taking college-level courses.[54] The *Daily Picayune* fittingly described it as:

Southern University
A Colored High School
With Grammar School Characteristics[55]

There was unconscious irony in the remark made by Governor Murphy J. Foster in 1896, that "this institution is a fair index to what is being done throughout the state for the education of colored people." [56] Inevitably, the failure of Negro higher education hurt the quality of instruction at lower levels. By 1893 there were 62,654 black children, about one-third of those eligible, who were enrolled in Louisiana's public school system. Forty-six of their teachers had some college training. Exactly fourteen held college degrees.[57]

Hostility against Negro education per se was probably always present. But it seldom reached print during the brief period of the "New Departure" immediately following Reconstruction. Later, however, toward the close of the 1880's, the frankest sort of attacks upon the very idea of instruction for blacks began to appear in numerous editorials and some public speeches. Dark-skinned people were simply out of place in a schoolhouse, according to a Catahoula Parish newspaper which was typical of many others. With divine insight, the

---

54 *Constitution of 1879*, Art. 231; *Report of the Secretary of State*, 1902, pp. 464–66; Baton Rouge *Daily Advocate*, July 1, 1898.

55 New Orleans *Daily Picayune*, March 18, 1881.

56 Baton Rouge *Daily Advocate*, May 14, 1896.

57 *Biennial Report of the State Superintendent of Public Education*, 1892–93, pp. 19, 22.

Trinity *Herald* commented: "God never intended the negro to be educated. Like the horse, he was destined to work for what he eats." Furthermore, the black man should be "put where he properly belongs, and to which the whites purchased him for—in the field and the wood pile." [58] The aptly-named Shreveport *Weekly Caucasian* agreed. Ignorant Negroes, it opined, were a pesky problem, but "education is the most dangerous remedy for the evil yet proposed. That education is a long stride toward social equality no sane man can doubt." [59] On the other hand, a correspondent for the *Morehouse Clarion* could find no fault with a particular Negro school in that parish; for the teacher, "unlike most of his kind . . . endeavors to learn [*sic*] them to be respectful to the white population. It is really amusing to meet about fifty of them, when they are returning home, to see them all pull off their hats and bow." [60]

A decaying school system was the most glaring of Bourbon shortcomings, but it was by no means the only blot on their social record. Another pernicious evil concerned the state's method of disbursing money to public institutions and employees. Under McEnery, the legislature failed to provide for any order or priority of payments; this had the effect of placing in the hands of State Treasurer Burke an arbitrary control over public funds and the payment of warrants. It was charged, and repeated without denial in the official journal of Louisiana's government, that Burke consistently gave priority to bondholders and by 1882 had deposited to their credit over one million dollars in a New Orleans bank. At the same time he refused to redeem on demand the state warrants issued to public institutions and employees, using the excuse of an emp-

[58] Trinity *Herald*, June 13, 1889; *ibid.*, quoted in New Orleans *Weekly Pelican*, September 21, 1889.
[59] Shreveport *Weekly Caucasian*, February 6, 1890.
[60] Bastrop *Morehouse Clarion*, July 9, 1880.

ty treasury. Warrants sent to the insane asylum at Jackson, according to the superintendent, were cashed by New Orleans brokers at only thirty-five cents on the dollar. Later, these same brokers bundled up the paper and sent it to Burke, who would suddenly discover that the treasury now had sufficient revenue for redemption.[61]

Conditions in the Jackson asylum were deplorable even by the standards of a callous age. In 1882 the angry superintendent threatened to open the gate and turn the starving inmates "loose on the highway" if he received any more thirty-five-cent-on-the-dollar warrants. This prospect appeared to stir the legislature into action; henceforth, the commercial value of the warrants was slightly increased by making them receivable for taxes due the state.[62] But the most hideous examples of state neglect of the insane were not to be found at Jackson. Considered worse off were the mentally ill from poor families in New Orleans. These urban insane were locked away in what the Louisiana Asylum Board blandly termed the "city prison for crazy people." In 1881, out of 170 in the New Orleans compound, 69 died. And 1881 was considered a healthy year for the city, since no epidemics were reported.[63]

A group of legislators, visiting the Jackson institution in 1888, were plainly shaken by what they found. Most wards had no furniture whatsoever, not even beds. No medical supplies of any sort could be discovered on the premises. Inmates wandered about in filthy rags; some were almost nude, and practically none had shoes. Inquisitively, the solons entered a cellar dining hall, but came up again hurriedly—the stench was overpowering.[64] Their blistering report to the General

---

61 Baton Rouge *Daily Capitolian-Advocate,* May 11, 17, 1882.
62 *Ibid.,* May 11, July 7, 1882.
63 *Ibid.,* June 20, 1882.
64 *Senate Journal,* 1888, pp. 330–33. The solons were also dismayed to observe racial integration among the inmates at Jackson.

Assembly brought some improvements. By 1890, steam heat was installed at Jackson; in earlier years, attendants had to walk the inmates about during cold weather to keep them from freezing to death.[65]

The mentally ill were not the only unfortunates whom the state neglected, a fact which could be attested to by the deaf, dumb, and blind who were confined at Baton Rouge. Since these latter three groups were all victims of serious lifetime handicaps, the legislature in 1888 decided to crowd them all under one roof. Instead of two dilapidated buildings as previously, the deaf, dumb, and blind, after 1888, occupied one dilapidated building. Governor McEnery, it must be said, objected to the idea of throwing all the handicapped together, for the reason that "centralizing them" would "propagat[e] a race of deaf mutes." [66] But legislative economy won out over gubernatorial theories of genetics.

While the insane and the physically helpless suffered through indifference and parsimony, another segment of the bottom rung of society received considerable legislative attention. The convicted criminals, unlike the others, were capable of yielding a profit and partly for that reason came up for frequent discussion in the General Assembly. It had been decided that lawbreakers should pay for their crimes in a literal sense: by renting penitentiary inmates to private contractors, the state was not only relieved of the financial burden of convict upkeep but also obtained a stipulated sum of money from businessmen who were willing to lease, and work, the criminal population.

Louisiana had pioneered the convict lease system in the South. Prisoners were leased to a private company as early as 1844. During Reconstruction, the state continued the system;

---

65 New Orleans *Daily Picayune*, January 14, 1877.
66 *Senate Journal*, 1888, pp. 178–80.

but instead of working inside the penitentiary walls as before, able-bodied prisoners were shipped across the state for levee and other construction work. Carpetbagger governments in other parts of the South made similar arrangements. In 1870, Governor Warmoth's administration signed a long-term convict lease agreement. At that time, S. L. James and two other contractors obtained the right to utilize the labor of all state prisoners for a period of twenty-one years.[67]

James emerged as the dominant lessee, and when the contract was renewed in 1890, no other name but his appeared on the agreement.[68] He did, however, sub-let many of the convicts to smaller contractors. A state "Board of Control" was supposed to inspect and report on the treatment of prisoners. But the effectiveness of this board was likely hampered by the fact that its members received their salaries not from the state, but from James. Thus for thirty years James and his lesser partners, in exchange for payments into the treasury varying from five thousand dollars to fifty thousand dollars per year, were given custody over the thousands of people who fell into Louisiana's penal system.[69] The lease arrangement was designed primarily for profit. but it did have an incidental deterrent value, of a grim sort. For a very high percentage of those under the care of Mr. James did not survive to commit other crimes.

According to Louisiana's best-known and ablest literary figure of the era, George Washington Cable, the penitentiary lease in his home state was probably the most brutal and corrupt example of the system to be found anywhere in the South. So completely did the state neglect its duties, Cable noted,

[67] Fortier (ed.), *Louisiana*, II, 296–97; *Biographical and Historical Memoirs of Louisiana*, I, 43; Blake McKelvey, "Penal Slavery and Southern Reconstruction," *Journal of Negro History*, XX (1935), 155; New Orleans *Daily Picayune*, June 15, 1877.

[68] *Calendar of the Senate of the State of Louisiana*, July 10, 1890, pp. 11–12.

[69] New Orleans *Daily Picayune*, June 15, 1877; *House Journal*, 1894, p. 14.

that no official report on the lessees and their charges was ever printed.[70] But any traveler who happened to observe convicts at labor needed no document to substantiate the horrors of the lease system. A Clinton newspaper described what was common knowledge:

The men on the [James] works are brutally treated and everybody knows it. They are worked, mostly in the swamps and plantations, from daylight to dark . . . punishment is inflicted on the slightest provocation. . . . Any one who has traveled along the lines of railroads that run through Louisiana's swamps . . . in which the levees are built, have seen these poor devils almost to their waists, delving in the black and noxious mud. . . . Theirs is a grievous lot; a thousand times more grievous than the law ever contemplated they should endure in expiation of their sins.[71]

Occasionally, information on the death rate among convicts was released. Fourteen percent of all prisoners were known to have died in 1881, and the annual death rate was seldom much lower. In 1882 the figure climbed above 20 percent; 149 of 700 prisoners expired that year. In 1884, 118 of 850 prisoners died.[72] Because of these statistics, it was estimated that for an able-bodied man, a sentence of seven years was the equivalent of capital punishment.[73] Toward the end of the 1880's prisoner mortality figures were not released at all; and Governor McEnery, in his last message to the legislature, insisted that the convicts "are well taken care of, humanely treated, well fed and clothed, and not overtasked in their labor." [74]

[70] George W. Cable, "The Convict Lease System in the Southern States," *Century Illustrated Monthly Magazine,* XXVII (February, 1884)) , 596–97.

[71] Clinton *East Feliciana Patriot-Democrat,* quoted in New Orleans *Daily Picayune,* March 22, 1886.

[72] Cable, *Century Illustrated Monthly Magazine,* XXVII, 596; New Orleans *Daily Picayune,* June 11, 1882; Baton Rouge *Weekly Truth,* June 4, 1886.

[73] Homer *Louisiana Journal,* June 30, 1886.

[74] *Senate Journal,* 1888, p. 23. In contrast to McEnery's view, see the mistreatment described in New York *Times,* May 22, 1886.

Approximately three-fourths of James's convicts were Negroes. Before the Civil War, whites had outnumbered blacks in the Louisiana penitentiary by about three to one. According to one specimen of Bourbon logic, this proved "very conclusively the improved moral condition of the blacks during the slave *regime*." [75] Negroes customarily received harsher sentences than did whites, unless their crimes were against other Negroes. In one case a black man named Theophile Chevalier was sentenced to five years for stealing five dollars, and while serving time he lost both feet to frostbite and gangrene. Notices of new arrivals into the penal system often revealed not only a disparity in sentences but a convoluted sense of values. For example, these two individuals entered the same day: Julia Brosset (white-female), manslaughter, sentenced to one hour; Clay Holly (colored-male), killing a hog, sentenced to one year.[76]

The lease system was disadvantageous to the state for reasons apart from its inhumanity. Economically and politically, it proved to be a mistake. The "penitentiary ring" was a power in government second only to the Lottery; mordant humorists, observing the influence of S. L. James and his associates, referred to them as the "James Gang." James was sometimes allowed to pay his annual fee to the state in depreciated back warrants rather than cash, and he was also permitted to make large deductions for so-called "repairs" to the old penitentiary at Baton Rouge, where convicts unsuited for hard work were kept. Moreover, in 1884 the legislature gave the James firm a monopoly on levee construction in Louisiana; the state paid a set price for it. James and his partners profitably sub-let much of this work to small contractors, and he was doubly protected by being privileged to turn down any levee con-

75 *Biographical and Historical Memoirs of Louisiana,* I, 150.
76 New York *Times,* May 22, 1886; Baton Rouge *Weekly Advocate,* August 5, 1881.

struction which he decided might be unprofitable.[77] By all ap-
pearances, in the one state in the Union where overflowing
rivers were most to be feared, the officeholding class believed
that a guaranteed return for a private firm took priority over
the need for adequate flood protection.

Blind and backward though they were in most matters,
Bourbon leaders would seldom admit to the charge that they
actually desired stagnation in the status quo. Probably many
of them sincerely believed that it was just and proper for government to set plantation and business interests ahead of
everything else; and also, they were probably convinced, as
was a young scion of the wealthy Gay family, that it took an
iron rule by the oligarchy to "keep back the mighty surge of
debased humanity that daily threatens to sweep over our fair
state." [78] But as evidence that they were really working for
the benefit of all Louisiana, the Bourbons cited, along with
their encouragement of business investment, their promotion of immigration.

Northern settlers as well as Northern money were welcome
in post-Reconstruction Louisiana. In particular did the young-
er Bourbons of the 1880's, such as Joseph E. Ransdell of Lake
Providence, speak of the good that would come from an influx
of Yankee "energy." [79] Immigration promoters were simultaneously to be heard throughout the South, but the Pelican
State's tubthumpers banged with a special intensity. They
realized that many outsiders regarded Louisiana "as an extensive burying ground, where mosquitoes, alligators and
'niggers' might thrive, but where 'white folks' inevitably

[77] Farmerville *Gazette,* February 19, 1896; New Orleans *Daily Picayune,*
November 2, 1887; *Compendium of Legislative Acts Relating to Levee Organization and Kindred Subjects: 1856–1918* (New Orleans, 1919) , 156.

[78] Andrew H. Gay, Jr., to Andrew H. Gay, Sr., April 18, 1893, in Gay Family
Papers, Department of Archives, Louisiana State University.

[79] Lake Providence *Carroll Democrat,* August 18, 1888.

passed in their checks after a brief sojourn." [80] For many years its yellow fever epidemics, not to mention its violent style of politics, had received extensive and unflattering coverage in the Northern press. When a Chicago writer remarked that Louisiana's people were "different from the inhabitants of any other State in the Union," no compliment was intended.[81] Prospective immigrants, reading these "slanders," feared to go.[82]

Louisiana's boosters strove to parry unfavorable publicity with fabulous accounts of her potential wealth, healthful climate and friendly citizenry. Heavy-handed attempts were made to eradicate the mephitic odor which clung to the state's reputation. Northern farmers were invited to "come and till where the south wind blows softly," and were informed that "the small farmer . . . in a few years . . . will grow rich, and with little severe labor." [83] And the climate! For it, no praise was too lavish. The state's weather was "deliciously delightful" since, by an imaginative reversal of seasons, the winters were "warm" while summers were always "cool." [84] As for public health, even epidemic-ridden New Orleans tried, lamely, to tell the world that its health and sanitation were "badly misunderstood." [85] Northern skeptics who wondered about "old scores connected with the war" received assurance from Tangipahoa Parish that its residents "rejoice that slavery is wiped out" and were sorry that the Civil War had occurred.[86]

Yet the welcome mat was not spread for everybody. Few

[80] New Orleans *Daily Picayune,* May 2, 1886.
[81] Chicago *Times,* quoted in Baton Rouge *Daily Capitolian-Advocate,* August 8, 1882.
[82] Lake Providence *Carroll Democrat,* August 4, 1888.
[83] Baton Rouge *Daily Advocate,* March 5, 1890.
[84] *Proceedings of the Ninth Annual Session of the Louisiana State Agricultural Society,* 77; *Southern Homeseekers' Guide and Winter Resorts on the Southern Division of the Illinois Central Railroad* (Chicago, 1887), *passim;* Brown, *Ascension Parish,* 2.
[85] *Official Souvenir and Program of the Louisiana Industrial Exposition and Jubilee* (New Orleans, 1899)), 69.
[86] *Southern Homeseekers' Guide,* 57.

favored the idea of Oriental immigration. And Negro newcomers, except to some large planters, were considered *per-
sonae non grata*. There were "too many colored people" as it
was, believed the Rayville *Beacon*. "Louisiana Needs Whiten-
ing." [87] Some went so far as to criticize the blacks for occupy-
ing space which might be put to better use by industrious
Yankees. As the Hammond *Leader* suggested: "All that is
needed down here to make the country a veritable 'gateway'
to paradise is the elimination of the colored population." [88]
The warning of George W. Cable, who said that the only way
to make the South a good place for white men to come in, was
to first make it fit for black men to stay in, failed to be heeded
by those in places of influence.

By 1886 the immigration societies, associations, and conventions, on both the state and parish level, had been fitfully active for a decade and more. But for all the windy resolutions
and brightly colored pamphlets, there was little proof of ac-
complishment. Since the early years of Reconstruction few
Northerners had arrived. True, thousands of people had
moved into Louisiana; but most of them were lower class
whites from the southeastern states, or Negro laborers of similar origin who had been lured in by the agents of great plantations. It was high time, asserted the Baton Rouge *Weekly
Truth*, to consider the fact that no intelligent person "would
desire to settle in a State where trade is affected with a palsy
and the people are poor and growing poorer." [89]

Suddenly, however, immigration prospects began to bright-
en. In 1886 the first trainloads of homeseekers from the North
and Midwest arrived in Lake Charles to investigate agricultural possibilities in the watery wilderness of southwestern
Louisiana. They had been attracted down by the promotional

activities of the Watkins Syndicate, an association of Northern and British investment corporations whose Louisiana holdings were managed by a Kansas banker, Jabez B. Watkins. The Syndicate had earlier purchased 1,500,000 acres of marsh and prairie land in the region, paying from 12½ cents to $1.25 an acre. Watkins had induced the president of Iowa Agricultural College, Seaman A. Knapp, to come to Lake Charles and take charge of prairie land development and sales.[90]

A phenomenal land boom was soon underway in the southwestern parishes. By 1890 thousands of farmers had arrived from Iowa, Illinois, Michigan, and other states. Those who came first, noticing that rice crops flourished even under the primitive methods used by Cajun farmers, decided to apply modern techniques and machinery to the local crop. The results were so impressive that subsequent immigrants entered with the specific intention of planting rice, and within a few years the prairie land of southwestern Louisiana would rightly be regarded as "the great rice center of America." [91]

State politics also took a more promising turn as the decade of the 1880's neared an end. For in January of 1888, Governor McEnery was defeated in his bid for renomination by a coalition of "Reform Democrats." The reformers had rallied behind the maimed war hero and former governor, Francis T. Nicholls. The change from McEnery to Nicholls would be an improvement, not by reason of any special virtues of Nicholls but because of the extraordinary failings of McEnery.

Those who directed the Nicholls wing of the party were sometimes referred to as "the more respectable Democrats of

[90] Edward Hake Phillips, "The Gulf Coast Rice Industry," *Agricultural History*, XXV (1951), 92–93; Stewart Alfred Ferguson, "The History of Lake Charles, Louisiana" (M.A. thesis, Louisiana State University, 1931), 68–71; Joseph Cannon Bailey, *Seaman A. Knapp: Schoolmaster of American Agriculture* (New York, 1945), 114–15.

[91] "Address of John Dymond," in *Proceedings of the Sixth Annual Session of the Louisiana State Agricultural Society,* 18.

the State." [92] The Burke-Wiltz-McEnery machine had, beginning in 1879, cast out much of the patrician class from the inner circle of power. McEnery, for a brief period after he succeeded to the governorship, had made vague gestures of conciliation to the genteel conservatives. But his actions belied his words. In 1884, efforts to stop McEnery's bid for the Democratic nomination to a full term had come to naught. But later, as it became evident that McEnery and State Treasurer Burke would seek reelection again in 1888, the grumbling which had been heard from patricians and from ordinary whites turned into wrathful clamor. "McLottery" was said to be surrounded by "buzzards and parasites." [93] He and his clique could no longer be endured.

Unseating McEnery from the gubernatorial chair could only be accomplished at the quadrennial party convention to nominate state officials. General elections had become a farce. Thus both the McEnery "Regulars" and the Nicholls "Reformers" devoted most of 1887, the year preceding the Democratic convention, to the business of lining up parish delegations. It was a prolonged, heated struggle. In Union Parish, to cite one bloody incident, both campaign managers of the rival factions died in the streets of Farmerville following a gun duel. Nicholls' strength lay in the small farm regions and among the Democratic sugar planters. McEnery's main support came from the parishes of great cotton plantations. New Orleans held the balance of power. [94]

[92] New York *Times,* April 22, 1884; Andrew Price to Edward J. Gay, January 19, 1888, in Gay Family Papers. Prominent among the "Reform Democrats" of 1888 were: Edward Douglass White, Randall Lee Gibson, Newton C. Blanchard and Robert N. Ogden. The venerable *Daily Picayune* and about half the rural press were anti-McEnery by 1887.

[93] New Orleans *Daily Picayune,* October 26, 1887; Homer *Claiborne Guardian,* quoted in Opelousas *St. Landry Democrat,* January 15, 1887.

[94] New York *Times,* December 21, 1887; Minden *Democrat-Tribune,* quoted in New Orleans *Daily Picayune,* January 24, 1887; Baton Rouge *Daily Capitolian-Advocate,* January 7, 1888; G. Montegut to Edward J. Gay, January 17, 1888, in Gay Family Papers.

The factional Democratic fight of 1887–88 glaringly revealed that the moral tone of Louisiana politics had not improved since Reconstruction. McEnery partisans dwelt upon the "imbecility and disastrous failure" of Nicholls' first administration. Major Burke, "the brainiest man in Louisiana," took the lion's share of credit for ending Radical Reconstruction. Governor McEnery, a Negro-baiter par excellence, solemnly pronounced Nicholls to be "unsound on the race question." [95] The powerful *Times-Democrat*, Burke's newspaper, kept up an editorial barrage on the theme that white supremacy and returning McEnery to the State House were indivisible. McEnery knew how to handle "bad and dangerous negroes." Nicholls, on the contrary, had proved himself in the Tensas trouble of 1878 to be "too honest" about such matters as vote fraud and intimidation.[96] One speaker for McEnery went so far as to suggest that if General Nicholls had been "smarter" he would not have been shot so frequently during the Civil War; McEnery, as it happened, had spent the war safely ensconced in a Confederate camp near his home town of Monroe.[97]

Nicholls' partisans dragged out an awesome array of skeletons from the McEnery closet. A moribund school system; awful conditions in state institutions; convict lease and levee contract scandals; fraud in state lands involving the Governor's brother, John McEnery; the ignoring of local sentiment in appointing parish officers—a list of ills which enraged the hill farmers and embarrassed "the best people of the state."

[95] *Biographical and Historical Memoirs of Louisiana*, II, 62; New Orleans *Times-Democrat*, October 15–16, 1887; Opelousas *Courier*, November 19, 1887; New Orleans *Daily Picayune*, November 4, 1887.

[96] New Orleans *Times-Democrat*, October 14, 1887, January 6, 1888; Thibodaux *Sentinel*, September 24, 1887; St. Martinville *Messenger*, quoted in New Orleans *Daily Picayune*, October 3, 1887.

[97] Opelousas *Courier*, September 17, November 12, 1887; Andrew B. Booth (comp.), *Records of Louisiana Confederate Soldiers and Louisiana Confederate Commands* (New Orleans, 1920), II, 1186.

The *Daily Picayune* wondered what nasty secrets Burke might be hiding in the books of the treasury office, and pointed out that a change in administration would give the public an examination of those records for the first time in a decade.[98] But one subject of mutual embarrassment was not discussed. The Louisiana Lottery Company, always a keen-eyed fisher in political waters, had contributed money to both Democratic factions.[99]

The "Reform" effort to oust McEnery was something less than an immaculate crusade. Speakers at Nicholls rallies replied to Negro-baiting with Negro-baiting. Stung by the assertion that Nicholls was "unsound on the race question," one of his friends related how the one-armed hero had once slapped a black man's face. Even so, Negroes looked upon Nicholls as the lesser of two evils; one group of them, participating in the Democratic campaign on servile terms, were reported by a Negro newspaper to have called themselves "Reform Nigger Democrats." [100] Nicholls, for his part, said little about race. Nor did he say much about anything else; he did not propose to end the medieval penitentiary lease, nor suggest that local officials should be elected rather than appointed. He criticized the harsh methods, but not the underlying philosophy, of Louisiana Bourbonism.

On January 5, 1888, one week before the nominating convention, Orleans Parish selected its delegation. The city gave Nicholls a majority, and the stand-off between the uplands and the cotton plantation parishes was broken. Major Burke, who saw his grip on state politics slipping away, worked des-

98 Opelousas *St. Landry Democrat,* January 1, 1887; New Orleans *Daily Picayune,* October 16, 1887.

99 Baton Rouge *Daily Advocate,* December 3, 1890; Opelousas *St. Landry Clarion,* December 27, 1890. Some of Nicholls' supporters later admitted that their side accepted Lottery money in 1887–88.

100 Arcadia *Record,* quoted in New Orleans *Daily Picayune,* October 29, 1887; New Orleans *Weekly Pelican,* September 10, 1887.

perately to block Nicholls' nomination. But Burke could not stop it. The convention went on to make a clean sweep of the incumbent administration, rejecting the state treasurer along with the rest.[101]

Nicholls' Republican opponent in the April general election was that insouciant carpetbagger, former Governor Henry Clay Warmoth. But, as had been the case in such contests since 1876, there seemed at first no reason for Democratic worry. Among other portents, Nicholls' revived popularity among rank-and-file whites was attested by the news that a patent medicine called "The Francis T. Nicholls Stomach Bitters" was "the sensation of the hour." [102]

Then lame duck Governor McEnery tossed out a bombshell by announcing that he would see to it that a "fair count" of ballots would take place in the general election. This, thought the Nicholls "Reformers," was a dastardly thing for McEnery to say. If the Governor's planter friends took him at his word, they might permit their Negro peons to vote, for once, unmolested. And Louisiana's black people were still at heart Republican.[103] Alarmed Nicholls supporters worked quickly to placate the aggrieved McEnery and a compromise was apparently reached. Later, as governor, Nicholls appointed McEnery to the State Supreme Court. The crisis was over. The "fair count" was called off. On election day, the Democratic commissioners in the bottomlands worked with customary zeal and Nicholls swamped Warmoth. The vote was 136,746 to 51,993.[104]

---

[101] New Orleans *Times-Democrat*, January 6–8, 1888; Baton Rouge *Daily Capitolian-Advocate*, January 7, 16, 1888.

[102] Baton Rouge *Daily Capitolian-Advocate*, March 30, 1888.

[103] Uzee, "Republican Politics in Louisiana," 82; Baton Rouge *Daily Capitolian-Advocate*, April 5, 1888. See also, New Orleans *Evening Truth*, quoted in Bayou Sara *True Democrat*, March 19, 1892.

[104] Warmoth later claimed that he had been personally encouraged by McEnery to try and beat Nicholls in the 1888 general election. Warmoth, *War, Politics and Reconstruction*, 251–52; *Report of the Secretary of State*, 1902, p. 561.

Nicholls' first inauguration, in 1877, had tolled the end of Reconstruction misrule. Now, eleven years later, he was being called upon to rescue this still unhappy commonwealth from the depths of Bourbon wrongdoing. And as Nicholls took the oath of office in May of 1888, his second administration began with one advantage which the first had lacked. Major Burke was no longer a power. Burke soon left the United States to attend to Central American mining stock, and his continued absence was guaranteed by an investigation which revealed irregularities in the state treasury totaling $1,267,905. No Reconstruction swindler had ever approached that figure. Toward the end of the century, enjoying a comfortable exile, Burke could boast to President William McKinley that he owned more property than any other American in Honduras.[105] Besides, Tegucigalpa bore a political resemblance to Baton Rouge. For Burke had discovered, in the person of President Louis Bogran, another McEnery.

---

[105] *House Journal,* 1890, pp. 20–21; Edward A. Burke to William McKinley, February 10, 1898, in E. A. Burke Papers, Department of Archives, Louisiana State University.

VII

The Louisiana Farmers' Union

E V E R Y S P R I N G, after plowing and planting were over, the upland farmers of North Louisiana had a short time for relaxation and neighborhood visits. One day might be spent at the local cemetery. By custom, on a designated morning, families would assemble where their dead were buried for what was called a "cemetery working": a poignant task of tidying up the churchyard and the grave plots within.[1] At noon, picnic baskets would be unpacked beneath the shade of nearby trees. Along with the food came a swapping of news and a discussion of mutual problems. If times were hard the faces would be grim and the talk bitter.

Near Bayou D'Arbonne, in Lincoln Parish, stood a little frame church and a cluster of weathered gravestones. There, the usual group of neighbors gathered one day in the spring of 1881. A skimpy year was in prospect; credit in the stores was tight because the previous cotton crop had turned out badly.[2] Conversation shifted to the need for an effective organization of farmers. Most of those present, remembering their disap-

1 A personal observation. The custom of an annual neighborhood "cemetery working" survived in portions of North Louisiana long into the twentieth century. This writer, as a child, participated in several such events at a village churchyard in Franklin Parish.

2 Louisiana's 1880 cotton crop was the smallest (359,147 bales) since the late 1860's. Watkins, *King Cotton,* 204; Boyle, *Cotton and the New Orleans Cotton Exchange,* 182.

pointment in the Grange, shrugged off all suggestions. But ten or twelve of the men agreed to meet again a few days later. They planned to create a new, secret society for the promotion of agrarian interests.

The minuscule organization that resulted was first called the Lincoln Parish Farmers' Club. Later it would be expanded as the Louisiana Farmers' Union. Under the latter name in January of 1887, it became merged with a society of like purpose in Texas, to form the National Farmers' Alliance and Cooperative Union—better known as the Farmers' Alliance. This order, spreading across the South and beyond, was destined to be the largest agricultural association of the nineteenth century. It had risen out of many sources and was fed by numerous wellsprings of discontent. Even the contemporary leaders of the movement were confused about its ultimate origins, because obscure men in obscure places had been involved in its genesis. But an important part of its mainstream can be traced back to a rustic churchyard in North Louisiana, in the year 1881.³

Lincoln was only one of several parishes to witness the creation of farmers' clubs in the early months of 1881.⁴ However, the little society near Bayou D'Arbonne was more ambitious

³ Recent historians who mention the Louisiana Farmers' Union (John D. Hicks, Theodore Saloutos and Carl C. Taylor) state that it began in 1880. Their source is a description of the Union's early history by John A. Tetts, which appeared in an old book by Nelson A. Dunning, *The Farmers' Alliance History and Agricultural Digest* (Washington, 1891), 219–22. Although this is the most important single source on the formation of the Union, either Tetts or the printer made a one-year error for every date in that description. Each date in Tetts's narrative is one year before the actual event. Another contemporary account, W. Scott Morgan, *History of the Wheel and Alliance and Impending Revolution* (Hardy, Ark., 1889), 370, gives the date 1861 for the founding of the Louisiana Union; this appears to have been a typographical error for *1881*. Regrettably, a close search of all available Louisiana newspapers for the years 1880 and 1881 yielded no direct information on the origin of the Union. But in 1881, unlike 1880, there were several vague references to the formation of "farmers' clubs" in parts of the state.

⁴ New Orleans *Daily Picayune,* February 14, 17, 1881.

than the others. Especially did one of its original members, John A. Tetts, hope that the club might become the nucleus of a statewide organization of dirt farmers. Louisiana's small agriculturists, Tetts surmised, were in their disunited condition "the natural prey of all kinds of speculation, and the subject of every class of fraud, from paper sole shoes to adulterated fertilizers, and from lying advertisements to false market reports." He also believed that the present conservative government in state and nation was doing "nothing to protect the farmers of our country from these thieving pirates of modern civilization." [5]

The constitution and by-laws of the Lincoln Parish Farmers' Club stressed the need for political action on the part of "the real farmers." Members were urged to work for the defeat of "all political rings and . . . machine candidates." Better representation "in the halls of legislation" was called for, so that laws more friendly to agriculture might be passed, and harmful measures defeated. Clubs in other parishes were requested "to write us and . . . make permanent the organization throughout the State." But only "practical farmers . . . of good moral character" need apply.[6] In what may or may not have been an oversight, Negroes were not specifically excluded from membership.

Trouble immediately developed over the question of the club's secrecy. In the neighborhood lived a number of prospective members who belonged to the Primitive Baptist Church, which did not permit its adherents to join any organization of a covert nature. Consequently, the original idea of secrecy was discarded.[7] But by the end of 1881 only about forty men, all from Lincoln Parish, had joined. Apparently the feelers

---

[5] Morgan, *History of the Wheel and Alliance,* 369–70; J. A. Tetts, "The Farmers and the Trust," *National Economist,* I (March 30, 1889) , 39.

[6] Dunning, *The Farmers' Alliance History,* 223.

[7] Later, attempting to spread into South Louisiana, the Union had to reiterate to doubting Catholics that it did not conflict with any religious beliefs. Opelousas *Courier,* May 21, 1887.

sent into other parishes had elicited no significant response. The proposed statewide association simply failed to materialize, and attendance at the club's meetings began to dwindle. By the summer of 1882 it had virtually disbanded.[8]

Three years later, in the autumn of 1885, Tetts, who had been secretary of the original club, happened to strike up a conversation with another bewhiskered farmer named Samuel Skinner on the streets of Ruston. "He had just sold his short crop of cotton for a short price," Tetts later recalled. "I had also disposed of my crop, and found that my receipts did not meet my expenses." [9] The two men decided that the time had come to resurrect the defunct society.

Tetts and Skinner were in many ways typical of the small landowner class of upland Louisiana. Skinner, fifty-eight years old in 1885, was a "hard-working farmer" who lived only four miles from his place of birth. He lacked formal education but laid claim to "a rich fund of useful information." During the 1870's he had been active in the Grange. Disgusted by Democrats and Republicans alike, Skinner considered himself a political independent. Tetts, thirty-eight years old, had come to Louisiana as a homesteader a decade earlier, leaving his birthplace in the unprosperous "sand hill" region of South Carolina. Tetts had some education, although he had been pulled out of school at fifteen and put to work in a grocery store owned by a relative. At seventeen he enlisted in the Confederate army; after the war he became a farmer, first in his native state and then in Louisiana. Like Skinner he was an ex-Granger.[10] The manuscript census returns for 1880 listed the total value of Tetts's 160-acre farm and all it contained at only $625.[11]

[8] Morgan, *History of the Wheel and Alliance,* 370.

[9] Dunning, *The Farmers' Alliance History,* 219.

[10] Morgan, *History of the Wheel and Alliance,* 369–72.

[11] Manuscript United States Census Returns, Tenth Census, 1880, Louisiana: Agriculture (Microfilm Document F–1, Roll 62, Louisiana State University Library) , 19.

Early in March of 1886, Tetts and Skinner conferred again; this time at the house of the former. After making some changes in the old club's constitution and by-laws, Tetts and Skinner sent word to their acquaintances that a meeting would be held on March 10, at Antioch Church, a place about fifteen miles from Tetts's home. Only nine people attended. But the Lincoln Parish Farmers' Club had thereby been reactivated. Simultaneously, a separate though virtually identical society came back into existence in neighboring Claiborne Parish; there, Negro as well as white agriculturists were becoming interested in organization. "There seems," one local editor observed in April of 1886, "to be a new life springing up among the farmers." [12]

During the next three months, subordinate units of the Lincoln Parish Farmers' Club were formed throughout that parish and John M. Stallings, a well-to-do farmer with political ambitions, took office as president. Tetts, who was actually the organizer and chief promoter, accepted his usual role as corresponding secretary. His hope of a statewide association was discussed and this time some action resulted. In August, the creation of the Louisiana Farmers' Union was announced, although as yet it did not extend beyond the borders of the parish. A new constitution was drawn up and one thousand copies printed for distribution. Somehow, a copy of the Texas State Farmers' Alliance constitution had found its way into the area, and many of its features were incorporated into the organic law of the Louisiana order. So as to lend solemnity to the meetings, an abbreviated version of the impressive Grange ritual was adopted. [13]

At the onset of expansion, Tetts had asked to be relieved of his duties because he was a working farmer "and had a

[12] Homer *Louisiana Journal,* April 21, 1886.
[13] Dunning, *The Farmers' Alliance History,* 220–21.

large family to support." But the other officials of the Union, needing his talents, persuaded him to stay on as corresponding secretary. Backwoods farmer though he was, Tetts could write with a certain picturesque vigor. The task of spreading word of the order was his, and during the late summer of 1886, Tetts made good use of his pen. He composed and mailed out scores of letters, and described the Union in an article or two which appeared in *Home and Farm*, an agricultural magazine with circulation in the lower Mississippi valley.[14] Tetts labored without salary. But he had earned the right to be pointed to, in later years, as "the founder of the Union in Louisiana." [15]

The Union grew slowly, but it did grow. A state convention of sorts was held in October of 1886; only four parishes sent delegates.[16] Yet already Greenbacker influence was beginning to show up in the new agrarian order as Jesse Moore Tilly, who had figured in the inflationist clamor of 1878, headed the Bienville Parish Union. Oddly, the nascent Farmers' Union had not yet taken root in the area where agrarian radicalism would, in succeeding years, prove strongest in Louisiana: the hill parishes of Catahoula, Grant and Winn.

By January of 1887 the Farmers' Union claimed ten thousand members.[17] This was a gross exaggeration. Not more than six or, at best, seven parishes were organized by that time; and the future heartland of the Union was still virgin

14 The only known copies of *Home and Farm* for 1886 are in the Duke University Library, and even these are in fragments. Upon request, a Duke librarian searched for the Tetts articles but found no trace of them.

15 Natchitoches *Louisiana Populist*, September 25, 1896.

16 By October, 1886, Farmers' Union subordinate units were operating in Lincoln, Bienville, Webster, and probably Union Parish. But information on the initial spread of the organization is of a vague and sometimes conflicting nature. Cf. *Biographical and Historical Memoirs of Northwest Louisiana*, 205, 690; Homer *Louisiana Journal*, December 8, 1886; Colfax *Chronicle*, October 4, 1886–April 30, 1887.

17 Opelousas *Courier*, May 21, 1887; *National Economist*, III (March 22, 1890), 15.

territory. Probably the actual membership did not exceed four thousand by the first month of 1887, when the merger with the Texas State Alliance took place. Apparently, only white farmers were being admitted. John Stallings continued as head of the order, and Tetts remained as corresponding secretary.

All the while, two farm organizations of greater numbers had been spreading across the neighboring states of Arkansas and Texas. And in the Midwest, the National Farmers' Alliance, with headquarters in Chicago, claimed to be operating in at least eight states. The Arkansas order titled itself the "Agricultural Wheel." It arose from origins similar to those of the Louisiana Union; by 1885 the Wheel boasted of units in twenty Arkansas counties and had begun to spread into all nearby states except Louisiana.[18] But the Texas Alliance was the largest and oldest of the group. It had first emerged in the mid 1870's among small cattle raisers. Faltering in its early years, the Texas Alliance almost disappeared after an abortive involvement in the Greenback Party effort of 1878. Then in 1885, with a sudden burst of energy, the movement spread into the farming counties of northern and eastern Texas and began voicing the grievances of dirt farmers.[19] Inevitably, politics again had a part. There was talk that a strong faction within the Texas Alliance wished to reach an understanding with the urban Knights of Labor, so as to create a proletarian bloc vote which could force concessions from the Texas Democratic Party. Word of this possible coalition reached Louisiana. The *Weekly Truth*, in May of 1886, prophesied that the un-

18 Roy V. Scott, "Milton George and the Farmers' Alliance Movement," *Mississippi Valley Historical Review*, XLV (1958) , 102–104; J. E. Bryan, *The Farmers' Alliance: Its Origin, Progress and Purposes* (Fayetteville, Ark., 1891) , 21.

19 C. W. Macune, "The Farmers' Alliance" (MS dated 1920 in University of Texas Library) , 3–5.

derdog farmers and city wage earners of the Pelican State would attempt a similar plan.[20]

The year 1887 marks a dramatic moment in the history of American agrarianism, for it was then that the Farmers' Alliance came to life at Waco, Texas. From 1887 to 1890, it would sweep across the cotton states and into the Great Plains with cyclonic fury; indeed, two historians have suggested that "one must go back to Medieval Europe, on the eve of the First Crusade, for an emotional situation comparable. . . ."[21] By the latter year, the Alliance would enroll between one million and three million members, and, although claiming to be nonpolitical, it was to form the basis of the Populist Party of the 1890's. In the words of its leading periodical, the *National Economist,* the Alliance represented an "ominous growl coming up from the people" against the conservative complacency of the late nineteenth century.[22]

Just prior to the Waco meeting the Texas Alliance, although at least ten times larger than the Louisiana Union in membership, had been in serious danger of dissolution because of internal political bickering. The man who has properly been given credit for saving the Texas order and, at Waco, transforming it into a powerful interstate association, was Dr. C. W. Macune. But it has also been presumed that Macune was most responsible for initiating the fusion with the Louisianians which marked the formal beginning of the Farmers' Alliance.[23] This point requires clarification. Because it was John

20 Baton Rouge *Weekly Truth,* May 21, 1886.

21 Louis M. Hacker and Benjamin B. Kendrick, *The United States Since 1865* (New York, 1934) , 301, quoted in C. Vann Woodward, *Tom Watson: Agrarian Rebel* (New York, 1938) , 137–38.

22 *National Economist,* III (April 19, 1890) , 76.

23 Saloutos, *Farmer Movements in the South,* 73–74; John D. Hicks, *The Populist Revolt: A History of the Farmers' Alliance and the People's Party* (Minneapolis, 1931) , 108–109. See also, Ralph Smith, "The Farmers' Alliance in Texas, 1875–1900," *Southwestern Historical Quarterly,* XLVIII (1945) , 356–57.

A. Tetts, and not the Texan, who came up with the idea and made the first overtures.

Tetts, it will be recalled, had in his possession a copy of the constitution of the Texas Alliance. On it were the names of the officials. During October of 1886, Tetts, at his own suggestion, was authorized by the Louisiana Union to correspond with the Texans to "try to bring about a consolidation" which would inaugurate a national alliance. He wrote to the individual whose name appeared first on the document, President Andrew Dunlap. But Dunlap did not reply, for the political schism among Texas agrarians presently forced his resignation. The powers of president fell, in November, to Dr. Macune. Then toward the end of the year Macune, having discovered the letter in Dunlap's files, wrote to Louisiana and, in Tetts's words, "he saw no reason why the two bodies should not unite and form a National as I had proposed. . . ." [24] Macune had previously corresponded with the loosely-organized "National" Farmers' Alliance in Chicago, but for various reasons he rejected a merger at that time with the Northerners. On the other hand, the information from Tetts indicated that the Louisiana Union was virtually identical in purpose with the Texas Alliance.[25]

Immediately, Tetts wrote back and asked Macune to send a Texas representative to the next meeting of the Farmers' Union, scheduled for January 11, 1887, in Ruston. Macune dispatched Evan Jones, who carried the news that the Texans were anxious to have the Louisianians join them and begin the work of proselytizing in other states. At the Ruston assembly, Tetts was selected as "a committee of one" to visit the

[24] Dunning, *The Farmers' Alliance History,* 221. See also, Morgan, *History of the Wheel and Alliance,* 370. Dr. Macune's manuscript account, "The Farmers' Alliance," 17, simply mentions that he "corresponded with" the Louisiana Union.

[25] Bryan, *The Farmers' Alliance,* 11–12.

Texas Alliance convention which was to be held at Waco on January 18; he had plenary powers to act for the Union in completing the amalgamation.[26]

Aside from the obvious need for interstate unity there was, from Tetts's standpoint, another good reason for initiating a merger with the Texans. For during the autumn of 1886 the Texas Alliance had infiltrated Louisiana territory; about fifteen lodges in De Soto Parish had joined their western neighbors rather than the Louisiana Union. Moreover, the Agricultural Wheel appeared to be considering a move into Louisiana.[27] Both these organizations were considerably larger than the Union. Tetts seems to have realized that his little association was destined, sooner or later, to be absorbed by one of the more powerful bodies. To approach one of them first, as he did, must have appeared the best course of action.

Attending the Waco gathering were five hundred Texans and John A. Tetts. At the closing session on January 21, the official merger into the Farmers' Alliance took place. Macune assumed the post of president; Tetts became first vice-president.[28] The formidable task of extending the order into other states now confronted them. Yet despite its significance, the birth of the Farmers' Alliance aroused little attention in the press. Louisiana's dailies mentioned it not at all, and to the Galveston *Daily News* the most notable event in Waco on January 21 concerned Jay Gould, who had that day taken a forty-minute tour of the town in the company of some prominent local businessmen. The last paragraph of the same story added, laconically, that some Texas farmers had met "with

[26] Macune, "The Farmers' Alliance," 17; Bryan, *The Farmers' Alliance,* 13; Austin *Daily Statesman,* January 19, 1887.

[27] Mansfield *Democrat,* quoted in Opelousas *St. Landry Democrat,* January 22, 1887; *Biographical and Historical Memoirs of Northwest Louisiana,* 244; Dunning, *The Farmers' Alliance History,* 221.

[28] *National Economist,* I (April 13, 1889) , 57; Morgan, *History of the Wheel and Alliance,* 370.

J. A. Fitts [*sic*] of Louisiana" to form a national association of farmers.[29]

The Farmers' Alliance next assembled at Shreveport in October of 1887. By that time the movement had taken root in eight states and for this reason an Alliance handbook described the Shreveport convention as "the first national meeting" of the order. Those in attendance included the distinguished North Carolina agrarian leader, Leonidas L. Polk. The rival Agricultural Wheel sent a delegation to discuss consolidation; the two would merge within a year.[30] And overtures were made by, and to, industrial labor. Tetts introduced the following resolution at Shreveport: "The National Farmers' Alliance . . . extends its fraternal good wishes to all labor organizations . . . and asks them to assist us in our battle for the rights of producers, and that each work to bring about a harmony of sentiment, and unity of action between the different organizations of labor." [31]

The resolution passed. But its vague phraseology gave a hint of the growing rift within the Farmers' Alliance over the question of combining with urban workers. A fundamental problem was involved: if the Alliance went headlong into "unity of action" with city labor, such unity would doubtless be expressed by pressures upon political parties, and perhaps even by third party action. But with the exception of Texas, a majority of the Southerners in the Alliance were landowners, albeit small ones; and most members in every state were still, during the late 1880's, considered as loyal Democrats.[32] Ma-

29 Galveston *Daily News,* January 22, 1887.

30 F. G. Blood, *Handbook and History of the National Farmers' Alliance and Industrial Union* (Washington, 1893) , 37; New Orleans *Times-Democrat,* October 13, 1887; New Orleans *Daily Picayune,* October 13–14, 1887; N. B. Ashby, *The Riddle of the Sphinx* (Des Moines, 1890) , 437.

31 Quoted in *National Economist,* I (April 13, 1889) , 57.

32 Macune, "The Farmers' Alliance," 11–14, 18–30; John T. Morgan, "Federal Control of Elections," *Forum,* X (September, 1890) , 35–36; Saloutos, *Farmer Movements in the South,* 76.

cune, and the relatively conservative element in the Alliance he represented, showed a willingness to stand with urban labor up to a point. Yet he and the more cautious Alliancemen did not look to the formation of an independent, proletarian political party.

At the time, the Knights of Labor was the only national association of wage earners which had a sizable membership in the South. The Knights embraced workers in the small towns and countryside as well as in the cities; this gave it a partially rural cast and seemed to encourage the prospects of Alliance-Knights cooperation. On the other hand, the Knights took in not only whites, but thousands of Negro laborers; this fact must have bothered many Alliancemen.[33] Within the Alliance, however, there was a poorer and more liberal substratum which anticipated rather than feared the economic and political possibilities of close accord with the Knights, even with the Negro Knights. It was as a spokesman for the left wing of his organization that Tetts wrote: "The labor in the field ought to be a friend to the labor in the factory and the mine. . . . They ought to unite to crush off the leeches that are sucking the life blood of all." [34]

In Louisiana, by the time of the Shreveport convention, the Alliance had entrenched itself in all the upland parishes north of the Red River. Over three hundred chapters were meeting each week. Total membership was now probably close to ten thousand, although claims ran much higher.[35] A few months earlier, in February of 1887, a newspaper which purported to

[33] Philadelphia *Journal of United Labor,* September 17, 1887; Jeanerette *Teche Pilot,* May 5, 1888; Frederick Meyers, "The Knights of Labor in the South," *Southern Economic Journal,* VI (1940), 479, 482.

[34] J. A. Tetts, "The Reason Why," *National Economist,* III (September 6, 1890), 398–99.

[35] Colfax *Chronicle,* March 5, 1887; H. L. Brian's "Farmers' Union Column," in Winnfield *Southern Sentinel,* September 16, 1887; New Orleans *Daily Picayune,* November 16, 1887.

be the state organ of the association, the Choudrant *Farmers' Union*, began weekly publication. Choudrant, a tiny hamlet in Lincoln Parish, did not even have a post office. As a mark of provincial pride, the designation "Farmers' Union," rather than "Farmers' Alliance," continued in popular usage within Louisiana; all state meetings into the 1890's took the previous name.[36] Even so, the allegiance of the Louisiana members to the interstate Alliance was understood by all.

During the following year, 1888, the Farmers' Union spread among the white agriculturists of southcentral Louisiana, and crossed the Mississippi into the old Grange strongholds of the Florida Parishes. By 1889 no less than fifteen thousand, perhaps twenty thousand, Louisiana farmers in thirty-five parishes were enrolled in local chapters; promotional literature in French had begun to be circulated among the Cajun farmers near the Gulf Coast. These Catholic farmers, however, were reluctant to join because of the strictures of their church against secret associations. Some meetings of the Farmers' Union were, in accordance with general Alliance policy, cloaked in secrecy. The fact that membership in the state, although growing, did not keep pace with that in other parts of the South was largely attributed to the hostility of the Catholic Church in the lower parishes.[37]

Surviving pockets of Grange activity were quickly swallowed up into the new order. During the early and mid-1880's the Patrons of Husbandry had taken on a frail second life through the efforts of its old leaders, including Dennett of the *Daily Picayune*. From 1882 through 1886, a prosperous plant-

---

36 Colfax *Chronicle,* March 5, April 30, 1887; Winnfield *Winn Parish Democrat,* September 11, 1888. Hereafter, the term "Farmers' Union" will be used whenever its activities on the state level are described. This will help avoid confusion with the national body and will be in keeping with the usage in contemporary sources.

37 Crowley *Signal,* quoted in Baton Rouge *Daily Capitolian-Advocate,* March 30, 1888; *National Economist,* I (May 25, 1889) , 155–56.

er of East Baton Rouge Parish, Daniel Morgan, assumed charge of what passed for the state Grange. Morgan's political affinity for the unpopular McEnery wing of the Democratic party was common knowledge, and this must have crippled the chances for a Grange revival among rank-and-file farmers.[38] After 1883, a good majority of the active Grangers in Louisiana were to be found in just one backland parish: Winn. In 1884, 1885, and 1886, Morgan came up from Baton Rouge to preside over the annual "state" conventions in Winn. But when the Farmers' Union entered Winn in February of 1887, Grange activity even there virtually ceased. Morgan then forsook it to play a minor role in the Farmers' Union.[39]

The self-help economic program of the Farmers' Union, like the Alliance elsewhere, followed in the main the path staked out by the Patrons of Husbandry. Between 1887 and 1890 about a score of retail stores, owned by farmer-stockholders, operated under the auspices of the Union. Most of these stores, and their state agency, would fail by 1893.[40] Oftener used was a simple device known as the "Farmers' Trade Committee," made up of Union members in various localities, which would meet with nearby merchants and agree to throw all the membership's trade to whichever businessman gave the best terms. A typical arrangement of this sort was found in Grant Parish, where C. C. Nash, a merchant in the town of Colfax, obtained the exclusive business of six Union chapters; Nash pledged to limit his net profit to 10 percent on

[38] New Orleans *Daily Picayune,* February 17–19, 1881; Willis, "The Grange Movement in Louisiana," 26–28; Winnfield *Southern Sentinel,* December 18, 1885; Baton Rouge *Daily Capitolian-Advocate,* December 7, 1887.

[39] Winnfield *Southern Sentinel,* December 18, 1885; Colfax *Chronicle,* September 29, 1888, January 4, 1890.

[40] This statement on the rise and subsequent failure of the Farmers' Union cooperative stores is based upon the following sources: the files of the *National Economist; Biographical and Historical Memoirs of Northwest Louisiana, passim;* Colfax *Chronicle,* April 30, 1887–April 9, 1892; New Orleans *Daily Picayune,* June 30, 1887–April 12, 1890.

cash sales and 20 percent on credit accounts.[41] The fact that the farmers appeared satisfied with this compact offers striking evidence of the severe credit terms which most of them had been enduring.

Most important of all cooperative activities was the creation of a Farmers' Union Commercial Association of Louisiana. It was set up in 1888, with headquarters in New Orleans. Differing little from the state agency of the Grange in the 1870's the association had both wholesale and retail functions. It supplied Farmers' Union retail outlets as well as individual farmers who were able to ship their crops directly to the New Orleans office. G. L. P. Wren, formerly the publisher of the Minden *Eagle-Eye,* presided over the board of directors. But actual control of the association's headquarters fell to state agent Thomas A. Clayton. A Scottish immigrant who had settled near Opelousas in the 1880's, Clayton was instrumental in spreading the Union into St. Landry Parish. Beginning in 1888, he divided his time between the New Orleans office and his farm.[42]

Inherent in the Union and the Alliance economic program was the farmer's conviction that he was being victimized by certain profit-mad business interests, the so-called "money power." Monopolistic businesses, according to the agrarian dialectic, grew rich off the sweat and agony of the "producers," these latter being the plain folk who labored with their hands. Despite the fact that most Alliancemen were landowners, engaging in commercial agriculture, their distress was such during the late nineteenth century that many viewed themselves not as rural capitalists, but as part of the downtrodden

41 Colfax *Chronicle,* March 17, 1888.

42 *National Economist,* I (April 13, 1889) , 59; Colfax *Chronicle,* October 6, 1888; *Biographical and Historical Memoirs of Northwest Louisiana,* 663; *Biographical and Historical Memoirs of Louisiana,* I, 351.

mass which capital exploited.[43] Mounting debts and declining crop prices loomed large in their complaints. A system of government (particularly in Louisiana) which seemed to cater to the desires of the more predatory interests of the commercial world, added to the farmer's woes and intensified his belief that a gigantic plot was afoot against the common man.

The conspiracy theory was, of course, an oversimplification. But it had some validity. And Louisiana's farmers were a provincial lot. They did not travel much. Thus it was natural for them to think that Wall Street was as selfish and immoral as the Carondolet Street brokers of New Orleans who had joined with Major Burke in milking the state, and to assume that Congress was merely an enlarged version of the cesspool of corruption to be found at Baton Rouge. Under the circumstances, it is not surprising that some of the most radical voices in the Farmers' Alliance were heard in Louisiana. John A. Tetts was one of them. But the man who most upset the Bourbon elite was the state lecturer of the Farmers' Union, Thomas J. Guice of De Soto Parish.

Guice's origins were as obscure as his circumstances were humble. He had drifted into Louisiana from Texas, where he was reportedly active in the Greenback Party during the late 1870's. His poverty and shabby clothes furnished much amusement for his conservative critics. At the same time, Guice's activities provoked some of the choicest of Bourbon expletives. He was characterized as a "dirty . . . greasy . . . ignorant" demagogue who possessed a "wide expanse of tobacco stained bosom." Snickering inquiries were made regarding his bathing habits. Yet many admitted the ability of "Greasy Guice"

---

43 Topeka *Advocate,* quoted in *National Economist,* III (March 22, 1890) , 15; Natchitoches *Louisiana Populist,* September 28, 1894. See also, Norman Pollack, *The Populist Response to Industrial America* (Cambridge, Mass., 1962) , 18, 68–69.

to sway rural audiences.[44] Once, while haranguing a crowd at Natchitoches, Guice carried the conspiracy theory to the length of implying that the Civil War itself had been a plot to enslave the white worker under the pretense of freeing the Negro. "The farmers and laborers should be the rulers," Guice insisted. Otherwise, the "moneyed aristocracy" would increase its power until "[we] will be reduced to the condition of the English and Irish peasantry." [45]

Rural anger sometimes exploded into violence. To a farmer deep in debt, the village merchant might be looked upon as a local manifestation of the satanic Baron Rothschild described in Guice's orations. The fact that so many of Louisiana's rural merchants happened to be Jewish made the comparison even more plausible. Beginning in 1879, years before the spread of the Farmers' Union, attacks upon the lives and property of Jewish tradesmen were reported rather frequently in parts of Louisiana. That year, for example, in St. Landry Parish the stores of Carl Wolff and P. Jacobs were destroyed by arsonists, as was the residence of another merchant named Sam Kaufman. In 1881, Lazarus Meyer, a prominent credit merchant in Catahoula Parish, was murdered by an irate customer. Five years later, to cite another instance, State Legislator Simon Witkowski, described as a "renegade Jew" and "one of Governor McEnery's satraps," was forced to depart from West Carroll Parish, where he owned thousands of acres and a number of stores. Witkowski's white tenants threatened his life, burned one of his business establishments and murdered two of his employees.[46] Oc-

44 Mansfield *Journal*, quoted in Colfax *Chronicle*, November 5, 1892; Bastrop *Morehouse Clarion*, quoted in Baton Rouge *Daily Advocate*, June 17, 1891; New Orleans *Daily Picayune*, August 7, 1891; Bastrop *Clarion-Appeal*, quoted in Shreveport *Evening Judge*, February 11, 1896.

45 Quoted in *National Economist*, I (June 15, 1889) , 198–99.

46 New Orleans *Daily Picayune*, May 22, 1879; Rayville *Richland Beacon*, October 8, 1881; Floyd *Messenger*, quoted in New Orleans *Daily Picayune*,

casionally, reports came in from the country of attempts made against gentile merchants. But these were less frequent.

Toward the end of the 1880's the number of reprisals by rural debtors against their Jewish creditors increased. The gun vied with the torch as a favored weapon. During the spring of 1887, rifles were discharged into the homes of Jewish tradesmen in Avoyelles Parish, while arsonists in Baton Rouge destroyed a gentile house of business as well as a Jewish one.[47] In 1889, during broad daylight, a "large band" of white farmers rode into the Richland Parish community of Delhi and shot up every mercantile establishment in town. All but one of Delhi's stores were owned by Jews. The farmers had taken this action, it was said, "to clear off old debts." Two months later the same Delhi merchants received several anonymous, threatening messages demanding that they leave town posthaste.[48]

A spectacular plan of agrarian violence was plotted by debtors in Bienville Parish early in 1888. They tried, unsuccessfully, to burn the entire business section of the town of Arcadia.[49] It is instructive to note that during the harvest season preceding the arson attempt, 16,116 bales of cotton were shipped from Arcadia and 15,000 of these had passed through the hands of local merchants.[50]

The Farmers' Union did not endorse such destructive outbursts. Nor was the organization ever accused of doing so by

October 12, 1887. For Witkowski, see also New Orleans *Weekly Pelican,* December 4, 1886. The above is by no means a complete list of instances found of attacks on Jewish businessmen in Louisiana.

[47] Colfax *Chronicle,* March 19, 1887; New Orleans *Daily Picayune,* November 12, 1887.

[48] Vicksburg *Commercial Herald,* quoted in Rayville *Richland Beacon,* November 2, 1889; Shreveport *Daily Caucasian,* January 4, 1890.

[49] Arcadia *Record,* quoted in Baton Rouge *Daily Capitolian-Advocate,* March 30, 1888.

[50] Arcadia *Louisiana Advance,* quoted in Baton Rouge *Daily Capitolian-Advocate,* February 1, 1888.

even the most critical Bourbon newspapers. But it is quite probable that many of the rifles and torches used against Jewish credit merchants were carried by men who were members of the Union. What should not be as readily assumed, however, is that anti-Semitic emotions played a significant role in these shootings and burnings. Possibly this was a factor in some cases. But that Jewish stores were hit oftener than those owned by gentiles proves nothing, since in many Louisiana communities Jewish merchants greatly outnumbered those of other faiths. As for the Farmers' Union, none of its orators or publicists appear to have ever attacked Jews as such; the references to Baron Rothschild as the head of the "money power" assailed him because he was an international banker, not because of his religion. Actually, the single overtly anti-Semitic diatribe to be found in a Louisiana publication of this era turned up in a Negro newspaper, the *Weekly Louisianian*.[51]

What the Union and the Alliance in various states did openly attack, and work against, was the power of certain business monopolies or near-monopolies. On one occasion a victory was won. In 1888–89, the Alliance undertook a boycott against the companies of the jute bagging trust, which manufactured the covering used on all cotton bales. This industry had aroused the ire of Southern farmers in 1888 by raising the price of the article to an allegedly "unreasonable" level. A Farmers' Union convention at Opelousas in August condemned the jute bagging trust and proposed "to take measures for the introduction of cotton bagging to be used in wrapping bales . . . instead of jute." [52] Farmers were jubilant when the Lane Company of New Orleans responded with the news that

51 New Orleans *Weekly Louisianian,* July 23, 1881.
52 New York *Times,* quoted in Lake Providence *Carroll Democrat,* July 28, 1888; Colfax *Chronicle,* August 11, 1888.

their firm had succeeded in making a cotton article which met the requirements for bale covering, yet would sell for a cheaper price than jute. Other state Alliances were equally interested. At Birmingham, in May of 1889, Alliance leaders from across the South voted unanimously to substitute coton bagging for jute. As it turned out, the makers of jute became thoroughly frightened by all this activity, and by 1890 the price of the article had gone down.[53] The triumph over the jute industry, important in itself, also gave Alliancemen a new sense of power.

As the decade of the 1890's began, inflated claims of membership in the Farmers' Alliance ran as high as 3,000,000, and this figure was reputed to directly "represent" a rural population of 10,000,000. More modestly, a census of the order listed 1,269,500 dues-paying adherents in twenty-two states.[54] Louisiana's membership was officially reported as 40,000 in 1890; and by that time Thomas Scott Adams, about whom more is to be said later, had replaced John Stallings as head of the Union.[55] Meanwhile, Dr. Macune's efforts to unite with the other National (Northern) Alliance had failed, but at a joint convention held in St. Louis in 1889 the agrarian leaders of Kansas and the Dakotas bolted the Northern organization to come into the stronger, primarily Southern, Alliance. Macune in 1889 stepped down as president, and

[53] *National Economist,* I (June 15, 1889), 208; William Warren Rogers, "Agrarianism in Alabama" (Ph.D. dissertation, University of North Carolina, 1959), 279, 287.

[54] Joseph R. Buchanan, "The Coming Cataclysm of America and Europe," *Arena,* II (August, 1890), 301; *Appleton's Annual Cyclopaedia, 1890* (New York, 1891), 301; New York *Times,* September 15, 1890; Haynes, *Third Party Movements,* 234–35.

[55] Shreveport *Daily Caucasian,* January 8, 1890; Shreveport *Weekly Caucasian,* January 30, 1890. It seems doubtful, however, that more than 25,000— or at most 30,000—Louisiana farmers were actually dues-paying members by 1890.

L. L. Polk presided from that year until his death in 1892.[56] Yet Macune, as editor of the *National Economist,* continued to hold a major influence in the affairs of the order. The Alliance, Macune insisted, "is a living, active . . . embodiment of the cause of Jesus Christ." [57]

Even as the Alliance claimed affinity with Jesus, so did a more worldly body than either, the Democratic Party of the South, assert that it was in communion with the cause of the farmer. Beyond question, most white Alliancemen in the South were, before 1890, dutiful Democrats. But from the beginning the agrarian movement had attracted some political heretics. A significant minority of the Louisiana Farmers' Union membership had a record of Greenbacker and even Republican activity. Most notably, the old Greenbacker-Republican coalition in Winn and Grant parishes, led by Benjamin Brian, wasted no time in joining the Union.[58] The fact that Parson Brian, and many others like him throughout the South, had gone into the Alliance worried conservative elements both inside and outside the order.

At first the Bourbon chieftains tended to scoff at suggestions that the dirt farmers of the Alliance might some day rebel against the party of home rule and white supremacy.[59] The real problem, as the more complacent Bourbons saw it, was to forestall the efforts of the Alliance to liberalize the Democratic Party from within. Benign platitudes and sympathy for the woes of agriculturists began to be expressed by Democratic leaders in practically every part of the South as the Alliance

56 *National Economist,* II (December 21, 1889) , 215–17; Herman C. Nixon, "The Cleavage Within the Farmers' Alliance Movement," *Mississippi Valley Historical Review,* XV (1928) , 22–33; Carl C. Taylor, *The Farmers' Movements: 1620–1920* (New York, 1953) , 255; Stuart Noblin, *Leonidas La Fayette Polk: Agrarian Crusader* (Chapel Hill, N.C., 1949) , 212.

57 Dunning, *The Farmers' Alliance History,* 260.

58 Colfax *Chronicle,* November 19, 1887, May 5, 1888; New Orleans *Daily Picayune,* August 7, 1891.

59 Morgan, *Forum,* X, 35.

grew to formidable size. Yet the entrenched officeholders, with few exceptions, had no real intention of acceding to the Alliance demands for government aid to agriculture. Nor were they willing to give ordinary farmers a larger voice in party councils. Typical was the attitude of the *Daily Picayune,* which maintained that although agrarians in Republican states might have ample cause for political independency, the rural folk of Dixie already enjoyed "a party which, while devoted to no special cause, nevertheless afford[s] the farmer every protection." [60]

Even the ultra-Bourbon regime of Louisiana was compelled to take notice of the rising spirit of agrarian unrest. Prior to 1886, however, statewide agricultural organizations had lacked either the inclination or the potency to disturb the status quo. For the Louisiana Sugar Planters' Association embraced the great land barons of the southern parishes, and its head, Duncan F. Kenner, was an "old line Whig" worth about $2 million.[61] While in the cotton parishes the National Cotton Planters' Association (first known as the Mississippi Valley Cotton Planters' Association) had been meeting since 1879; membership in it was also confined to the larger landlords, together with some merchants.[62] And the Grange had been too weak to disturb professional politicians.

But late in 1886 the efforts to create the Louisiana Farmers' Union began to merit Bourbon attention. As the young order started taking shape in the northwestern parishes, an announcement was made in Baton Rouge to the effect that His Excellency Samuel D. McEnery had become concerned with the need for agricultural unity. On December 2, 1886, Gover-

60 New Orleans *Daily Picayune,* December 8, 1890.
61 New Orleans *Weekly Pelican,* July 9, 1887; *Dictionary of American Biography,* X, 337–38.
62 St. Joseph *North Louisiana Journal,* May 10, 1879; Saloutos, *Farmer Movements in the South,* 57–59.

nor McEnery issued a proclamation which read, in part: "As Governor of Louisiana [I] do hereby request the planters and farmers of Louisiana to meet at the city of Baton Rouge, in the agricultural hall of the State University [on January 26, 1887] for the purpose of organizing a State Agricultural Society." [63]

McEnery had been urged by a certain "Farmers' and Planters' Club" of the Baton Rouge area to issue this call. Significantly, Daniel Morgan, a political supporter of the Governor, was a leading member of this club.[64] Morgan, who at the time was also the Master of the moribund state Grange, was in a position because of his trips upstate to have knowledge of the Farmers' Union; the Union had not as yet been noticed by the New Orleans or Baton Rouge newspapers. McEnery made no public mention of the Farmers' Union. But there is a suspicious coincidence about the date of the Governor's proclamation, and the date for which he set the organizational meeting of the proposed State Agricultural Society: the former was issued during the time that Tetts and his friends were discussing amalgamation with the Texas order; the latter missed by five days the birth of the Farmers' Alliance at Waco.

An oration by the Governor opened the first session of the Louisiana State Agricultural Society. "Labor has organized," declared McEnery, "and it is opportune, yea even a necessity, for agriculture to combine." But the nature of the association which the Governor visualized can best be judged by the names of those who were presently chosen to fill the society's offices. General Joseph L. Brent, a very conservative sugar planter and Democratic legislator from Ascension Parish, served as president from 1887 until 1890. Brent also

[63] *Proceedings of the First Annual Session of the Louisiana State Agricultural Society* (Baton Rouge, 1887) , 3.
[64] Baton Rouge *Weekly Truth,* April 16, December 17, 1886.

headed a parish branch of the Sugar Planters' Association.[65] Other sugar planter Democratic politicians served as district vice-presidents or as members of the society's executive committee. Among the more prominent were John Dymond, Emile Rost and Donelson Caffery, Sr.

None of the Farmers' Union leaders were listed on the society's committees, nor were any of them reported as attending the organization meeting. McEnery expressed disappointment that "every parish in the State was not present." [66] He obviously hoped that the state's small agriculturists would accept the leadership of the large planters who headed the society. Also it was probable that McEnery desired to use the society as a fulcrum to pry the farmer vote away from Francis T. Nicholls and toward himself. For the gubernatorial campaign of 1887–88 was then beginning.

The Shreveport *Times,* temporarily at odds with McEnery, made the snide observation that "such sturdy farmers as Governor McEnery and Editor Jastremski" were at the society's first convention, along with Major Burke and other "horny handed sons of toil." It added that these gentlemen were, to be sure, interested in "cultivation"; they wished to cultivate the farm vote for the incumbent regime.[67] More abrupt was the reaction of the Homer *Claiborne Guardian,* which blasted the society as a "sinister" maneuver by McEnery; it was "another contemptible rope-in." [68] An Opelousas editor predicted that "the great mass of farmers" would wisely shun it.[69] Yet none of the Farmers' Union ac-

<hr />

[65] *Proceedings of the First Annual Session of the Louisiana State Agricultural Society,* 6, 33–34; Brown, *Ascension Parish,* 28.

[66] *Proceedings of the First Annual Session of the Louisiana State Agricultural Society,* 6.

[67] Shreveport *Times,* quoted in New Orleans *Daily Picayune,* January 24, 1887.

[68] Homer *Claiborne Guardian,* quoted in Opelousas *St. Landry Democrat,* January 15, 1887.

[69] Opelousas *St. Landry Democrat,* February 5, 1887.

tivists publicly denounced the society. While McEnery was governor they simply kept away from its meetings.

After Nicholls' return to the State House in 1888 a number of small farmers commenced participating in the society. North Louisiana came in for special attention; in 1888 the annual convention was held at Shreveport, in 1889 at Monroe, in 1890 at Arcadia, and in 1891 at Alexandria. Still, conservative Democratic sugar planters remained at the society's helm. On one or two occasions, however, a radical managed to insert a word into its sessions. At the third convention, a farmer named G. V. Soniat was scheduled to read a paper with the innocuous title: "Review of the Rice Industry of Louisiana." But he shocked the staid society's officials with a closing, off-the-subject tirade: "Arise, ye agriculturists. . . . The legislators are against us. The speculators are against us. The agriculturist is about turned beggar in the land of plenty; the sweat of his brow is turned into pearls by that grinding despot, monopoly. . . . The time is now ripe for a leader to call us together and beckon us to enter one grand association or party of agriculturists, to control the destinies of this nation." [70]

Quite the contrary were the opinions held by society president Brent, who spoke for those who dominated the order. He expressed horror at any proposal to form a "new party." In almost the same breath he defended that bane of the small farmer, the crop-lien. "Credit," asserted Brent, "is the flower and blossom of good government," and he argued that toilers who were hurt by the system ought to blame their "individual frailty." [71] Toward the Farmers' Union,

[70] G. V. Soniat, "Review of the Rice Industry of Louisiana," in *Proceedings of the Third Annual Session of the Louisiana State Agricultural Society*, 39–40.

[71] General J. L. Brent, *Annual Address Delivered January 25, 1888, at Shreveport. Before the Louisiana State Agricultural Society* (New Orleans, 1888), 15.

Brent took a friendly but cautious approach. In 1888 he "expressed a desire to hear an explanation of [its] objectives and purposes" and invited its members to attend the society's next state convention.[72] By the following year, Brent had concluded that the Farmers' Union was a "beneficent organization," and he implied that it was really in partnership with the society. "We," he proclaimed, "are so numerous that if we organize in politic[s] . . . all the powers and functions of the State would pass under our control." Of course, he added, Louisiana's agriculturists should never take advantage of their electoral majority. To do such a thing would be, he said, "inexpedient." [73]

In the end, the Nicholls "Reform" wing of the Democratic Party would prove more adroit than the McEneryites in blunting the thrust of agrarian unrest. The transparent ploy of the state society accomplished little in that direction for either McEnery or Nicholls; but beginning in 1890 a different and more subtle effort was made by the Nicholls gentry to capture the Farmers' Union. To achieve this goal the "Reform" Democrats required a stalking horse within the Union. They discovered him in the person of Thomas Scott Adams.

Adams, a prosperous cattleman and planter of East Feliciana Parish, had come to Louisiana in 1853 at the age of thirteen. His South Carolina birthplace was not far from that of John Tetts. A college graduate and an officer in the Confederate army, Adams had been reared in the genteel tradition of *noblesse oblige*. He entered politics in 1884. Elected to the state legislature that year, Adams quickly became "disgusted with the corruption" he discovered at Baton Rouge.[74] When Farmers' Union organizers visited the Florida Parishes, Ad-

72 Baton Rouge *Daily Capitolian-Advocate,* January 28, 1888.
73 *Proceedings of the Third Annual Session of the Louisiana State Agricultural Society,* 4–8.
74 *Biographical and Historical Memoirs of Louisiana,* I, 246–47.

ams was one of several substantial planters who joined. He was elected president of the state Union in 1888, and was reelected at each of its next three annual conventions. And by the end of his fourth term in 1892, the Union was all but dead.[75] Through ineptness and political naivete, and perhaps a touch of his own mendacity, Adams figured largely in that decline.

The Feliciana planter did give enthusiastic support to most of the economic program urged by the Farmers' Alliance. But in the all-important area of politics, he remained an unswerving Democrat. More conservative than most of the Alliance leaders in other states, Adams did not even suggest a change of personnel within the dominant party: "We ask for a change of measures, not of men," he told his fellow Louisianians.[76] Adams seemed particularly anxious to put down third-party talk among the rank and file. Gratefully, the Nicholls administration sought him out.

In August of 1890, shortly before his second reelection as president of the Farmers' Union, Adams was appointed state commissioner of agriculture by Governor Nicholls. Ominously, the *Daily Advocate,* which steadfastly opposed almost any conceivable sort of reform, agrarian or otherwise, thought Adams's appointment "an excellent one." [77] And the Nicholls conservatives were raising other signs of pretended friendship to the Union. By official invitation, the Farmers' Union held its 1890 convention inside the State House.

As the rustic delegates gathered in the State House on a hot August day in 1890, a few blocks away another and better dressed convention of "the leading citizens of Louisiana" had simultaneously begun. The latter was the first meeting of the

75 New Orleans *Times-Democrat,* August 2, 1892.
76 "Address of President Adams at the State Meeting," *National Economist,* III (August 30, 1890) , 381.
77 Baton Rouge *Daily Advocate,* August 3, 1890.

Anti-Lottery League.[78] Wealthy gentlemen from New Orleans and the sugar parishes, including Edgar Farrar, Donelson Caffery, Sr., and Murphy J. Foster, had set up the League for the primary purpose of fighting the Louisiana Lottery Company's bid for constitutional recharter in the forthcoming state election of 1892.

It was expected that the Lottery, while seeking an extenuation of its life, would also strive to return its friend, McEnery, to the governorship. The men of the Anti-Lottery League in 1890, preparing for the fight against the hated company and McEnery, implored the Farmers' Union to join forces with them. From the standpoint of the patricians such a coalition would have the incidental benefit of averting the agrarians' attention away from more basic and radical reforms. Some of the Unionmen were suspicious of the Anti-Lottery League's motives, and more should have been. Because one of the most Machiavellian maneuvers in the long, squalid history of Louisiana politics was about to commence.

---

[78] *Ibid.*, August 7–8, 1890; Sidney James Romero, "The Political Career of Murphy James Foster," *Louisiana Historical Quarterly,* XXVIII (1945), 1150–52.

VIII

Black Protest and White Power

W H Y   W A S   I T, wondered a Bourbon leader of Opelousas, that Negroes kept on trying to rise above their station in life. He knew of some who were "scared to death" of visits from white vigilantes and yet, paradoxically, even the most frightened of them persisted in taking an interest in politics and other matters which did not concern them. This was odd behavior for a sub-human species. All he could surmise was that "niggers are strange animals any way you take them." [1]

This view of the black caste as something outside the pale of humanity was heard all too frequently in post-Reconstruction Louisiana. The fierce Negrophobia of Hearsey's *Daily States* became the standard response of a predominant portion of the political and journalistic elite; and the supposed horrors of "rapine and robbery" of Reconstruction's "negro rule" were constantly recalled,[2] although the state had never at any time been under the control of blacks.[3] During the 1880's and 1890's individual instances of paternalism toward the Negro were still discoverable, but the ruling classes' public attitude, being one of contempt and cruelty, militated

[1] Opelousas *St. Landry Clarion,* April 4, 1896.
[2] For prime, but not unusual, examples of this continuing theme, see St. Joseph *North Louisiana Journal,* October 30, 1880; Plaquemine *Iberville South,* April 18, 1896.
[3] Highsmith, "Louisiana During Reconstruction," 188.

against the humane instincts of *noblesse oblige.* Sometimes even acts of presumed kindness revealed racial discrimination in its shabbiest forms. In a typical example, the Shreveport *Times,* in offering to give away mutilated coins to local children, thought it necessary to add: "the white babies can have the large pieces and the colored ones the nickels." [4]

Not many Louisiana Negroes of the time were able to leave written evidence of their reaction to the increasingly hostile environment in which they lived. There was, to be sure, an articulate and relatively well-to-do black minority in and near New Orleans; their recorded opinions show a grim cognizance of what was happening and a helpless rage against Bourbonism.[5] While on occasion, the actions of the poverty-stricken black majority spoke as loudly as words. The "Kansas Fever" of 1879 gave strong proof of their discontent. In the decade which followed, although few attempted emigration, mass black protests against conditions within the state by no means ceased.

In 1880 and again in 1887, Negro wage earners in the sugar parishes engaged in strikes which brought down upon them the wrath of their employers and the state government. Upstate, the blacks appeared more docile. The sharecropping system prevalent in the cotton parishes held out less hope for economic advancement than did the meager wages paid cane field workers, but the decentralized nature of cotton plantations limited the possibility of unified protests by Negro families. In the sugar country, on the other hand, the gang labor system and the existence of an active (though white-run) Republican Party encouraged cohesion among Ne-

[4] Shreveport *Times,* quoted in Natchitoches *People's Vindicator,* October 22, 1881.

[5] Based on the files of Louisiana's two leading post-Reconstruction Negro newspapers, the New Orleans *Weekly Louisianian* and the New Orleans *Weekly Pelican.*

groes; they were allowed a modicum of choice in politics as well as in place of employment. Blacks in the cotton parishes generally had little free will in anything.

The 1880 sugar strikes commenced in the fields of St. Charles Parish on March 17. Plantation owners immediately accused the Negro ringleaders of trespassing upon private property "and inciting the laborers to stop work in the fields." According to the parish judge, the instigators were armed with weapons and had been "forcing workers to join their band by assaults and threats." Judge James D'Augustin admitted, however, that most of the black population of St. Charles was in sympathy with the "rioters." For that reason, D'Augustin claimed that local authorities could not handle the disturbance, and so he called upon the state for militia.[6]

Richard Gooseberry, spokesman for the St. Charles strikers, denied the allegations of violence. The colored people, he said, "had simply struck for one dollar a day, as they could no longer work for seventy-five cents." Nevertheless, the planters maintained that Gooseberry's followers threatened to kill white people, burn down dwellings, and seize control of the entire parish. As it turned out, there were no specific acts of violence against the white minority of St. Charles.[7] It must also be said that the strikers displayed remarkable forbearance when they gathered, on March 19, to listen to speeches by Judge D'Augustin and others who "expounded the law to them." One official passed this compliment on to the black audience: "The great arm of the great wheel of agriculture is the nigger. Next is the mule."[8]

A battalion of state militia presently arrived in St. Charles. No resistance was met. Twelve strikers were arrested, sent

[6] New Orleans *Democrat,* March 19, 1880; New Orleans *Daily Picayune,* March 19, 1880.
[7] New Orleans *Democrat,* March 18–21, 1880.
[8] New Orleans *Daily Picayune,* March 20, 1880.

to New Orleans, and sentenced to jail terms. Ostensibly they were guilty of trespass; but more to the point, they had run afoul of the Bourbon position that "all strikes are wrong, criminally wrong, both in theory and act." [9] The trouble in St. Charles appeared to be over, and as yet there had been no outbreaks reported elsewhere.

But labor discontent soon extended to other parishes along the lower delta. By March 29, the situation in St. John the Baptist Parish looked more serious than had the previous disturbance in neighboring St. Charles. The same demand was voiced: daily wages must be raised from the present level of seventy-five cents. But the St. John Negroes struck a more militant pose. They proclaimed that "the colored people are a nation and must stand together." Indeed, the ringleaders set up a governing council, complete with a constitution. All strikers in the parish took an oath to obey this constitution, which stated that none would work for less than one dollar a day, and any who violated the oath "shall be punished with a severe thrashing." A correspondent for the *Daily Picayune,* though hostile to the strike, was impressed by the earnestness of the blacks. "Strange to say," he wrote, "they have kept sober." [10]

Governor Wiltz responded to the pleas of the St. John landowners with a warning to "these evil doers and mischievous persons to desist from their evil doings." He also sent in state troops. The militia, it was explained, was being used to "protect the laborers" from harm. Despite a number of arrests, the disturbance in St. John continued for several days. Blacks paraded along the dusty parish roads, carrying banners which read: "A DOLLAR A DAY OR KANSAS," and "PEACE—ONE DOLLAR A DAY." But no violence, outside

9 Opelousas *St. Landry Democrat,* September 24, 1881.
10 New Orleans *Daily Picayune,* March 29, 31, 1880.

of the whipping of Negroes by Negroes, was reported. One of the instigators of the strike, when arrested, remarked that he was "glad to go to jail," for at least there he would get "enough to eat." [11]

It was not entirely a coincidence that the St. John strike occurred during the same week that ex-President Ulysses S. Grant paid a visit to Louisiana. The strike leaders knew of it, and apparently timed their activities accordingly. Grant arrived in New Orleans at the peak of the trouble in nearby St. John. "The deluded laborers," one report noted, anticipate that "Grant will come up and make the planters pay extra wages." [12] As the *Weekly Louisianian* rather sadly put it, the unlettered black masses viewed Grant as a kind of superman.[13] At the opposite extreme, his visit touched off a predictable editorial tirade in the *Daily States*.[14]

The hero of Appomattox was, in one sense, concerned with Negro affairs in Louisiana. During his stay in New Orleans, he attended a reception at the home of P. B. S. Pinchback, where he met "the cream of Negro society." [15] Pinchback and a number of his guests were scheduled to be delegates to the upcoming Republican national convention. And Grant hoped to return to the White House in 1881. Other than that, he demonstrated no interest in local matters except when he said that "I think the South is better suited [for the black man] than any other place. . . . I want him to have the right to stay where the climate suits him." [16]

[11] New Orleans *Democrat*, March 27–April 2, 1880; New Orleans *Daily Picayune*, March 31, 1880.

[12] New Orleans *Daily Picayune*, April 1, 1880.

[13] New Orleans *Weekly Louisianian*, April 3, 1880.

[14] New Orleans *Daily States*, quoted in Bastrop *Morehouse Clarion*, April 16, 1880.

[15] Uzee, "Republican Politics in Louisiana," 97.

[16] New Orleans *Weekly Louisianian*, April 10, 1880. When James Garfield, rather than Grant, was nominated by the Republicans in 1880, Louisiana's Negroes expressed marked disappointment. Uneducated blacks had never heard of Garfield and asked "who 'Garfish' was." Uzee, "Republican Politics in Louisiana," 100.

Shortly after Grant's departure from New Orleans, the strike in St. John was broken. Later in the month of April, however, sporadic strikes by cane field laborers were reported in Ascension, St. James, St. Bernard, Jefferson, and Plaquemines parishes. But in these instances the presence of the militia was not required. Local authorities broke up the disturbances by summary arrests of the ringleaders. Thus the strikes of 1880 had totally failed. During the next few years, wages generally remained at seventy to seventy-five cents a day for "first class" adult males. Only in the busy harvest and grinding season (from around late October to the end of the year) was there a wage raise, usually to ninety cents or one dollar.[17]

Localized labor disturbances, poorly organized and barren of results, sprang up at intervals in the sugar country during the years from 1881 through 1886. Until the latter year, black workers were not affiliated with any recognizable labor organization. Even in the relatively serious strikes of 1880, there seems to have been no effort to unify the laborers of the several parishes. Those in one locality may have taken their cue from events elsewhere, but no attempt at interparish coordination was observed by correspondents on the scene.

In New Orleans, meanwhile, a degree of cooperation among laboring groups was slowly being achieved—including some unity between black and white—but as yet there were no tangible benefits from it. Late in 1880 a vague "Association" of thirteen city unions was formed, embracing whites and Negroes, skilled and unskilled.[18] In September of the following year the various orders within the Association all threatened to strike for higher wages; and the more than ten thousand dockworkers, of whom 30 percent were Negro, carried the threat into action. Negro strikebreakers were hired and

17 Andrew H. Gay, Jr., to Andrew H. Gay, Sr., January 19, 1888, in Gay Family Papers; Sitterson, *Sugar Country*, 248, 319.
18 Pearce, "The Rise and Decline of Labor in New Orleans." 25.

brought in from as far away as Savannah, but for once the local dockworkers of both colors stood together in demonstrations and attacks against the "scabs." [19] The strike eventually subsided without significant concessions to the laborers, but even so an unprecedented degree of biracial harmony had been revealed. When a black demonstrator was killed by police, "it was a source of satisfaction" to the Negro press to see great numbers of white workers march in his funeral procession.[20]

In 1883 the Knights of Labor entered Louisiana. One of the most ambitious and visionary associations in American labor history, the Knights advocated a uniting of all working people, of whatever skill, color, or sex, into one gigantic order. At the same time, however, the Knights shunned the Marxist and anarchistic radicalism of the time; their national leaders did not seek the extinction of capitalism.[21] But the very fact that the Knights promoted class consciousness and organized Negroes along with whites made the order, in the eyes of Southern Bourbons, a dangerous disturber of the status quo.

At first confined to New Orleans, and inconsequential there, the Knights drew little attention in the Pelican State until 1886. Nationally, the order reached its peak membership that year, then began to decline. Yet contrary to the trend elsewhere, the Knights developed new strength in the rural South; losses in Northern cities during the late 1880's were partially offset by fresh adherents from the Southern towns and countryside. Particularly was it growing in North Carolina and Louisiana.[22] New Orleans provided most of the leadership for the Knights' plan of expansion in the Pelican

[19] New Orleans *Daily Picayune*, August 26, September 1–13, 1881; New Orleans *Weekly Louisianian*, August 13, September 17, 1881.

[20] New Orleans *Weekly Louisianian*, September 17, 1881.

[21] Meyers, *Southern Economic Journal*, VI, 483; Foster Rhea Dulles, *Labor in America* (2nd ed.; New York, 1960), 126–27.

[22] New Orleans *Daily Picayune*, March 26, 1886; Meyers, *Southern Economic*

State. At least five thousand urbanites joined it by mid 1887, and a Knights newspaper, *Southern Industry,* had commenced weekly publication.[23]

It was from the city that Knights organizers fanned out into the lower delta parishes in 1886, to impress upon cane field Negroes the need for unity in obtaining concessions from their landlord-employers. Higher wages and payment in regular currency "instead of commissary paste board" were the prime rallying points. The Knights simultaneously recruited artisans of both races in South Louisiana's towns. Early in 1887 the Knights were potent enough in Morgan City to run a slate of candidates in the municipal election, and every man on the labor ticket won office. Conservative planters and businessmen were beginning to take alarm.[24]

Louisiana's sugar growers, after experiencing a bad crop in 1886, reduced wages for the following year to sixty-five cents per day, without rations. Most workers averaged twenty days out of every month in the fields. The larger planters paid wages in commissary script, redeemable only at the plantation stores. Actually, a Negro family with one employed member would receive what amounted to six or seven dollars in real wages per month during the ten-month growing season. Workers without rations had to feed and clothe their families out of this small amount, although usually no rent was charged for the cramped living quarters. Pay for the grinding season of 1887 was set at rates varying from seventy-

Journal, VI, 485–86; Richard J. Hinton, "Organizations of the Discontented," *Forum,* VII (July, 1889) , 550.

23 New Orleans *Southern Industry* was edited by William I. O'Donnell. It was one of twenty-one Knights newspapers published at that time in the United States. Philadelphia *Journal of United Labor,* April 9, 1887; New Orleans *Weekly Pelican,* July 9, 1887.

24 Hall, "Labor Struggles in the Deep South," 31; New Orleans *Daily Picayune,* January 4, 1887; Letter from "W. W. F.," Springfield, La., in Philadelphia *Journal of United Labor,* August 27, 1887.

five cents to $1.15 per day for "first class" adult males; and for six hours of overtime night work, called a "watch," the planters offered fifty cents.[25]

During August of 1887, ten weeks before harvest, the Knights leadership requested a conference with local branches of the Louisiana Sugar Planters' Association. They wanted to discuss wages for the approaching busy season. Association officials sent no reply. Later, on October 24, the Knights District Assembly 194 addressed a circular letter to planters in Iberia, Lafourche, St. Martin, St. Mary and Terrebonne parishes, insisting that wages be raised for the November-December months of harvesting and grinding. The scale drawn up by the Knights proposed $1.25 per day without rations, or $1.00 per day with rations. For a night watch, no less than sixty cents would be accepted. Furthermore, instead of monthly payments, the Knights demanded that wages for day work be received every two weeks, and "watch" money each week. The District Assembly of the Knights comprised about forty locals in the five parishes. Planters were informed that they must meet the terms by November 1, or face a general strike.[26]

An estimated six thousand to ten thousand laborers went on strike when the deadline date arrived with no sign of acquiescence from the planters. Nine-tenths of the strikers were Negroes. All were said to be members of the Knights of Labor. The planters, although refusing to negotiate, were visibly disturbed; the growing season of 1887 had been one of near-perfect weather, and a large crop yield was in pros-

---

25 Cf. Philadelphia *Journal of United Labor,* September 17, 1887; New Orleans *Times-Democrat,* November 6, 1887; New Orleans *Weekly Pelican,* November 19, 1887; Sitterson, *Sugar Country,* 319–20.

26 New Orleans *Daily Picayune,* October 29, 1887; New Orleans *Weekly Pelican,* November 5, 1887; Philadelphia *Journal of United Labor,* November 26, 1887.

pect.[27] Conservative newspapers depicted the strikers' demands as "unreasonable" and "reprehensible," and insisted that the current market price of sugar precluded any increase in wages.[28] As for biweekly or weekly paydays, the planters claimed that this "would demoralize labor." Because it was "a well known fact that as long as the average laborer has money he will not work." [29]

The local officials of the Knights, who were white men and literate blacks, received the brunt of landowner wrath. Special bitterness was expressed toward J. R. H. Foote and D. Monnier, white laborers of the town of Thibodaux, in Lafourche Parish. Other leaders among the Lafourche Knights included Henry Cox, George Cox and P. O. Rousseau. The Cox brothers were Negro artisans. Rousseau, a white man, had once been a planter but "times [had] changed" for him.[30] In Terrebonne Parish, a light-skinned Negro named Jim Brown led the strike, while in St. Mary, black men took the lead in labor agitation among the sugar workers. They, together with Negroes who urged the strike in other parishes, were categorized by Major Burke's *Times-Democrat* as "bad and dangerous . . . relic[s] of Radical days." [31]

Planter spokesmen also vented anger upon the New Orleans Knights who had first organized the lower sugar country. These urban "communists," as the *Daily States* termed them, were blamed for arousing "passions" among the usually

27 Hall, "Labor Struggles in the Deep South," 32; New Orleans *Weekly Pelican,* November 5, 1887; William C. Stubbs, *Sugar Cane: A Treatise on the History, Botany and Agriculture of Sugar Cane and the Chemistry and Manufacture of Its Juices Into Sugar, and Other Products* (Baton Rouge, 1897), I, 37–38.

28 Thibodaux *Sentinel,* November 12, 1887; Baton Rouge *Daily Capitolian-Advocate,* November 4, 1887; New Orleans *Times-Democrat,* November 3–6, 1887.

29 New Orleans *Daily Picayune,* October 29, 1887.

30 *Ibid.,* November 9, 1887. See also, New Orleans *Weekly Pelican,* November 26, 1887; *Biographical and Historical Memoirs of Louisiana,* I, 133.

31 Hall, "Labor Struggles in the Deep South," 32; New Orleans *Times-Democrat,* November 6, 1887.

tractable Negroes.[32] Concerning the attitude of rank-and-file laborers, it was obvious that they placed great faith in the Knights of Labor. One wealthy planter, W. W. Pugh, used the word "veneration" to describe Negro attitudes toward the labor society. When directives came down from Knights head-quarters, said Pugh, the workers "generally obey at whatever sacrifice it may prove to their own welfare." [33] A leader of the strike remarked, when the trouble began, that the white employers "had never met the negroes united before," and he predicted that every one of the four hundred laborers in his group would lay down their lives before giving in to the planters.[34]

On the morning of the first day of the strike a battery of state militia arrived in Lafourche Parish. Members of the Sugar Planters' Association—not the local government—had asked for the troops. For the landowners perceived that "serious trouble" would result from their announcement that all laborers who refused to work must vacate the plantation cabins. By November 10, Governor McEnery had ordered ten companies and two batteries of state militia into the troubled parishes. At least one unit brought along a Gatling gun.[35] These militiamen were assigned the work of eviction.

Some critics of Governor McEnery asserted that he "had acted hastily" in sending out the militia; the New Orleans *Mascot* suggested that His Excellency's action "was caused by his eagerness to curry favor with the . . . wealthy sugar planters in the hopes that he can transfer their allegiance from

32 New Orleans *Daily States,* quoted in Baton Rouge *Daily Capitolian-Advocate,* November 24, 1887.

33 Letter from W. W. Pugh, in New Orleans *Daily Picayune,* November 20, 1887.

34 New Orleans *Daily Picayune,* November 2, 1887.

35 *Senate Journal,* 1888, p. 22; New Orleans *Mascot,* quoted in New Orleans *Weekly Pelican,* November 12, 1887; Philadelphia *Journal of United Labor,* November 19, 1887.

CUTHBERT VINCENT

A roving reporter for the leftist Winfield (Kansas) *Non-Conformist*, Vincent arrived in 1890 to help familiarize Louisiana with a new political name, "the People's Party." The Baton Rouge *Advocate* referred to his rural speeches as "rantings."

REVEREND BENJAMIN BRIAN

Brian presided over the first state convention of the People's Party on October 2, 1891. In 1892 he was the only Populist in the Louisiana Senate.

HARDY BRIAN

Populist legislator and editor, Brian could retort in kind
to Bourbon abuse. The son of the Reverend Benjamin
Brian, he boasted that his Winnfield *Comrade* was the first
Populist newspaper in the South.

SAMUEL D. McENERY

McEnery, of Monroe, was governor from 1881 until 1888.
His friends called him "the levee governor" and "the
farmers' friend." His enemies called him "McLottery"
because he supported the infamous Louisiana Lottery.

MURPHY J. FOSTER

The successful reform candidate for governor in 1892, Foster fought the Lottery, which was supported by his factional Democratic opponent, Samuel D. McEnery. At his inaugural ball, Governor Foster danced the first set with Mrs. McEnery.

JOHN A. TETTS

Although Tetts earned the title "founder" of the Farmers' Union in Louisiana, he was not a man equipped to hold his own in the Byzantine arena of Louisiana Democratic politics.

B. W. BAILEY

Bryant W. Bailey, an unsuccessful Populist candidate for Congress in 1894, became editor of Hardy Brian's Winnfield *Comrade*. A youthful but powerful stump speaker, he was called "simpering dolt" and "bellowing Bailey" by the Democrats.   COURTESY OF JOHN PRICE

BATON ROUGE
DAILY ADVOCATE
CARTOON
OCTOBER 27, 1896

In 1896 the attempted fusion by the sugar planters with Negro voters prompted angry newspaper comments describing the ticket as, "mongrel" and a combination of "canejuice . . . and malodorous nigger wool."

LSU ARCHIVES

THE SIAMESE TWINS.

Joined Together by Mark Hanna and Greed.

Nicholls to himself."[36] Major Burke's newspaper, on the other hand, dwelt upon McEnery's alleged knowledge "of the negro character," which allowed the Governor "to appreciate the danger." The trouble in the sugar country, philosophized this administration organ, was not a mere labor dispute. It was a racial matter.[37]

The first report of bloodshed came on November 2, from Terrebonne Parish. According to pro-planter sources, the blacks shot down four of their race who refused to join the strike. More severe was the disturbance which followed in St. Mary Parish: near the town of Berwick, on the night of November 4, Negroes fired upon and wounded four unidentified white men; the next day, militiamen killed "four or five" strikers outside of Pattersonville community.[38] Each side had its own version of the St. Mary shootings. Spokesmen for the Knights claimed the militia shot without provocation; other reports said the troops were forced to act in self-defense.[39] A St. Mary newspaper accused "leading colored men" in the Pattersonville area of making "incendiary speeches . . . that would put the Chicago anarchists to shame," and it quoted one Negro Knight as saying that "if the planters do not come to our terms we will burn the damn sugar houses."[40] Elsewhere, by November 20, at least one black laborer was killed and several wounded in Lafourche Parish.[41]

The sugar strike reached its violent climax during the last week of November. As some had feared, the town of Thibo-

36 New Orleans *Mascot,* quoted in New Orleans *Weekly Pelican,* November 12, 1887.

37 New Orleans *Times-Democrat,* November 6, 1887.

38 *Ibid.,* November 3, 1887; New Orleans *Daily Picayune,* November 3, 1887; Philadelphia *Journal of United Labor,* December 3, 1887.

39 Cf. New Orleans *Daily News,* quoted in New Orleans *Weekly Pelican,* November 19, 1887; New Orleans *Times-Democrat,* November 7–8, 1887.

40 Morgan City *Free Press,* quoted in Baton Rouge *Daily Capitolian-Advocate,* November 12, 1887.

41 New Orleans *Daily Picayune,* November 21, 1887.

daux then was the scene of a bloody riot. For Thibodaux had become a refugee center for the strikers; hundreds of Negro families, evicted from the plantations where they refused to work, were crowding into its dingy backstreets. A *Daily Picayune* correspondent described the spectacle: "Every vacant room in town tonight is filled with penniless and ragged negroes. All day long a stream of black humanity poured in, some on foot and others in wagons, bringing in all their earthly possessions which never amounted to more than a frontyard full of babies, dogs and ragged bed clothing. . . . On many of the plantations old gray-headed negroes, who were born and have lived continually upon them, left today." [42]

Residents of Thibodaux who were members of the Knights of Labor attempted to provide food and shelter for the homeless blacks. One observer, sympathetic to the refugees, said they behaved peaceably and tried to avoid incidents with local whites. But an opponent of the strike wrote that a number of the incoming male Negroes were armed and that the women "made threats to burn the town down." [43] By late November the atmosphere was growing more tense each day.

Judge Taylor Beattie, who had once been a defender of Negro rights—at least voting rights—when he ran for governor on the Republican ticket in 1879, took the lead in setting up a committee of local planters and Thibodaux property owners for the purpose of keeping the town's new residents under control. Beattie described the black refugees as "ignorant and degraded barbarians." [44] He said flatly that "the question

[42] *Ibid.*, November 3, 1887.

[43] Cf. Thibodaux *Sentinel,* November 12, 1887; New Orleans *Weekly Pelican,* November 26, 1887; New Orleans *Daily Picayune,* November 25, 1887.

[44] Letter from Judge Taylor Beattie, in New Orleans *Daily Picayune,* December 3, 1887.

of the supremacy of the whites over the blacks" had become the paramount issue.[45]

Actually, from the planters' point of view the situation was becoming desperate, but for another reason. The entire sugar crop was in immediate danger of ruin. On November 21, the first ice of the season formed in the puddles and ponds around Thibodaux; cane in the fields showed considerable damage and it was feared that the remainder of the crop would soon "be lost through the senseless . . . strike of laborers." [46] The day of the freeze Judge Beattie declared martial law in the town. The militia had recently been withdrawn. In place of the troops were armed bands of white vigilantes, composed of local "organized citizens" plus a number of grim-visaged strangers to the community. These newly arrived men were alleged to be "Shreveport guerrillas, well versed in killing niggers." [47]

Reports of the gruesome events that followed are conflicting. All dispatches agreed that the shooting began on the night of November 22. But the planters' and the Knights' versions of who commenced it were, as might be expected, quite different. Each blamed the other.[48] For what it may be worth, the conservative *Iberville South,* which sided with the planters, in later years accused Judge Beattie of having "instigated" the riot "which resulted in the death of so many sons of Africa." [49] There is no question that many were killed.

When the firing ceased at noon the next day at least thirty

[45] Opelousas *Courier,* November 26, 1887.

[46] Thibodaux *Sentinel,* November 26, 1887.

[47] New Orleans *Daily Picayune,* November 25, 1887; New Orleans *Weekly Pelican,* November 26, 1887.

[48] Cf. New Roads *Pointe Coupee Banner,* November 26, 1887; Thibodaux *Sentinel,* November 26, 1887; New Orleans *Weekly Pelican,* November 26, 1887; Philadelphia *Journal of United Labor,* December 3, 1887.

[49] Plaquemine *Iberville South,* April 18, 1896.

Negroes lay dead or dying in Thibodaux. The injured list ran into the hundreds, of which only two people were white.[50] One planter journal stated that "quite a number of darkies" were unaccounted for and might also have been killed.[51] The *Daily Picayune's* reporter told of additional bodies being found in nearby swamps, and related an ugly story about a large, dark canine which one vigilante supposedly shot by mistake, because it "looked like a negro lying down." [52] A member of one prominent planter family, Lavina Gay, cryptically wrote in a letter that "they say the half has not been published." [53]

The massacre at Thibodaux virtually ended the sugar strike of 1887. As a sequel, the two Cox brothers were taken from jail a day or so later and they "disappeared." By the beginning of December, most Negroes were back at work, harvesting and grinding the cane at wages previously set by the planters. Yet the violent repression of the strike appeared to stimulate a shortlived revival of Exodus talk among Louisiana's black population. One group did leave the state to seek, they said, more humane surroundings. Their destination was the state of Mississippi.[54]

Having dealt with the strike, planter interests now gave attention to what was considered the root of the trouble, the Knights of Labor. During the subsequent year a determined effort was made to eradicate the order from the sugar region. As the Jeanerette *Teche Pilot* made plain: "The darkey who steers clear of that organization will always find himself better off in this section." Those who persisted in holding

---

[50] New Orleans *Times-Democrat*, November 24–26, 1887; Baton Rouge *Daily Capitolian-Advocate*, November 24, 1887; Hall, "Labor Struggles in the Deep South," 40.

[51] Opelousas *Courier*, November 26, 1887.

[52] New Orleans *Daily Picayune*, November 24–26, 1887.

[53] Lavina Gay to Edward J. Gay, December 10, 1887, in Gay Family Papers.

[54] Opelousas *Courier*, November 26, 1887; New Orleans *Weekly Pelican*, November 26, 1887.

membership in the Knights were likely to find their household goods unceremoniously dumped on the levees and themselves blacklisted.[55] In 1888 minor strikes broke out in four sugar parishes, but were quickly put down. Whites there and elsewhere in the state had meantime put into motion a new "Regulating Movement" aimed at discouraging economic or political assertiveness on the part of Negroes. And so failed the attempt to unionize the field hands of rural South Louisiana. By 1891, state membership in the Knights of Labor was not of any size outside of its original base in New Orleans.[56]

Viewed in perspective, the Thibodaux bloodletting was simply a deadlier-than-usual example of a much broader phenomenon. The lot of the Louisiana Negro, although never good, was growing harder. Indeed throughout the South, during the late 1880's and the 1890's, repression and discrimination against the black race was on the rise.[57] Nor was this unlovely trend confined to the states of the late Confederacy. As the American nation took up imperialistic adventures in the Pacific and the Caribbean, the Northern public came increasingly to accept the doctrine of the natural superiority of Anglo-Saxons over dark-skinned peoples. Doubtless the expatriate Louisianian George W. Cable was grieved to discover that his pleadings on behalf of the black man, which had fallen upon deaf ears in his native state, now received little better attention in the North.[58]

But it is unlikely that Negroes in any other state suffered

[55] Jeanerette *Teche Pilot,* May 5, 1888; New Roads *Pointe Coupee Banner,* quoted in *ibid.*

[56] New Orleans *Weekly Pelican,* May 11, 1889; Sitterson, *Sugar Country,* 321–22; New Orleans *Daily Picayune,* August 7, 1891.

[57] C. Vann Woodward, *The Strange Career of Jim Crow* (2nd ed.; New York, 1957), 51–56; Arthur S. Link, *American Epoch: A History of the United States Since the 1890's* (3rd ed.; New York, 1967), I, 30–31.

[58] For Cable's liberal views on race, see especially George Washington Cable, *The Negro Question* (New York, 1890), *passim.*

more than those in Louisiana. That they received less in the way of education has already been demonstrated. Available evidence also points to the conclusion that Pelican State blacks were subjected to a greater degree of violence than Negroes in other parts of the South during the late nineteenth century. Why was this so? The answer lies partially hidden in the labyrinthine social history of antebellum and colonial Louisiana. Somehow, the commingling of English-speaking and Creole-Cajun cultures had resulted in a milieu of political instability and unusual insensitivity to human rights. Long before the Civil War, the state had been notorious for its lawlessness and for its maltreatment of slaves.[59] When Harriet Beecher Stowe tried to portray the cruelest side of slavery in *Uncle Tom's Cabin,* it was not by chance that she located Simon Legree's plantation up the Red River, near Shreveport.

Upper class conservatives in the post-Reconstruction South have been regarded as being, relatively speaking, the black man's best friends among the white population. Presumably they believed that he was due some protection; that though an inferior, he should not be deliberately hurt or degraded.[60] This generalization, whatever its worth elsewhere, was hardly valid for Louisiana. The ruling class of the Pelican State continued, as in the days of slavery, to hold an extraordinarily circumscribed view of Negro "rights." The most rabid Negrophobes in the state were as consistently vehement in defense of upper class white privileges. Some of the white elite did, to be sure, sincerely try to uphold the ideals of *no-*

[59] Clement Eaton, *The Growth of Southern Civilization: 1790–1860* (New York, 1961), 125–33; Ulrich Bonnell Phillips, *Life and Labor in the Old South* (Boston, 1929), 151–53; John Hope Franklin, *From Slavery to Freedom* (2nd ed.; New York, 1956), 191; Alfred H. Conrad and John R. Meyer, "The Economics of Slavery in the Ante-Bellum South," *Journal of Political Economy,* LXVI (1958), 92–122.

[60] Woodward, *The Strange Career of Jim Crow,* 29; Simkins, *A History of the South,* 509–11; Coulter, *The South During Reconstruction,* 162–64.

blesse oblige. But, as Daniel Dennett once remarked about honest politicians in the state, "they [were] lonesome." [61]

Editorial diatribes and mob outrages against the black people grew to such proportions by 1890, that at least a few whites thought the time for a moratorium had arrived. "Heavens," exclaimed the Welsh *Crescent,* "how we would enjoy a rest on the 'nigger' question! It seems that four-fifths of the State [newspapers] can't come out without a long-winded article . . . with the negro as their target; and what's more, they have been at it for the Lord only knows how long." [62] Many Negroes, however, bore the brunt of something more hurtful than mere words.

Lynchings not only occurred with growing frequency, but those who died at the hands of mobs might consider themselves fortunate if they expired quickly by a bullet or the rope. For some reason, 1881 marked a turning point toward extreme cruelty; several of the sixteen reported lynchings in the state that year involved brutal tortures. One of the dead had been accused of only stealing a chicken. Another victim, a Negro woman of Claiborne Parish named Jane Campbell, was burned at the stake.[63] At the same time, a mob in Morehouse Parish was congratulated for discovering a "new and original mode" of punishment for a black man guilty of cattle theft. He was trussed up inside the carcass of a cow, "leaving only his head sticking out," so that buzzards and crows would pick out his eyes. The Rayville *Beacon* joked that this amounted to "COW-PITAL punishment," but added that "a great many worse things are . . . being done in our vicinity." [64]

Between 1882 and 1903, according to a Chicago *Tribune*

61 New Orleans *Daily Picayune,* February 19, 1881.
62 Welsh *Crescent,* quoted in Baton Rouge *Daily Advocate,* March 4, 1890.
63 New Orleans *Daily Picayune,* September 19, 1881; New Iberia *Sugar Bowl,* quoted in *ibid.,* October 8, 1881.
64 Bastrop *Morehouse Clarion,* September 2, 1881; Rayville *Richland Beacon,* October 1, 1881.

survey, Louisiana lynchings accounted for 285 deaths. Of this number, 232 victims were black.[65] Records kept by Tuskegee Institute corroborate the *Tribune* figures.[66] Not included are the numerous deaths resulting from the sugar country riot of 1887, but even without these Louisiana ranked third in the nation in total lynchings for the period. The two states with higher totals had larger populations. Also, the above statistics failed to include many cases reported by the local press. For example, the Tuskegee records for 1888 list seven lynchings for the state, but a contemporary account from just one parish, Iberia, told of no less than ten blacks murdered by vigilantes. The Negroes were described as "vagrant and lewd."[67] Some instances were probably not reported anywhere. The Monroe *Bulletin* refused to print any stories about lynchings in Ouachita Parish because white citizens in the area regarded such matters "not only with indifference but with levity."[68]

Blacks were usually, but not always, the victims of lynch law. Notable among the white sufferers were the eleven Italians murdered by a mob in downtown New Orleans in 1891; this event was praised by much of the leadership of the state, including the editor of the *St. Mary Banner,* who hailed "the killing of the Dagoes" as "the greatest event of the year."[69] Three others of that nationality were strung up in Hahnville in 1896. In reply to the protests of the Italian government over these murders, the *Times-Democrat* thought it well to point out that residence in the Pelican State entailed, for any-

[65] James Elbert Cutler, *Lynch Law: An Investigation Into the History of Lynching in the United States* (New York, 1905), 179, 183.

[66] The Tuskegee records begin with 1885, but bear out the *Tribune* figures quoted in *ibid.* for 1885–1902. Monroe N. Work (ed.), *Negro Yearbook: An Annual Encyclopedia of the Negro, 1918–1919* (Tuskegee, Ala., 1919), 374–75.

[67] Lake Providence *Carroll Democrat,* August 25, 1888.

[68] Monroe *Bulletin,* quoted in New Orleans *Daily Picayune,* September 28, 1886.

[69] Franklin *St. Mary Banner,* March 23, 1891.

body, a certain amount of danger, and that "foreigners who come to this country must take the same risk with natives." [70] More often than not, serious acts of violence against Negroes in Louisiana were committed by men of some substance in the white community. Contemporary sources make it clear that the poorer whites were not involved in a majority of cases reported. To cite one of the most notorious instances of persecution, a reign of terror was conducted in 1890 against "industrious, reliable" Negroes near Baton Rouge by certain white landowners; only those blacks who had managed to accumulate property were shot, whipped, or otherwise molested. The black farmers were told to sell their property cheaply or be killed. The Bourbon *Daily Advocate* strongly condemned the whites responsible.[71] But almost never did conservatives publicly criticize the many lynchings in which the black victims had been accused of some crime. Often they praised such events, and demurred only if a trivial offense had been involved. "Lynch law," said a prudent gentleman of the town of Arcadia, "should not be resorted to except in very aggravated cases." [72]

"A crowd of the most worthy citizens of our Parish . . . took charge of the prisoner, and in a short time he was launched into eternity." [73] This report from Abbeville in the summer of 1881 would be repeated, like a dreary refrain, by other localities in the years which followed. As one example among many, in 1898 "hundreds of the most prominent citizens in Bossier Parish" conducted a dual lynching near the town of Benton.[74] A Tangipahoa Parish group known as the "Phan-

70 New Orleans *Times-Democrat,* quoted in *Chautauquan,* XXIV (October, 1896) , 92.
71 Baton Rouge *Daily Advocate,* November 26–27, 1890; letter from Anna M. Harris, in Opelousas *St. Landry Clarion,* February 14, 1891.
72 Arcadia *Louisiana Advance,* May 31, 1889.
73 Abbeville *Meridional,* August 20, 1881.
74 Natchitoches *Enterprise,* December 8, 1898.

tom Riders" molested Negro families without fear of the law because, it was stated, "good" citizens rode with the band.[75] And upper class participation was most obvious in the lynching which attracted the greatest notice outside Louisiana: the killing of the eleven Italians in New Orleans in 1891. Included among the prominent citizens who headed that mob was none other than the District Attorney. The *Nation* was forced to conclude that New Orleans was unique among American cities in that "even the more respectable and sober-minded portion of the community are in a constant state of readiness for remedial violence." [76]

At least one Bourbon spokesman seemed to fear that the murder of the Italians had momentarily diverted attention away from the more pressing need for lynching Negroes. The *Morehouse Clarion,* which posed as an aristocratic journal, advised its readers shortly after the New Orleans massacre that more "little 'neck tie' parties" would "do a lot of good" among the black population around Bastrop. Years earlier it had similarly urged an increase in "swingings." [77] But it took a Shreveport newspaper to describe a lynching as "beautiful." This was "the right way," the *Evening Judge* decided, "to deal with every such black brute. Before the war they kept their places like the other beasts of the field." [78]

Shreveport advertised itself as a city of New South "energy, push, and vim." [79] Yet at the same time its businessman elite, together with the planters around the town, supported or condoned the most pitiless forms of social injustice to be found anywhere in the state. The "Shreveport Plan" of 1889

75 New Orleans *Weekly Pelican,* July 16, 1887.

76 "The New Orleans Massacre," *Nation,* LII (March 19, 1891), 232. See also, Philadelphia *Journal of the Knights of Labor,* March 14, 1891.

77 Bastrop *Morehouse Clarion,* quoted in New Orleans *Daily Picayune,* August 10, 1891. See also, Bastrop *Morehouse Clarion,* February 5, 1881.

78 Shreveport *Evening Judge,* March 23, 1896.

79 Shreveport *Times,* quoted in New Orleans *Daily Picayune,* March 21, 1887.

was a representative specimen. Conceived by a local publication, the *Daily Caucasian,* the proposal revolved around the old concept that the Negro was a sub-human species and should be treated accordingly. Specifically, Negroes were not to hold "easy jobs." Under this heading were listed the occupations of bootblacks, waiters, porters, cooks, clerks and teachers. But the plan also implied intimidation of whites. For "no white man" was to "be permitted to employ a colored man . . . in any other manner than at the hardest and most degrading tasks." Apparently an exception could be made for the staff of Shreveport's Negro newspaper, *Bailey's Free South,* because they were supposed to be conservative Democrats.[80]

One New Orleans Negro leader, hearing of the plan, described it as "an old mummy" exhumed from "the Shreveport pyramids." He added: "The pernicious idea must be limited to the mean locality in which it had its origin. It would not live in more generous soil, and there are few places in this wide world so sterile in noble sentiments as that which immediately surrounds the publication office of the *Caucasian.*" [81]

The extent to which the "Shreveport Plan" was actually practiced in the area is problematical. Almost certainly, many residents of the city continued to hire blacks for tasks which were proscribed by the *Daily Caucasian.* But that "white supremacy" was "always . . . the motto" of Shreveport there was never any doubt.[82] Of course "we are kindly disposed to the negro race," said one prominent citizen in 1896, "wherever and whenever they properly demean themselves." [83]

80 Shreveport *Daily Caucasian,* quoted in New Orleans *Weekly Pelican,* July 27, August 17, 1889; Baton Rouge *Daily Advocate,* February 14, 1892.
81 New Orleans *Weekly Pelican,* July 27, 1889.
82 Shreveport *Evening Judge,* February 24, 1896.
83 *Ibid.,* March 25, 1896.

The indications are that the city's gentry often acted in a barbarous fashion toward the less fortunate of both races. This must have been the impression of two white men who once appeared in municipal court on a charge of vagrancy. Both were one-legged. The judge, who was also the mayor of Shreveport, enjoyed a grotesque sense of humor. He gave the crippled derelicts a sporting chance. If they could hop outside the city limits within twenty-five minutes, they would not have to serve one hundred days in jail.[84]

In other parts of Louisiana, well-to-do conservatives such as Howard G. Goodwyn of Colfax, occasionally complained that Negroes "were shamefully and needlessly bulldozed, and could hope for no legal redress." [85] But the most explicit plea for racial justice was voiced by a man who represented lower class whites. He was Aurel Arnaud, a legislator from St. Landry Parish. Arnaud was a political independent and of poor Cajun ancestry.

One day in 1886, Representative Arnaud stood up in the State House to speak on the unfairness of the method by which Louisiana maintained her public roads. His opening remarks were aimed at a statute of 1880 which instructed parish officials to impose twelve days of "road work," or a stipulated cash assessment, upon all adult males. He pointed out that this law worked a special hardship upon Negro tenants and laborers, since most black families seldom had as much as forty dollars a year to spend on clothes, medicine, and fresh meat. Arnaud expanded on his theme with blunt language: "Can you not see that this amount is not sufficient to support the laborer? And every day you divest him from a chance of earning something is a robbery of his daily bread? Should any one familiar with these facts, be surprised to hear

---

84 *Ibid.*, March 4, 1896.
85 Colfax *Chronicle,* January 9, 1892.

that the negroes steal? *I am only surprised that they do not steal more."* [86]

Arnaud raised the possibility of another, more serious, Kansas Exodus of the state's black population, if their sufferings continued. He hastened to add that he was not a "leveller"; he offered no socialistic proposals. He merely believed that Negroes "must be treated with as much consideration as we treat our mules." That, he indicated, would be a vast improvement over present conditions. Finally, in what must stand as among the most candid words ever uttered by a white Louisiana official, Arnaud said:

I have treated the subject entirely as from a . . . negro standpoint. But are there only negroes involved . . . ? And if there were only negroes involved, would I be here defending their cause? That is a question I have often asked myself, but I have never dared to probe my heart sufficiently to answer it, for fear I would perhaps find myself selfish enough to answer: no, because they are negroes. . . . But in what way is the white laborer treated with more consideration? Does the law give him any more protection? Is he paid better wages? Does he get more or better goods for his money? Do his children get more schooling? Yes, there is an immense difference between the two classes; but this difference exists only in the fancy of unscrupulous and rascally politicians: in every respect the white laborer stands exactly on the same footing with the negro. . . .[87]

Not quite so frank, but to the same point, were statements made by leaders of the more liberal element in the Louisiana Farmers' Union. Especially, John A. Tetts and Thomas J. Guice spoke up for the Negro. "What we want distributed to all men, 'regardless of race, color, or previous condition of servitude,' " Tetts wrote, "is the opportunity for the pursuit

[86] Baton Rouge *Weekly Truth,* May 28, 1886 (Italics mine).
[87] *Ibid.* Rep. Arnaud's outspokenness naturally irritated the defenders of the status quo. According to a conservative paper in his home parish, Arnaud belonged in either "prison garb" or "a straight jacket." Washington (La.) *Argus,* quoted in Shreveport *Times,* May 29, 1887.

of happiness." Tetts believed that the Alliance movement was doing what "the sword, the press and the pulpit" had failed to do: it was forcing the "half Ku Klux and half desperado" white cotton farmer of the South out of his provincial shell, and into an awareness of class interest which transcended racial or regional boundaries. In his typically quaint style, Tetts optimistically reported that "the horns of the Ku Klux were knocked off . . . and the [bloody] shirt that has been waved so faithfully has been torn up . . . and cast into the Mississippi, and by this time no doubt [is] in the maw of some cat-fish, or making a nest for some mud-turtle of a politician who will have to crawl into his shell when he sees the result of the next election." [88]

Guice, the state Lecturer of the Farmers' Union, agreed with Tetts on the need for biracial unity and joint protest. According to Guice, the "spirit of fairness," if nothing else, required that white agrarians include poor blacks in their drive to ameliorate economic and political evils. He believed that working people, "be they white or black," must act together because the "liberties and happiness" of both were at stake.[89] The old agrarian activist from Winn and Grant parishes, the Reverend Benjamin Brian, who was now prominent in the Farmers' Union, had been proposing the same thing since the latter days of Reconstruction.

The Louisiana Farmers' Union was, however, exclusively a white organization. Neither were Negroes admitted to the interstate Alliance proper. But there was a subsidiary association, the Colored Farmers' Alliance, which existed as a means of bringing the South's black agriculturists into the movement. It was founded in Houston County, Texas, in

[88] J. A. Tetts, "The Good the Alliance Has Done," *National Economist*, III (April 12, 1890), 64.

[89] Letter from Thomas J. Guice, in New Orleans *Daily Picayune*, October 3, 1891.

1886. Spreading across the South with the white Alliance, the Negro order claimed 1,200,000 members by 1890. Though separate, the white and colored Alliances pledged "fraternal regard" for each other. Both orders held their annual national conventions at the same date and in the same city, beginning at St. Louis in December of 1889. The following December, both met at Ocala, Florida.[90]

Fifty thousand Louisiana Negroes were reported on the membership rolls of the Colored Farmers' Alliance by the time of the Ocala convention. In 1891, at the peak of activity, the state's Negro Alliance claimed to be organized in twenty-seven parishes.[91] Detailed information regarding it is lacking, but the alleged fifty thousand membership was probably far above the actual number. The Colored Alliance may have entered the state as early as 1887; but the first report discoverable tells of a Grant Parish lodge which was set up in October of 1889.[92] Black Alliancemen were most numerous in the cotton parishes along the Red River. Apparently, few if any Negroes in the Mississippi River delta joined the order.[93] Neither was there much activity in the sugar country; the recent suppression of the Knights of Labor, and the weakness of even the white Alliance there, must have negated organizational efforts among the Negroes. Below the Red River, the Colored Farmers' Alliance was strongest in St. Landry Parish, where it did not take root until 1891.[94]

90 Frank M. Drew, "The Present Farmers' Movement," *Political Science Quarterly*, VI (1891), 287–89; Dunning, *The Farmers' Alliance History*, 289, 291–92.

91 *Western Rural and American Stockman*, XXVIII (December 13, 1890), 789, quoted in Saloutos, *Farmer Movements in the South*, 81; Opelousas *St. Landry Clarion*, October 10, 1891.

92 *Biographical and Historical Memoirs of Northwest Louisiana*, 503.

93 The two leading journals of the northeastern delta parishes, the Lake Providence *Carroll Democrat* and the St. Joseph *Tensas Gazette*, reported no Negro Alliance activity between 1888 and 1892. Neither paper was in the habit of ignoring signs of unrest or organization among local blacks.

94 Opelousas *St. Landry Clarion*, June 27, 1891.

L. D. Laurent, an Alexandria Negro, was the first superintendent of the state's Colored Alliance. He held the post until succeeded by Isaac Keys of Catahoula Parish in 1891. Another significant black Allianceman was state secretary J. B. Lafargue. These men were rather circumspect in their activities; conservative whites seldom noticed anything they said or did. The mass of Louisiana Negroes, in or out of the Alliance, tended toward caution in their dealings with local whites, and Laurent, Keys, and Lafargue were probably no exceptions. Certainly, the rising racial bitterness of the late 1880's hampered attempts at biracial agrarian protest. White Alliancemen who came to offer advice at Negro farmers' meetings were said to be received "with great courtesy," but were likely received with suspicion as well. Many blacks in St. Landry Parish refused to join the Colored Alliance because they believed that the white Farmers' Union included men who were anti-Negro "regulators." [95]

Race relations within the Alliance movement were not helped by the fact that the Farmers' Union president, Thomas S. Adams, in 1889, selected the Shreveport *Weekly Caucasian* as the official state organ of the white agrarians.[96] From the Negroes' standpoint, a more insulting choice could scarcely have been made. Equally inauspicious was the fact that in 1890, most of the Democratic state legislators who happened to be members of the Farmers' Union (including ex-president John M. Stallings and G. L. P. Wren) voted for a bill which made racial segregation compulsory on all railroad coaches within the state. Upper class Bourbons were, as a Negro legislator pointed out, the prime movers behind this bill; but the Farmers' Union solons had, with few exceptions, quietly supported it.[97]

95 *Ibid.*, June 27, August 8, 15, October 10, 1891.
96 Shreveport *Weekly Caucasian*, January 24, 1890.
97 *House Journal,* 1890, pp. 200–204.

Even so, the possibility of white and Negro agrarian unity was still alive. During the year 1890, a third-party revolt against the conservative leadership of both the Democratic Party and the Farmers' Union began to reverberate among the hills of North Louisiana, and the white farmers who led the protest immediately sought the support of the Colored Alliance.[98] The Negro Alliancemen were more than willing to help. At the Ocala gathering of the Alliances in December, three of the seven Louisianians present signed a call for a national third-party convention, scheduled to meet the next year at Cincinnati: they were L. D. Laurent, J. B. Lafargue and I. Miller. All three were Negroes. The state's white delegation at Ocala, dominated by Thomas S. Adams, refused to sign this birth certificate of the Populist Party.[99]

[98] Baton Rouge *Daily Advocate,* October 5, November 18, 1890; New Orleans *Daily Picayune,* November 8, 1890.

[99] Alexandria *Farmers' Vidette,* quoted in Colfax *Chronicle,* January 10, 1891.

IX

The Rise of Populism

LOUISIANA'S conservative Democrats faced no serious third-party challenge in the twelve years between the Greenback agitation of 1878 and the birth of Populism in 1890. The decline of the earlier inflationist party had been rapid; in 1880, their presidential candidate, James B. Weaver, was credited with less than 500 votes out of a total 100,000 reported in the statewide returns.[1] And when Benjamin F. "Spoons" Butler became the party's nominee in the national election of 1884, the ranks of Louisiana Greenbackers became even thinner. Butler received only 120 votes in the Pelican State.[2] Finally, a sort of funeral for the party was held at New Orleans in 1888, when local Greenback Labor Party members met and announced the demise of their organization.[3]

The little Union Labor Party became the immediate heir of Greenbackism. Nationally, the Greenbackers merged with this newly-created political fragment in 1887. That same year a Union Labor Party committee took shape in New Orleans under the chairmanship of J. E. Sweeney, a Knights of Labor activist. But for Louisiana, the talk of running state and con-

[1] New York *Times,* November 16, 1880; Edward Stanwood, *A History of the Presidency: 1788 to 1897* (New York, 1898) , 417.

[2] *Biographical and Historical Memoirs of Northwest Louisiana,* 457; New York *Times,* November 1, 1888.

[3] New Orleans *Times-Democrat,* September 20, 1888.

gressional candidates came to naught in 1888. The presidential nominee of the party obtained a mere 39 votes out of the total 115,000 in the state's official returns.[4] In all likelihood, the Union Laborites did have a thousand or more supporters in New Orleans whose votes were simply not counted. At any rate, Louisiana was an exception to the third-party pattern of 1888; in most states, the Union Laborites drew what strength they possessed from rural areas, for third-party politics in the Northern cities had reached a condition of virtual collapse.[5]

The apparent lack of third-party interest in rural Louisiana during the decade of the 1880's afforded much comfort to Bourbon Democrats.[6] But agrarian unrest was, in fact, always present in one form or another. Hill country whites frequently demonstrated their anger against Democratic officeholders by either voting Republican or backing "independent" candidates for local posts. Governor McEnery's Republican opponent in 1884, John Stevenson, carried four upland white parishes; and Stevenson's vote greatly exceeded the number of Negro registrants in other localities.[7] On more than one occasion between 1879 and 1888, seven predominately white farming parishes—Catahoula, Grant, St. Helena, St. Tamma-

---

[4] New Orleans *Daily Picayune,* November 13, 1887; Jeanerette *Teche Pilot,* October 3, 1888; *Report of the Secretary of State,* 1902, p. 573; Frank L. McVey, *The Populist Movement* (New York, 1896), 197.

[5] John R. Commons and others, *History of Labour in the United States* (New York, 1918), II, 469; Haynes, *Third Party Movements,* 211.

[6] Colfax *Chronicle,* April 21, 1888; Lake Providence *Carroll Democrat,* June 23, 1888; Many *Sabine Southron,* quoted in Baton Rouge *Daily Capitolian-Advocate,* February 22, 1888.

[7] In 1884, a Northern correspondent described the anti-Democratic vote in the backland parishes as "astonishingly large." McEnery lost Grant, Livingston, St. Helena and St. Tammany parishes to the Republican candidate, and the Republicans came close to winning other white parishes that year. New York *Times,* April 23, 1884; *Report of the Secretary of State,* 1902, pp. 546–53, 561. See also, Donaldsonville *Chief,* April 26, 1884.

ny, Washington, and Winn—elected Republicans or pro-Republican "independents" to legislative or parish office.[8]

By 1888 the Farmers' Union had become the focus of agrarian activity. The Union, like the Alliance in other states, immediately took on a dual political significance: it held out to farmers the prospect of taking over, by sheer weight of numbers, the state Democratic organization; but it also created the framework for a possible third-party revolt in case the Democratic leadership refused to make room for agrarian demands and candidates. By 1890, because of a mounting belief that the established order would not change, many farmers were asking themselves the question that John Tetts posed in a *National Economist* article: "A New Party, or Not?" [9]

Between the summers of 1890 and 1891, the Louisiana variety of the People's (Populist) Party came to life. The circumstances which led to the founding of this newest political association in the Pelican State were many, and they grew out of decades of agrarian frustration. But there were three proximate reasons for its emergence at that particular time.

One was the refusal of Louisiana's Democratic congressmen, with a single exception, to endorse the cherished economic panacea of the Farmers' Alliance—the subtreasury plan. Even the sole congressman who supported it later reversed himself.[10] The subtreasury plan, conceived by Dr. Macune and others, was a precursor of the New Deal agricultural legislation of the 1930's; it proposed that the federal government set up warehouse storage facilities and provide low-cost loans

---

[8] Cullom to Hayes, February 6, 1879, in Hayes Papers; Richardson to Currie, August 1, 1882, in Chandler Papers; Colfax *Chronicle,* December 6, 1879, May 3, 31, 1884; Baton Rouge *Daily Capitolian-Advocate,* April 25, 28, May 7–9, 1888.

[9] J. A. Tetts, "A New Party, or Not?" *National Economist,* III (June 28, 1890) , 237.

[10] Congressman Samuel M. Robertson of the Sixth District at first approved, then refused to support, the subtreasury plan. Rayne *Ranger,* quoted in Clinton *Southern Watchman,* April 14, 1894.

to farmers. The plan was designed to free agriculturists from crop-lien mortgages and allow them to withhold their produce from sale until such time during the year when prices went up. Moreover, the subtreasury loans would have put more paper money into circulation. Twenty-nine parishes in the state—817 counties in the nation—raised enough crops to have qualified for subtreasury facilities. Conservatives throughout America deprecated the whole concept as paternalistic class legislation; some called it "hayseed socialism." [11] The official journal of Louisiana's government reacted with an apoplectic tirade against the "crack-brained" subtreasury "monstrosity," and then fumed that all "the complaints of the downtrodden are simply bosh and nonsense." [12]

A second inadvertent contributor to the birth of Louisiana Populism was the capture of the Farmers' Union by the Nicholls administration and its extra-official arm, the Anti-Lottery League. This envelopment began in August of 1890 with the appointment of Union president Thomas S. Adams as state secretary of agriculture, and with the League's proposal to the agrarian order that the two groups join hands against the Louisiana Lottery Company in the approaching 1892 state election. Respectable conservatives despised the Lottery. Aside from its corrupting political influence, it reportedly "demoralized" Negro laborers, many of whom became obsessed with the dream of winning a fortune. It "was indubitably a nuisance." [13]

By 1890 the Lottery was taking in, from bettors throughout the nation, somewhere between twenty million dollars and thirty million dollars each year. Approximately 47 per-

[11] For details of the subtreasury plan, see *National Economist*, II (December 21, 1889), 216–17; *ibid.*, III (April 19, 1890), 72. See also, New York *Sun*, quoted in *ibid.*, III (March 22, 1890), 1.

[12] Baton Rouge *Daily Advocate*, September 30, November 11, 1890.

[13] Thomas Beer, *The Mauve Decade: American Life at the End of the Nineteenth Century* (New York, 1926), 103–105.

cent of its gross receipts was retained as profit. The remainder went out for prizes, advertisements, and other expenses such as bribes to Louisiana lawmakers. But its charter was due to expire in 1894. At the 1890 session Governor Nicholls at last took a public stand against the gambling syndicate; his veto, however, was unable to stop the submission of a pro-Lottery constitutional amendment to the voters in 1892. The amendment, if passed, would renew the life of the Lottery for another twenty-five years.[14] A gubernatorial election was also slated for 1892. As to the position of the Farmers' Union, it had been against the Lottery before the formation of the patrician Anti-Lottery League. Yet many of the agrarian rank and file were more deeply concerned with other social and economic evils. For that reason, the militants within the Union were "far from friendly" to the Anti-Lottery League's proposition that a partnership be formed within the state Democratic Party.[15]

Adams, on the other hand, was enthusiastic about a League-Farmers' Union political alliance. A trap was baited, and he along with numerous other Unionmen fell into it. At the next Farmers' Union annual convention, held at the town of Lafayette in the summer of 1891, the League made a specific and seemingly generous offer: if the two groups, acting together, could win control of the next state Democratic convention, then the nominations for governor, treasurer, and superintendent of public education would go to men of the Farmers' Union; the League was to have the other state offices. Their announced candidate for governor in 1892 was Adams himself. Seventy-three delegates at Lafayette voted to accept

[14] Frank McGloin, "Shall the Lottery's Charter be Renewed?" *Forum*, XII (January, 1892) , 555–58; White, "The History of the Louisiana Lottery," 26; *Congressional Record*, 51st Cong., 1st Sess., 8706–8713; *Senate Journal*, 1890, pp. 413–15, 423–24.

[15] New Orleans *Daily Picayune*, August 6, 1891; Winnfield *Comrade*, quoted in Colfax *Chronicle*, August 20, 1892.

the League's proposal. A minority of twenty-two opposed it. Nearly all of the twenty-two were, or soon would be, members of the Populist Party.[16]

One among the dissenting minority spoke of the "Lafayette Compact" as an attempt to herd the farmers "back into the old party to be robbed and enslaved as of yore. It is only a question of time. . . ." [17] Subsequent events gave weight to this assessment. Late in December, 1891, the state Democratic convention met at Baton Rouge and split in two. "Pro-Lottery" and "Anti-Lottery" Democratic delegates met in separate buildings, while each faction angrily accused the other of being an illegitimate rump convention. The pro-Lottery nominee for governor was, as anticipated, State Supreme Court Justice Samuel D. McEnery. The gathering of Anti-Lottery and Farmers' Union Democrats gave their nomination, as had been promised, to Adams. But then something happened. Adams arose to make an announcement. He wished to "emphatically decline" the honor. "For the sake of the great cause," he said, another man should be chosen. He went on to name several men as possibilities; at the top of his list was Murphy J. Foster.[18]

Exactly what had gone wrong was revealed later. The gentlemen of the Anti-Lottery League had held several "harmonizing conferences" with the Farmers' Union president just prior to and during the Democratic conventions. They told Adams that he could not possibly beat McEnery in the general election. It was widely assumed that Governor Nicholls also brought pressure to bear upon Adams, and had urged the nomination of Foster. Pointed questions were asked about

16 Lafayette *Advertiser,* quoted in Opelousas *St. Landry Clarion,* August 15, 1891; New Orleans *Daily Picayune,* August 6, 8, September 17, 1891; Colfax *Chronicle,* December 26, 1891.

17 L. A. Traylor, quoted in New Orleans *Daily Picayune,* September 19, 1891.

18 New Orleans *Times-Democrat,* December 17–20, 1891; Opelousas *St. Landry Clarion,* December 26, 1891.

the ability of Adams's rural supporters to provide campaign funds. Reluctantly, he capitulated. His pride, however, prompted him to insist on a sham nomination. And as part of the bargain, Adams obtained a lower place on the ticket: that of secretary of state. Foster, who was sometimes referred to as "the Saint from St. Mary," thereupon became the Anti-Lottery convention's gubernatorial nominee and went on to face McEnery in the general election of April, 1892.[19] This rank betrayal of the agrarian cause served to confirm the worst suspicions of the militant reformers, and it added new converts to the People's Party. As for the Farmers' Union, it began to fade into nothingness.

The third catalyst for Populism in Louisiana was a visitor from Kansas named Cuthbert Vincent. He arrived in Baton Rouge one midsummer day in 1890. A roving reporter for a leftist paper called the *American Non-Conformist,* he delivered an address before that year's convention of the Farmers' Union. Conservative Democrats had heard something about the man, and they feared him. For although Vincent "disclaimed that he was the agent for any political party," [20] the *Non-Conformist,* published at Winfield, Kansas by his two brothers, was widely recognized as a potent source of radical agrarian ideas. The Vincents had been leading spokesmen for the Union Labor party of 1888, which was stronger in the plains states than elsewhere. But by 1890, the third-party men of Kansas were jettisoning the laborite designation in favor of one more attractive to rural voters. While Cuthbert spoke in Baton Rouge, the other Vincents were familiarizing the public with a new political name: "the People's party." [21]

[19] Henry E. Chambers, *A History of Louisiana* (Chicago, 1925) , I, 709; Romero, *Louisiana Historical Quarterly,* XXVIII, 1154, 1159; Baton Rouge *Capitol Item,* quoted in New Orleans *Louisiana Review,* February 3, 1892.

[20] Baton Rouge *Daily Advocate,* August 7, 1890.

[21] Winfield (Kan.) *American Non-Conformist,* quoted in *National Economist,* III (August 16, 1890) , 355. For the background of the Vincents, see

Louisiana's Bourbons had cause to worry about the presence of Cuthbert Vincent. After the Farmers' Union convention at Baton Rouge ended on August 8, 1890, the man from Kansas spent several weeks visiting and lecturing in the rural parishes of North Louisiana. The *Daily Advocate*, keeping its eye on his travels, wondered if it were possible that the "conservative spirit" of the Anglo-Saxon yeomanry was being perverted by "the rantings of lecturer Vincent." [22] Actually, in several upland parishes—particularly Catahoula, Grant, and Winn—conservatism had already become a rather scarce commodity. Vincent was finding enthusiastic audiences. Winfield, Kansas, and Winnfield, Louisiana, were alike in more than name.

Thomas J. Guice and Benjamin Brian were among those who eagerly discussed the nascent Populism with Cuthbert Vincent in the late summer and early fall of 1890. [23] Another participant was the Reverend Brian's twenty-five-year-old son, Hardy Lee Brian, who would later become Louisiana's outstanding Populist leader. Hardy Brian had seen his father challenge Democratic candidates in every state senatorial election since Reconstruction; he had been "rocked in an 'Independent' cradle." [24] According to young Brian, the 1890 visit of the Kansas spellbinder did much to stir the farmers to action. Vincent "was the first to break the ice for a new party," Brian later wrote.[25]

The farmers of North Louisiana were particularly ready

Elizabeth N. Barr, "The Populist Uprising," in William E. Connelly (ed.) , *A Standard History of Kansas and Kansans* (Chicago, 1918) , II, 1140–59; Martin M. La Godna, "Kansas and the Ocala Convention of 1890: Groundwork of the People's Party" (M.A. thesis, Florida State University, 1962) , 6–7, 20–21.

22 Baton Rouge *Daily Advocate*, September 3, 1890.

23 Cf. Colfax *Chronicle*, September 20, October 4, 11, 25, 1890; Winnfield *Comrade*, quoted in *ibid.*, October 11, 1890; Baton Rouge *Daily Advocate*, October 30, 1890.

24 Colfax *Chronicle*, September 12, 1891.

25 Natchitoches *Louisiana Populist*, September 28, 1894.

for third-party action in the autumn of 1890 because of their anger against their two congressmen. Representatives Newton C. Blanchard (Fourth District) and Charles J. Boatner (Fifth District) had both firmly refused to lend support to the sub-treasury bill which the Alliance desired from Congress. In August, Blanchard and Boatner had won out over strong Farmers' Union opposition in their respective districts' Democratic nominating conventions. Immediately afterward, the Winn Parish Union called upon the agrarian order in every parish of the Fourth District to send delegates to a special convention at Natchitoches on October 1, for the announced purpose of nominating a man to oppose Blanchard in the November general election.[26]

The hostility toward Blanchard involved more than the subtreasury plan. A member of Congress since 1881, Blanchard by his own admission had not overworked himself to defend the claims of upland homesteaders against the "Backbone" land grant of Jay Gould's New Orleans Pacific Railroad.[27] The Congressman was a wealthy Shreveport lawyer. The fact that he could and did sojourn in Europe "for his health" was another reason for his unpopularity among "those of his constituents who have to scuffle around peartly to get a quarter to buy a box of Wright's pills to work the malaria out of their systems." [28]

Seven of the twelve parish Unions of northwestern Louisiana sent delegates to the Natchitoches gathering in October. Five of the parish delegations then voted in favor of "inde-

[26] Colfax *Chronicle,* September 20, 1890. The *Chronicle,* although hostile to the third-party movement, is the most important extant source on the early development of Populism in Louisiana.

[27] Letter from Congressman Newton C. Blanchard, *ibid.,* February 17, 1883; New Orleans *Times-Democrat,* quoted in Farmerville *Home Advocate,* October 30, 1885.

[28] Baton Rouge *Capitol Item,* quoted in Natchitoches *Louisiana Populist,* September 14, 1894.

pendent" political action (as yet the appellation "People's Party" was not being used). Frantically, the president of the state Union, Adams, wired them: "Do not, under any circumstances, nominate an independent candidate for Congress. Your honor . . . is pledged to the support of the Democratic nominee. . . . Go forth like men and rally your entire forces to the flag of the Democracy. Stand by the colors of the party, and bide your time with patience. T. S. Adams, President." [29]

Adams's plea was ignored by the delegates from Grant, Rapides, Sabine, Vernon, and Winn, who selected a Farmers' Union-Independent candidate for the Fourth District congressional race. Thomas J. Guice was their nominee. At once, Guice was hit by a flood of vituperation; the Democratic journal in Grant Parish described him as being "afflicted with a diarrhoea of words and a constipation of ideas," and the journal opined that the "bolting farmers" who selected him were under the spell of that meddlesome outsider, Vincent of Kansas.[30] But Guice, after some hesitation, declined the nomination. He still held the position of state lecturer in the Farmers' Union. President Adams put heavy pressure on Guice, and the fact that only four parish Unions, the Rapides group having changed its mind, were endorsing him, sobered Guice's obvious desire to make the race.[31] The *Daily Picayune* had previously referred to him as plain "Guice," but after his refusal to run, the paper styled him "Colonel Guice." Not to be outdone, the official journal of the state government offered him the title "General Guice," if he would leave third-party politics alone.[32]

On election day, November 4, 1890, Blanchard received

---

29 Colfax *Chronicle*, October 4, 1890.

30 *Ibid.*, October 11, 1890.

31 Lake Providence *Carroll Democrat*, October 11, 1890; Opelousas *St. Landry Clarion*, October 18, 1890.

32 New Orleans *Daily Picayune*, quoted in Baton Rouge *Daily Advocate*, October 14, 1890.

8,307 votes in the District. Guice, although not a candidate, was credited with 277 protest ballots. But discontent showed up in the returns in another way. Two years before, Blanchard had garnered 16,302 votes against a weak Republican opponent. The totals from Winn Parish were especially revealing. There, in 1890, almost the entire electorate acted upon Hardy Brian's suggestion that they show opposition to Blanchard by staying away from the polls.[33]

In northeastern Louisiana's Fifth District, there was even greater reason for the Farmers' Union to be unhappy with the incumbent Congressman. Charles J. Boatner, an ultraconservative, occupied his seat only because of the disproportionate strength given the plantation parishes in the District's Democratic conventions. A lawyer and a planter, Boatner was firmly allied with the McEnery wing of the party. Hill people were haughtily told to "quit grumbling" at Boatner and the apportionment system which foisted him upon the region.[34] At least Blanchard spoke kindly of the Farmers' Union, while Boatner scorned it as a "secret political organization" which no true Democrat should join.[35]

A convention of "dissatisfied farmers" of the Fifth District met at Monroe in October of 1890, but they failed to name an opposition candidate. Yet Boatner's path was not entirely clear. The head of the Union in Lincoln Parish urged members to "ignore Mr. Boatner" in the coming election, and the congressman's strength throughout the district sank from his 1888 level by about 10,000 votes.[36] The Union in Catahoula

[33] *Report of the Secretary of State*, 1902, pp. 573–74; Winnfield *Comrade*, quoted in Baton Rouge *Daily Advocate*, October 31, November 18, 1890.

[34] Winnsboro *Franklin Sun*, March 2, 1884; *Biographical and Historical Memoirs of Louisiana*, I, 301; Lake Providence *Carroll Democrat*, October 27, 1888. Boatner began his political career in Catahoula Parish in 1876, when he defeated Benjamin Brian for the state senate. Boatner moved to Ouachita Parish in 1884.

[35] New Orleans *Daily Picayune*, September 4, 1891.

[36] Ruston *Progressive Age*, quoted in Lake Providence *Carroll Democrat*,

Parish, said to be dominated by "the poorer class of farmers," concluded that boycotting was not enough, and by way of protest, offered a man named T. E. Pritchard as their congressional candidate. Pritchard carried Catahoula, with 587 votes to 435 for Boatner. The local unit of the Colored Farmers' Alliance ignored the Republican nominee and supported Pritchard.[37] Thus, in the only parish in the state where a Democratic congressman faced an active agrarian opponent in 1890, the Democrat lost.

Third-party sentiment in Louisiana, as registered in the congressional races of 1890, seemed almost nonexistent outside the northern hill parishes, and, obviously, it was not yet organized even there. The small farmers of the southern districts had put up no opposition to Democratic candidates, while in New Orleans, the nominee of the Union Labor Party, Carson Mudge, drew less than two hundred votes out of the reported total cast in the First Congressional District.[38]

Nevertheless, the more astute conservatives were now uneasy. The McEnery Bourbons and the Nicholls gentry might disagree over the Lottery, but both feared and resented any movement of protest, however slight, on the part of ordinary whites. The close attention which the hill country stirrings of 1890 aroused in Baton Rouge and New Orleans proved that the Democratic establishment well understood that a major challenge to them was in the making. Special notice was taken of the emergence of a third-party newspaper in Winn Parish. The Winnfield *Comrade* began publication on October 3, 1890, and soon had readers in distant parishes. Hardy Brian

September 4, 1890; Baton Rouge *Daily Advocate,* October 3, 1890; *Report of the Secretary of State,* 1902, pp. 573–74.

37 Trinity *Herald,* quoted in Colfax *Chronicle,* August 1, 1891; *Report of the Secretary of State,* 1902, p. 574; Baton Rouge *Daily Advocate,* October 30, 1890; New Orleans *Daily Picayune,* November 8, 1890.

38 New Orleans *Daily Picayune,* November 16, 1890.

was the editor. Brian boasted that the *Comrade* was the first Populist newspaper in the South.[39]

The *Comrade* was owned by the Winn Parish Farmers' Union. Its arresting name came about by unusual circumstances. The battered old press and type cases had previously been used by the *Winn Parish Democrat* which, after selling its shop and equipment, ceased publication. The new management was at once faced with the problem of renaming the paper; the old title simply would not do. But to order a new nameplate from New Orleans might take weeks and besides, money was scarce. The youthful editor, Brian, thought for awhile and then said: "We'll see how we can change the title we already have." Luckily, all the letters in "Democrat" were upper case. By shuffling them about, and discarding the "t," Brian found a combination that made some sense: *Comrade*.[40] At that, it sounded better than the other possibilities, such as "Tarcomed," or "Ratodem."

One month after the elections of 1890, the annual conventions of the Farmers' Alliance and the Colored Farmers' Alliance were held at Ocala, Florida. Many Southern states had gone though gubernatorial as well as congressional campaigns. The Alliance appeared to some to be making great progress toward taking over the Democratic Party of the South. Four new governors (in Georgia, South Carolina, Tennessee, and Texas) had won with Alliance backing. Eight

[39] Colfax *Chronicle,* November 8, 1890, July 11, 1891; Baton Rouge *Daily Advocate,* December 30, 1890; Natchitoches *Louisiana Populist,* December 7, 1894. The *Comrade* may well have been the South's first People's Party newspaper. It was an avowed third-party organ from the date of its first issue, although it did not begin using the Populist label until after its editor, Brian, returned from the party's Cincinnati convention in May of 1891. The *Comrade* was published until 1911. Regrettably, no copies are extant prior to 1910, and by that time the paper was in Democratic hands.

[40] Brian recalled how the *Comrade* was named in an interview a half-century later, which appeared in the Shreveport *Times,* March 13, 1939. See also, *Biographical and Historical Memoirs of Louisiana,* II, 168; Colfax *Chronicle,* October 11, 1890.

Southern legislatures were said to be under the control of the agrarian order. About forty-four congressmen in Dixie purportedly endorsed the subtreasury plan.[41] By comparison, Louisiana seemed woefully behind her sister states in Alliance success within the Democratic framework; but Thomas S. Adams, who took the chastened Guice along with him to Ocala, was still pinning his hopes on the 1892 state election.[42]

The more conservative Alliancemen at Ocala hailed the supposed victories of 1890 as proof of the efficacy of remaining inside the traditional political structure. But the Kansas delegation, the Negro Alliance, and a handful of Southern white delegates took a contrary view. The new People's Party in Kansas was booming. Less than six months old as a state organization, it had elected a majority to the state legislature, five congressmen, and a United States Senator. Prominent among the Kansans at Ocala were the three Vincent brothers. They were credited with drawing up and circulating among the assembled farmers the call for a subsequent "conference" at Cincinnati, destined, in 1891, to set in motion the national People's Party. About seventy-five of the five hundred or more individuals present at Ocala signed the call. Dr. Macune and Farmers' Alliance president L. L. Polk tried to arrange a compromise which would delay any decision on a third party until February of 1892.[43] But the militant minority, mostly Kansans and Negroes, refused to wait.

At Cincinnati, in May of 1891, there assembled 1,412 delegates from over 30 states and territories. Inevitably, the three

41 Norman Pollack (ed.), *The Populist Mind* (Indianapolis, 1967), xxxvi; Saloutos, *Farmer Movements in the South,* 116; Roscoe C. Martin, *The People's Party in Texas: A Study in Third Party Politics* (Austin, 1933), 36.

42 Alexandria *Farmers' Vidette,* quoted in Colfax *Chronicle,* November 29, 1890.

43 La Godna, "Kansas and the Ocala Convention of 1890," 31–37; New York *Times,* December 5, 1890; Jacksonville *Florida Times-Union,* December 8, 1890; Philadelphia *Journal of the Knights of Labor,* December 11, 1890; Blood, *Handbook and History of the National Farmers' Alliance,* 66–67.

Vincents were on hand. So were such veteran reformers as Ignatius Donnelly of Minnesota, James B. Weaver of Iowa, and Anson J. Streeter of Illinois—men who were no strangers to third-party causes. There also, but as interested spectators, were Terence V. Powderly of the Knights of Labor and Samuel Gompers of the American Federation of Labor. But the attendance at this first People's Party national convention was geographically lopsided. An overwhelming majority of delegates came from the Midwest and plains states; Kansas alone sent 411, while only 36 were mustered from the entire South. Two of the Southerners were from Louisiana: Hardy Brian of Winnfield and I. J. Mills of Lake Charles.[44]

Hardy Brian was described by one correspondent as "the temporary lion of the hour" at the opening day of the Cincinnati convention.[45] The *Comrade* editor was a more outspoken Populist than any other Southerner interviewed; in fact, most of those who had come up from the South followed the lead of Congressman Leonidas F. Livingston of Georgia, who said he was present "to fight this third party move." [46] Brian's credentials also drew comment. The Winn Parish agrarians, in authorizing him as their representative, had attached 1,200 signatures; this was a number just 131 shy of the total adult male population of the parish.[47] Around Winnfield, Brian told reporters at Cincinnati, the people would not be intimidated by Bourbon outcries over "the negro menace" and the need for white Democratic solidarity. He added that "the race cry doesn't scare us." [48]

44 Cincinnati *Enquirer*, May 18–21, 1891.

45 Philadelphia *Journal of the Knights of Labor*, May 21, 1891. For one thing, Brian entertained the more urbane delegates by telling of his departure; he rode a pony for fifty miles to catch the nearest train which would make connections to Cincinnati.

46 Cincinnati *Enquirer*, May 19, 1891.

47 Philadelphia *Journal of the Knights of Labor*, May 21, 1891; *Compendium of the Eleventh Census, 1890,* I, 782–83.

48 Cincinnati *Enquirer*, May 19, 1891.

After formally proclaiming the birth of the national People's Party, the Cincinnati convention of 1891 adjourned. Their platform was not an original document. It embodied the program of the Farmers' Alliance as drawn up in the so-called "Ocala Demands" of 1890: the major planks being the subtreasury plan, the unlimited coinage of silver at a ratio of 16 to 1 relative to gold value, abolition of the national banking system, prohibition of alien ownership of land, a graduated income tax, government control (or ownership) of communications and transportation facilities, the eight-hour day for labor, and the direct election of United States Senators.[49] These would continue to be the major proposals of Populism during the 1890's.

The Cincinnati convention had been cleverly directed. It permitted old agrarian warhorses such as Donnelly and Weaver to be "in on the ground floor" as the Populist Party emerged.[50] And the majority element of the Farmers' Alliance, which had wished to defer any third-party decisions, was quickly and carefully placated. The managers at Cincinnati set up a national committee to smooth the way for a union of Midwest and Southern white agrarian forces at the proposed St. Louis convention in February of 1892. By that latter date the president, L. L. Polk, and many other Alliance leaders in the South were ready for Populism. The Democratic Party of Dixie had not been, and was not likely to be, captured by the agrarians. The alleged victories of 1890 proved hollow. The subtreasury plan was being sabotaged in Congress by Southern Democrats.[51] As for Louisiana, it was during 1891 that the Farmers' Union fell into the snare set by the Anti-Lottery Democrats.

49 *Ibid.*, May 21, 1891.
50 Hicks, *The Populist Revolt*, 217.
51 Philadelphia *Journal of the Knights of Labor*, May 28, 1891; Noblin, *Leonidas La Fayette Polk*, 270–73; Woodward, *Origins of the New South*, 239.

By July of 1891, within a month of Brian's return from Cincinnati, the majority of Farmers' Union members in Catahoula, Grant, and Winn parishes had openly renounced all ties to the Democratic Party and, while gathered at Union meetings, pledged their support to the People's Party. Soon, Populist activity was visible among the farmers of Calcasieu, Natchitoches, Rapides, Sabine, and Vernon parishes.[52] Conservative Democrats grew increasingly disturbed and angry over these mass defections, and the choler of the *Daily Caucasian* was raised even more by the news, late in July, that "Professor Vincent" of Kansas had returned "to preach his third party heresy to Louisiana farmers." [53]

The Populist groundswell attracted a number of restless misfits. L. A. Traylor, a physically dwarfish man whose political history included Radical Republicanism and Greenbackism, was one such individual. Traylor was an ordained Baptist minister. He had also taught school in several hill parishes and, at various times, sold insurance for the Famous Life Association and peddled "some sort of patent medicine." During the summer of 1891 Traylor took to the road as an organizer for the People's Party in northern and central Louisiana. He seemed to be most effective in swaying Negroes from Republicanism to Populism.[54] Accused by the Colfax *Chronicle* of preaching "communistic ideas," Traylor replied: "The wealth of the country, like the oil from the Standard Oil Trust, flows through a thousand pipes into the vaults of capitalists, making the rich richer and the poor poorer. . . . It is

[52] Baton Rouge *Daily Advocate,* June 21–23, 1891; Colfax *Chronicle,* June 20, 27, 1891; Lake Charles *Echo,* quoted in *ibid.,* August 1, 1891; New Orleans *Daily Picayune,* October 3, 1891.

[53] Shreveport *Daily Caucasian,* quoted in Baton Rouge *Daily Advocate,* July 28, 1891.

[54] For Traylor's background and activities, see Baton Rouge *Daily Advocate,* October 5, 1890; Homer *Guardian-Journal,* quoted in Colfax *Chronicle,* August 1, 1891; Colfax *Chronicle,* August 8, 1891.

unnatural, unrighteous and damnable, and if I must preach the doctrine of communists to arouse the people from their lethargy, then make the most of it." [55]

Traylor's Populist work made him an object of attention, probably for the first time in his life. He was appointed president of what was described as a "college" in Grant Parish, and was named state chairman of the Committee of Organization of the Louisiana People's Party. In September of 1891, when the Populists of Grant Parish raised money to start a party organ at Colfax, Traylor became its editor. His paper was christened the *Ocala Demand*.[56] Traylor then had the opportunity to use his acid pen on what he called the "vindictive, villainous and arrogant . . . Louisiana aristocrats." His prime local target was the Democratic Colfax *Chronicle*, which frequently reprinted anti-Populist diatribes from other papers; Traylor assailed it as a chamberpot into which was emptied "the filth and slush" of the state's Bourbon press.[57]

But Traylor's days as a crusader were numbered. Late in 1891, money from the Louisiana Lottery Company began trickling into Colfax, and the *Ocala Demand* underwent a startling reversal of policy; Traylor now implored his Populist readers to "enlist under the banner" of Samuel D. McEnery in the current gubernatorial campaign.[58] On this sour note did Traylor close his brief third-party career. Obscurity again claimed him.

From the summer of 1891 until April of 1892, political activity in Louisiana, Populist or otherwise, revolved around the

[55] Letter from L. A. Traylor, in Colfax *Chronicle*, August 1, 1891.

[56] James S. Penny, "The People's Party Press During the Louisiana Political Upheaval of the Eighteen-Nineties" (M.A. thesis, Louisiana State University, 1942), 67; New Orleans *Daily Picayune*, October 3–5, 1891.

[57] Colfax *Ocala Demand*, quoted in Colfax *Chronicle*, October 17, 1891.

[58] *Ibid.*, January 9, 1892. Hardy Brian confirmed reports that Lottery money was at work among Populist leaders in Grant Parish, and he called Traylor "the arch traitor and cats-paw." Winnfield *Comrade*, quoted in Colfax *Chronicle*, February 6, 1892; Natchitoches *Louisiana Populist*, August 2, 1895.

election of a successor to Governor Francis T. Nicholls. The Populists at first offered qualified support to Thomas S. Adams. As Hardy Brian explained it in the *Comrade,* the Populists desired most of all a governor and a legislature sympathetic to the Farmers' Alliance program; if Adams would stand by the "Ocala Demands" and not become a mere tool of the Anti-Lottery League patricians, then the third-party men stood ready to vote for an Adams-headed state Democratic ticket in 1892. But Adams fulfilled none of these Populist provisos. He even began expressing doubts about the subtreasury plan.[59]

It was at the Lafayette convention of the Farmers' Union, in August of 1891, that the break between Adams and the left-wing agrarians became irrevocable. The latter not only feared the outcome of the "compact" between Adams and the Anti-Lottery League, but they also resented the fact that Adams' speech before the gathering at Lafayette was confined to two main topics: the Lottery evil and the unwisdom of straying from the Democratic Party. A number of hitherto faithful Adams men, including Thomas J. Guice, then proclaimed themselves Populists.[60]

The first state convention of the People's Party was slated for October 2, 1891, at Alexandria. Populist organizers were meanwhile busy. Hardy Brian and Guice spent much of September talking with workingmen's organizations in New Orleans; the *Daily Picayune,* observing their progress, reported that the Knights of Labor "are in hearty sympathy with the movement." [61] The People's Municipal Party, as Populism's

59 Winnfield *Comrade,* quoted in Baton Rouge *Daily Advocate,* July 30, 1891; New Orleans *Times-Democrat,* quoted in Colfax *Chronicle,* October 31, 1891.

60 New Orleans *Daily Picayune,* August 8–9, September 17, 1891; Winnfield *Comrade,* quoted in Baton Rouge *Daily Advocate,* August 13, 1891; Opelousas *St. Landry Clarion,* August 15, 1891.

61 New Orleans *Daily Picayune,* September 16–20, October 3, 1891.

urban affiliate was designated, had been holding meetings since midsummer. Moreover, the New Orleans *Issue*, a laborite weekly founded in the spring of 1891, presently endorsed the Populist cause. Thomas A. Clayton, manager of the Farmers' Union Commercial Association of Louisiana, reportedly provided the funds for the party in the Crescent City.[62]

Seventy-eight delegates from seventeen parishes were present at the Alexandria convention. Most surprising was the size of the urban delegation. Thirty-five, almost half of the total Populists assembled, had come up from Orleans Parish. Winn Parish, by comparison, occupied five seats. All those present at the morning session were white men; however, Superintendent Isaac Keys of the state's Colored Alliance, along with another black Allianceman, arrived later in the day and the two were admitted to the speaker's platform.[63]

The Reverend Benjamin Brian presided over the convention preliminaries. The elder Brian, facing the assembled farmers and laborers, expressed "great satisfaction" at seeing the movement he had worked "for the last fifteen years" to create, finally organized on a statewide basis. He also spoke of the growing Populist sentiment among Negro people. The big planters, Brian prophesied, would try to stop their black sharecroppers from joining the new party; yet he indicated confidence that this obstacle "would be attended to at the proper time." [64] His curious optimism on this point was not well grounded in reality.

The Alexandria convention adjourned without making nominations for state office. That would be done later, in

[62] New Orleans *Issue*, August 1, 1891; Colfax *Chronicle*, October 31, 1891. The *Issue* was owned and edited by J. B. Cameron and J. R. Hoening, Jr. Both were active third-party workers in the city.

[63] New Orleans *Daily Picayune*, October 2–4, 1891; Opelousas *St. Landry Clarion*, October 10, 1891.

[64] Colfax *Chronicle*, October 10, 1891; New Orleans *Daily Picayune*, October 3, 1891.

February of 1892. A state organization was, however, set up; Thomas Clayton was named as chairman of the state executive committee, and Hardy Brian became secretary of the party. Also, on October 3, the public read the striking "Address to the People of the State of Louisiana . . . Irrespective of Class, Color, or Past Political Affiliation." This first platform of the state People's Party read, in part:

> None can yet tell whether this revolution shall be accomplished by peaceable means, by appeals to the reason of the dominant element of our population . . . or whether a deaf ear will still be turned . . . until . . . the people rise in their mighty wrath, and with swift retributive strokes, beat down the gates of . . . monopoly . . . and corruption. . . .
>
> You colored men . . . you must now realize that there is no hope of any further material benefit to you in the Republican party, and that if you remain in it you will continue to be hewers of wood and drawers of water in the future as you have been in the past.
>
> Democrats. . . . Have you not the experience of uninterrupted Democratic rule in this State? What has it done for you? Are your children growing up better equipped for the battle of life than you were? Are your institutions equal to the demands made upon them? Have your public finances been honestly administered? The spectre of negro supremacy has been used to keep you in the toils of the scheming machine politicians as effectively as the voudou is employed to terrify the credulous negroes themselves.
>
> But now the machine politicians have put a new slide in the magic lantern . . . and show you on their screen the hideous figure of lottery rule, to intimidate you and prevent you from grasping the hand held out to help you escape from your political dungeon. Must a man be bound hand and foot in Democratic fetters before he can be trusted to vote against the lottery . . . ? Cast your ballot against this lottery and all . . . gambling on the product of your labor.
>
> Will you still remain the willing serfs of machine politicians?

Shall Louisiana not join in that ringing shout for liberty and reform that started in Kansas . . . ? [65]

After studying this platform and examining the signatures
suffixed thereto, the *Daily Picayune* headlined: "IT MAY BE
RIDICULOUS, BUT IT IS REVOLUTION." Nothing like
the Alexandria Populist convention, said the old New Orleans
paper, had ever been witnessed in Louisiana before; "It is a
gathering of all the discontented, dissatisfied and unprosperous
elements of the population. . . . It is easy to laugh at, but . . .
there is nothing absurd in the fact that half the delegates . . .
were from this city. When the city and country unites, the results may be serious." [66]

The Alexandria convention lacked, however, one bewhiskered face that had shown up at almost every significant agrarian meeting in the state during the past decade, including the
forlorn little gathering at the cemetery near Bayou D'Arbonne
in 1881. John Tetts was in Alexandria in October of 1891.
But he stayed away from the Populist convention. Tetts, since
1889, had steadily fallen under the conservative influence of
Thomas S. Adams; late in that year the Farmers' Union president had appointed Tetts as editor of the "Union Department" of the newspaper selected as their official state journal,
the Shreveport *Weekly Caucasian*. Not long afterward, the
two men concluded that a paper "wholly owned and controlled by the Order" was an imperative need. This decision
led to the founding of the Alexandria *Farmers' Vidette* in the
autumn of 1890. Tetts was at first co-editor, then editor-in-
chief.[67]

During 1891 the *Farmers' Vidette* boomed Adams for the

[65] New Orleans *Daily Picayune,* October 4, 1891.

[66] *Ibid.,* October 5, 1891.

[67] Shreveport *Weekly Caucasian,* January 30, 1890; *National Economist,* III
(August 30, 1890), 382; *Biographical and Historical Memoirs of Northwest
Louisiana,* 533; New Orleans *Louisiana Review,* January 27, 1892.

governorship and praised the Anti-Lottery League as much or more than it dwelt upon the problems of small agriculturists. Editor Tetts also castigated the third-party movement, as it spread outward from Winn Parish, with heated language. The Populists returned his fire. Tetts was inaccurately accused of being the prime fulcrum behind the Farmers' Union-League's "Lafayette Compact"; Traylor of the *Ocala Demand* once referred to the *Farmers' Vidette* as "Tetts, Adams & Co.," and vowed to "eat up Tetts, bloody raw." [68]

But Tetts, whatever his purposes may have been—he reportedly was hoping for the lucrative state printing contract—was not a man equipped to hold his own in the Byzantine arena of Louisiana Democratic politics. In April of 1892, three days after the state election, Tetts resigned as editor of the fading *Farmers' Vidette*. His usefulness to the Anti-Lottery League had terminated. Tetts, along with his wife and son and three unmarried daughters, prepared to move to the village of Robeline, in Natchitoches Parish. He had saved enough money to buy some second-hand newspaper equipment. One month later the Robeline *Battle Flag* made its first appearance. Tetts had become a Populist.[69]

In the state election of 1892, Louisiana's voters had a choice, in theory at least, among five separate parties. This fragmentation bemused all but the most seasoned and cynical political veterans. As noted before, the pro-Lottery "Regular" Democratic ticket was headed by McEnery, while the anti-Lottery "Reform" Democrats ran a slate topped by Murphy J. Foster. The Republicans, not to be outdone, spoiled any chance they might have had by likewise putting out two state tickets;

[68] Alexandria *Farmers' Vidette*, quoted in Colfax *Chronicle*, November 7, 14, 1891; Mansfield *De Soto Democrat*, quoted in New Orleans *Louisiana Review*, January 27, 1892; Colfax *Ocala Demand*, quoted in Colfax *Chronicle*, November 14, 1891.
[69] Penny, "The People's Party Press." 50; Colfax *Chronicle*, May 7, 1892.

Albert H. Leonard was the pro-Lottery (Kellogg faction) and John E. Breaux the anti-Lottery (Warmoth faction) Republican candidate for governor. Finally, in February, the People's Party nominated Robert L. Tannehill of Winn Parish for the governorship, along with a slate of aspirants for the lesser state offices.[70] "Political nomenclature," remarked the *St. Landry Clarion*, "is becoming numerous and complex." Equally muddled were the positions taken by some of the nominees. The McEnery Democrats, though recently indifferent toward virtually everything that would have uplifted the state, were now wringing their hands in pious dismay over the woeful condition of Louisiana's schools and institutions. For the McEneryites were supporting the Lottery's bid for constitutional recharter; and in exchange for the right to exist another twenty-five years, the Lottery was offering to pour $1,250,000 for each of those years into the state treasury. Therefore, McEnery partisans attacked the Foster Democrats as cruel "rich men" who cared nothing for the poor school children who would benefit from the proffered Lottery largess. On the other hand, the fact that the Foster ticket included Thomas S. Adams and two other members of the Farmers' Union, prompted Hearsey's *Daily States* and other Bourbon organs to categorize the entire "Reform" Democratic slate as "red revolutionists."[71]

70 Romero, *Louisiana Historical Quarterly*, XXVIII, 1154–60; Uzee, "Republican Politics in Louisiana," 89–91; New Orleans *Times-Democrat*, February 19–21, 1892. The Populist state ticket in 1892 offered: for governor, Robert L. Tannehill of Winn; for lieutenant governor, I. J. Mills of Calcasieu; for secretary of state, D. McStravick of Orleans; for treasurer, John Mahoney of Orleans; for auditor, John Hendricks of Caddo; for superintendent of education, J. D. Patton of Grant; for attorney-general, Wade Hough of Concordia.
71 Opelousas *St. Landry Clarion*, quoted in Penny, "The People's Party Press," 29; New Orleans *Daily Picayune*, August 24, 1891; New Orleans *Louisiana Review*, January 6, 1892; New Orleans *Daily States*, quoted in Baton Rouge *Daily Advocate*, February 12, 14, 1892.

The Foster Democrats hammered away at the moral evil of the Lottery and reminded the public of its carpetbagger origins. They also spoke of the possibility that a "McLottery" victory in 1892 might bring Major Burke back in triumph from his Honduras exile. Nor were some of the shortcomings of Governor McEnery's 1881–88 administration allowed to be forgotten.[72] Yet the Fosterites, while rejecting the idea of Lottery money being used to upgrade the state's schools and institutions, suggested no improvement plan of their own. All the while, the Leonard and Breaux Republican tickets were too absorbed in their internecine squabble to trouble the Democrats.

"This newborn babe," as Hardy Brian termed the Louisiana People's Party, hoped to benefit from the family fights taking place within the Democratic and Republican households. The Populists, during their nominating convention at Alexandria in February, revised their earlier platform in such a way as to make an even stronger bid for Negro support. "We declare emphatically," read the document, "that the interests of the white and colored races of the South are identical. . . . Equal justice and fairness must be accorded to each." Of the 171 delegates present, at least 24 were black.[73]

Considering the time and place, and the fact that the white Populists were mostly from the small farmer class, this second Alexandria convention was a remarkable gathering. Rural white Louisianians had been taught contempt or hatred for the Negro practically since birth, but here in 1892 some of them were attempting to lay aside the animosities of a life-

---

72 Bayou Sara *True Democrat*, March 9, 1892; Opelousas *St. Landry Clarion*, January 23, 1892; Bunkie *Blade*, quoted in Baton Rouge *Daily Advocate*, January 27, 1892.

73 Winnfield *Comrade*, quoted in Lucia Elizabeth Daniel, "The Louisiana People's Party" (M.A. thesis, Louisiana State University, 1942), 32; New Orleans *Times-Democrat*, February 19, 1892.

time for the sake of biracial class interests. That many were still deeply prejudiced may be taken for granted; that they needed and wanted the black man's vote was obvious; yet Louisiana Populism, for all its limitations, represented a brave and essentially sincere effort to break down some of the awful barriers which lay between ordinary whites and blacks.

Two of the Negro delegates at Alexandria were placed in nomination for a position on the state ticket. Charles A. Roxborough and L. D. Laurent were both candidates for the Populist nomination to the office of state treasurer. Others among the blacks present, however, urged them to withdraw their names because "it was not the proper time" for Negro Populists to run for office. The white Populists did not take part in the argument, preferring to let the Negroes settle it themselves. Shortly before the convention balloted, both Laurent and Roxborough withdrew as candidates. But they did receive positions within the party, becoming members of the Populist state executive committee. Roxborough had recently resigned from the Republican Party after deciding that "in this State" it as well as the Democratic organization tended "towards that same goal—white supremacy." [74] For him, Populism gave at least some new hope.

Robert L. Tannehill, the only genuine Populist the party would ever nominate for the governorship of Louisiana, was a relatively prosperous resident of Winnfield. He owned a saw mill and a cotton gin. Forty-four years old in 1892, Tannehill had previously been sheriff of Winn Parish, but he had held no other public office. He served as treasurer of the state Farmers' Union and presided over the parish Union

---

[74] New Orleans *Times-Democrat*, February 19, 1892; Charles A. Roxborough to J. S. Davidson, July 31, 1890, in Department of Archives, Louisiana State University.

from 1887 to 1890.[75] Actually, Tannehill was almost unknown outside the borders of Winn. The other members of the ticket were similarly obscure.

The McEnery Democrats tended to ignore the Populist candidates, although one Bourbon journal, the *Daily Advocate,* described Tannehill's platform as "little short of flat communism." McEnery's partisans assumed, correctly, that the small agrarian party would draw most of its votes from men who would have otherwise supported Foster. The Fosterites understood this as well. Consequently, the Populist ticket was treated most hostilely by the "Reform" Democrats; the latter insisted that Lottery money financed the Populist campaign and that the third party was making the race "in order to help the Lottery as much as possible." In fact, there was little of any kind of financing for the People's Party; and as to the Lottery, Tannehill took the view that it was a great evil, but not the only one which plagued the state. The New Orleans *Issue,* Populism's urban voice, suggested that the Foster Democrats had taken up the anti-Lottery crusade primarily to herd working people away from other fields of reform.[76] In other words, according to this view, the Lottery was a sacrificial wolf being thrown to the lambs.

That Foster was to be the next governor became evident several weeks before the election. By February of 1892, the federal government had forced the Lottery to discontinue its use of the United States mail, and McEnery's obvious lack of popularity convinced the officials of the gambling syndicate that their cause within the state was also hopeless. The company withdrew its request for recharter and also its offer of

75 *Biographical and Historical Memoirs of Northwest Louisiana,* 492; Winnfield *Southern Sentinel,* August 28, 1885, September 16, 1887.

76 Baton Rouge *Daily Advocate,* March 31, 1892; Alexandria *Town Talk,* quoted in Opelousas *St. Landry Clarion,* October 3, 1891; New Orleans *Issue,* June 4, 1892.

$1,250,000 per year. McEnery's chances faded with the Lottery. On election day, April 19, Foster obtained 79,388 votes against 47,037 for McEnery. The two Republicans divided 41,-818 votes. Populist Tannehill brought up the rear with 9,804.[77] Of course, "official" returns from any Louisiana election of that era were subject to question, and everyone but the Fosterites claimed that gross frauds had occurred. Nonetheless, it was clear that Populist sentiment had not yet made much headway either in the rural parishes or in the city. Six percent of the state vote was not an auspicious beginning.

Tannehill ran ahead of his Democratic and Republican opponents in just four parishes: Catahoula, Grant, Vernon, and Winn. One-tenth of the Populist candidate's total strength came from his home parish, where he received 1,001 votes against 305 for all the others; but, as one Bourbon jokingly observed, when the total from 59 parishes was added up it became quite clear that "Tannehill didn't *Winn.*" He made a respectable showing in nine other parishes: Bienville, Calcasieu, Caldwell, De Soto, Jackson, Natchitoches, Rapides, Red River, and Sabine. But the urban returns were discouraging to the extreme. Out of almost 40,000 ballots reported from New Orleans, Tannehill received 71. His support in the city was hampered by the fact that in no Orleans Parish precinct were the Populists allowed to have commissioners.[78]

Four People's Party men were elected to the legislature in 1892. Benjamin F. Brian was the sole Populist member of the upper house; the seat he had once held (1880–84) as an independent, and had run for a total of six times, would now be his for the remaining years of his life.[79] Hardy Brian,

77 Ezell, *Fortune's Merry Wheel,* 266–67; Romero, *Louisiana Historical Quarterly,* XXVIII, 1160; *Senate Journal,* 1892, p. 21.

78 Lake Providence *Carroll Democrat,* April 30, 1892; New Orleans *Times-Democrat,* April 18–22, 1892.

79 Benjamin Brian died in 1896, at the age of 63. Natchitoches *Louisiana Populist,* November 6, 1896.

his son, represented Winn Parish in the lower house. Albert Shelby of Grant Parish, who was an ex-Republican, and John Franklin of Vernon Parish were the other Populist representatives.[80] It became the strategy of the four Populist legislators to refrain from introducing bills on their own, for anything advanced by a non-Democratic member had little chance of ever reaching the floor for a vote; instead, they quietly backed the bills introduced by those Democratic solons who belonged to the Farmers' Union. But at best, the agrarian coalition of Populists and Farmers' Union Democrats could count on only four senators out of thirty-six in the Senate, and twenty-two out of one hundred members in the House of Representatives.[81] The session was notably lacking in reform legislation.

During the summer and autumn of 1892, as the presidential and congressional races drew near, the People's Party of Louisiana came to realize the enormity of the task which confronted them. Factionalism within the Democratic Party was ending. The Lottery question was settled, and Governor Foster's intense conservatism on matters of economics and race began to win plaudits among the old McEnery Bourbons.[82] In fact the previous distinction between Bourbon and patrician Democrats no longer really applied at the political level; Foster had emerged from the *noblesse oblige* class, but his entire administration, because of circumstances and natural inclinations, would represent a patrician shift into the Bourbon camp.

United, the conservative Democracy of Louisiana scrutinized their agrarian challengers and found them weak but po-

[80] The official journal erroneously listed all but Senator Brian as Democrats. Cf. *House Journal,* 1892, pp. 698–700; Colfax *Chronicle,* April 23, August 6, 1892.

[81] See Hardy Brian's later recollection in Shreveport *Times,* March 13, 1939.

[82] Romero, *Louisiana Historical Quarterly,* XXVIII, 1164–66; Baton Rouge *Daily Advocate,* October 7, 1892.

tentially dangerous. As one of McEnery's friends phrased it, "a spirit of political insubordination" was abroad in the land.[83] Foster's handling of the New Orleans general strike in November of 1892 increased his popularity among upper class Louisianians; he took a "firm position," threatened to use the state militia, and in general "gave the strikers to understand that protection would be given the business interests."[84] Luckily for the Governor, the twenty-five thousand or more striking laborers confined their protests to conditions of wages and hours of work and, with few exceptions, were apathetic toward the idea of political union with the rural Populists.

Despite the lack of response from the city, the People's Party decided, in October of 1892, to set up its permanent state headquarters in New Orleans. An urban resident named Andrew B. Booth was named chairman of the state executive committee. A young and rather ineffectual man, Booth served more as a clerk and errand-boy for the party than as a molder of policy. He continued as chairman until 1896. Booth's work in the shabby New Orleans office was hampered by an almost total lack of money; often, he was unable to mail out Populist literature because the headquarters could not afford postage stamps. Booth, in the meantime, earned a living as a lecturer for something called the Knights of Honor, which had no political affiliation but appeared to be an insurance company disguised as a benevolent and fraternal lodge.[85] Hardy Brian, who served as state secretary of the party, resided at Winnfield and edited the *Comrade* until 1894, when

83 Lake Providence *Banner Democrat,* September 10, 1892.

84 Crowley *Signal,* Lake Charles *American,* St. Joseph *Tensas Gazette,* quoted in Baton Rouge *Daily Advocate,* November 23, 1892. See also, the article by Roger W. Shugg, "The New Orleans General Strike of 1892," *Louisiana Historical Quarterly,* XII (1938), 547–60.

85 Colfax *Chronicle,* October 15, 1892; Natchitoches *Louisiana Populist,* July 12, 1895; Lake Providence *Banner Democrat,* February 1, 1896.

he moved to Natchitoches and began publishing the *Louisiana Populist*. Booth and Brian seldom had a chance to meet and plan strategy. An effective statewide organization did not exist.

Shortly before the national election of November, 1892, Populists announced for Congress in four of Louisiana's six districts. The mere fact that they were running provoked a torrent of Bourbon abuse which surpassed all previous expletives used against the agrarian rebels. The *Daily Advocate* and the *Daily States* led the attack. Populists, according to the former, were "political hermaphrodites," and their party "a bastard organization. . . . We appeal to the patriots of Louisiana to shun this monstrous political gangrene as they would a leper at the gates." Moreover, the Baton Rouge paper was "quite tired" of the Populist "mouthings and whinings" about vote fraud, saying, "if . . . they . . . can't protect themselves from being 'counted out,' they should move . . . and go to some place where people don't 'count out.' " Not bothering to deny that such stealings took place, this official journal of the state government half-jokingly proposed that "India rubber" ballot boxes be used in elections, since the tin depositories would not take stuffing beyond a certain limit.[86] In similar vein, Hearsey's *Daily States* indicated that the methods used to defraud Republicans worked equally well against agrarians, and described the latter as "sore heads, demagogues, agitators . . . rainbow chasers"; in sum, "miserable excrescence of the Democratic and Republican parties." Later, in a moment of supreme candor, Hearsey advocated dictatorship as the most suitable form of government for Louisiana.[87]

There were vast differences between Populists and the white leadership of the Republican Party of Louisiana, but

[86] Baton Rouge *Daily Advocate,* October 5–6, 27, 1892. See also, *ibid.,* April 22, 1892.

[87] New Orleans *Daily States,* quoted in Colfax *Chronicle,* August 13, 1892, and in Baton Rouge *Daily Advocate,* August 27, 1897.

in the autumn of 1892, common necessity began driving them together. Both were the victims of Democratic robbery; both could at least agree on the overriding need for "honest elections, and a fair count." As a Republican had grimly observed earlier, the state's Democratic rulers had devised a cunning substitute for representative government. It was, he said, "an oligarchy by arithmetic." [88]

One month prior to the November election, Thomas J. Guice went to New Orleans to open political negotiations with both the Kellogg-Leonard and the Warmoth-Breaux factions of the G.O.P. By October 20, the bargain was sealed. The Populists would nominate candidates in the Fourth, Fifth, and Sixth Congressional Districts; Republicans would run their men in the Second and Third; while an independent in the First District was to be supported by both parties. The Republicans were to endorse the Populists in the Fourth, Fifth, and Sixth; the agrarians were to return the favor in the downstate districts. At the same time, an agreement was reached on presidential electors. A "fusion" ticket would be issued. Four Populist electors pledged to James G. Weaver and four Republicans pledged to Benjamin Harrison were to appear on the ballot.[89]

National leaders of the Republican Party were seemingly much in favor of the Louisiana fusion arrangement, although some G.O.P. partisans inside the state voiced misgivings. Highly critical, on the other hand, was the national People's Party. Populist National Chairman H. E. Taubeneck said the fusion in Louisiana was made "against my protests." [90] Else-

88 New Orleans *Weekly Pelican,* January 5, 1889.

89 Melvin J. White, "Populism in Louisiana During the Nineties," *Mississippi Valley Historical Review,* V (1918–19) , 9–11; New Orleans *Times-Democrat,* October 21–23, 1892.

90 Robert Lowery to J. Ernest Breda, October 14, 1892, in Breda Family Papers, Department of Archives, Louisiana State University; H. E. Taubeneck, quoted in New Orleans *Issue,* December 10, 1892.

where in the South in 1892, Populists and Republicans tended toward informal understandings in local, state, and sometimes congressional races. But only in Louisiana were the presidential electors fused and the congressional agreement so positive.[91]

The Populist-Republican coalition of 1892 was, of course, not without precedent in Louisiana. The National Party movement of 1878 had tried something of a similar union of yeoman white and Negro Republican voters. But that effort, falling as it did under conservative white Republican direction, was a standing lesson to the Populists of the 1890's. Everyone understood that Warmoth, Kellogg, and other remnants of carpetbaggism were not the most trustworthy of allies. Many Populists reacted negatively to the 1892 fusion. Hardy Brian, though he accepted it, wrote in a shamefaced manner when he asked his upland neighbors to share their Weaver votes with a "plutocrat" like President Harrison.[92] But with Bourbon Democrats for foes, the Louisiana People's Party could not spurn allies from any quarter.

The hottest agrarian campaign in the Pelican State that year was waged in the Fourth District, where Thomas J. Guice was the Populist congressional nominee. He now made the race against Democrat Newton C. Blanchard which the Farmers' Union militants had urged him to make two years before. Guice's stature among the Populists was rising sharply; for in August of 1892, at the Farmers' Union annual state convention, held at Monroe, he had captained the third-party forces in a take-over of the Union organization. Union President Adams, who had recently been sworn in as secretary of state under Governor Foster, resigned as head of the Union and walked out of the Monroe convention. Populists thereupon

---

[91] Rogers, "Agrarianism in Alabama," 390–99; Alex M. Arnett, *The Populist Movement in Georgia* (New York, 1922), 152–53; Martin, *The People's Party in Texas,* 77; Hicks, *The Populist Revolt,* 245–47.

[92] Winnfield *Comrade,* quoted in Colfax *Chronicle,* October 29, 1892.

took over most of the offices in the agrarian order, which then became nothing more than an adjunct of the People's Party.[93] As expected, Guice's congressional candidacy aroused special Democratic ire: "Greasy Guice," "Garrulous Guice," "this statistical old ass," "the ignoramus candidate," "the great unwashed from the forks of the crick," and "veritable scum," were a few of the epithets applied. Hardy Brian, who was not a stranger to Bourbon invective himself, once remarked that no other agrarian reformer of his acquaintance was ever subjected to as much slander and personal abuse as fell upon Thomas J. Guice.[94]

Robert P. Webb, the veteran Greenbacker from Claiborne Parish, ran as a Populist against Congressman Boatner in the Fifth District. Also in that race was an independent candidate with a Populistic program: Andrew Augustus Gunby, publisher of the Monroe *Bulletin*. In the Sixth District, Josiah Kleinpeter, an East Baton Rouge planter, accepted the Populist congressional nomination but did not conduct an active campaign. The Republicans having decided not to enter a man in the Third District contest, Populist I. J. Mills announced his candidacy there. In the metropolitan First and Second districts, the Populists, as had been agreed, supported independent James Wilkinson and Republican Morris Marks, respectively.[95]

Populist presidential candidate James B. Weaver toured

93 John Pickett was named president of the Farmers' Union at the 1892 convention. Like Thomas S. Adams, Pickett was a member of Governor Foster's cabinet; he had been elected treasurer of Louisiana on the Foster ticket in 1892. But by the time of the Monroe convention of the Farmers' Union, Pickett had broken with the Democrats and was a Populist. Daniel, "The Louisiana People's Party," 42–43; Colfax *Chronicle*, August 13, 1892.

94 Colfax *Chronicle*, July 30, September 3, November 5, 1892; Lake Providence *Banner Democrat*, September 10, 1892; Baton Rouge *Daily Advocate*, September 4, November 1, 1892, March 9, 1894; Natchitoches *Populist*, September 2, 1898.

95 Mer Rouge *Vidette*, quoted in Lake Providence *Banner Democrat*, October 29, 1892; Bayou Sara *True Democrat*, October 22, 1892; Baton Rouge *Daily Advocate*, October 11–12, 1892; New Orleans *Issue*, December 10, 1892.

Louisiana and several other Southern states during the autumn of 1892. The fact that Weaver had been a Union general in the Civil War was emphasized by the Bourbon press; his actions against the Confederacy were described as "merciless ... brutal ... cruel." When this theme was exhausted, the *Daily Advocate* went on to call Weaver an anarchist and a "prostitute," and after he departed, said that he should "thank his stars" that he got out of the Pelican State in one piece.[96]

While attacking Weaver and the local Populists, the state's Democratic spokesmen also flailed away at the already dead "force bill." A Republican measure which had been placed before Congress in 1890, it proposed Federal controls over elections and voter registration. The bill had failed to pass. Yet it had summoned up the ghost of military Reconstruction. Though defeated in Congress, the force bill performed a valuable function for Southern Democrats, because "force bill and nigger domination" became a potent shibboleth in coming elections. Louisiana's Populists were accused of supporting a revival of the measure in Congress. Guice was quoted, probably inaccurately, as saying that "Bourbonism is doomed. If they don't give us a fair count, they'll get the force bill or hell." [97]

None of the four Populist congressional nominees were able to unseat Democratic incumbents in the November 8 election. The official returns showed a topheavy victory for the majority party in all six districts. But Populist leaders were able to see a few bright signs. Tannehill's vote in April had been less than 10,000 for the entire state; seven months later, the party's congressional candidates, although none ran in two

---

[96] Colfax *Chronicle*, August 13, 1892; Baton Rouge *Daily Advocate*, September 27, October 7, 1892.

[97] Morgan, *Forum*, X, 23–26; Natchitoches *Louisiana Populist*, December 20, 1895; Lake Providence *Banner Democrat*, November 5, 1892.

districts, almost doubled that figure. In the presidential race, the Cleveland Democratic electors polled 87,922 against 26,132 for the Harrison-Weaver slate. How much of the Harrison-Weaver vote was Populist and how much was Republican could only be guessed.[98]

Little of the Populist gain in the congressional races could be attributed to Republican help. In the Third District, wealthy Republican sugar planters supported the protectionist-minded Democratic incumbent rather than the Populist Mills. While in the Fourth, Fifth and Sixth districts, the Democratic machine refused to relax its grip on plantation parish ballot boxes. The G.O.P. organization in these latter regions, although presumably willing to help the Populists, was impotent. Said the New Orleans *Issue,* with only slight misstatement: "We owe nothing to the Republicans." [99]

Populism in the Pelican State next awaited the congressional races of 1894 and, of most concern, the gubernatorial election of 1896. In the interval, the lot of ordinary whites and blacks worsened as a disastrous nationwide depression commenced; Governor Foster's administration became more closely identified with Bourbon reaction; and a sudden politico-economic split within the upper class began to shake the self-assurance of the ruling oligarchy. It was then that the Bourbons of Louisiana would face their sternest challenge in the half century between Reconstruction and Huey Long.

98 Populist candidates for Congress carried seven parishes in 1892: Grant, Jackson, Lincoln, Sabine, Union, Vernon and Winn. *Report of the Secretary of State,* 1902, pp. 575–76; W. Dean Burnham, *Presidential Ballots: 1836–1892* (Baltimore, 1955) , 487, 918.

99 Uzee, "Republican Politics in Louisiana," 125; *Report of the Secretary of State,* 1902, pp. 575–76; New Orleans *Issue,* December 10, 1892.

X

Rob Them! You Bet!

L O U I S I A N A' S Bourbons were not always nicely logical, but they could boast of a certain consistency between their words and deeds. The official journal of the state once remarked, apropos of vote fraud, that the victims—not the perpetrators —were mostly to blame; that those unable to prevent their ballots from being falsely counted "are not worthy of the rights of citizenship." [1] Through such reasoning, and because of a fear that the dispossessed might not always be held down by existing methods, the Foster administration decided, in 1894, to work toward fundamental changes in the state's suffrage laws.

What Governor Foster proposed was plainly aimed at the poor of both races. It was imperative, he explained, that "the mass of ignorance, vice and venality without any proprietary interest in the State" be totally disfranchised.[2] Until such a time, the attempted coalition of poverty under the People's Party banner would be held in check at all costs, and the customary practices of fraud and intimidation became intensified. Nowhere else in the South did Populism encounter so many obstacles or as much brutality.

The Constitution of 1879 placed no unusual restrictions on

[1] Baton Rouge *Daily Advocate,* January 27, 1892.
[2] *Senate Journal,* 1894, p. 28; Baton Rouge *Daily Advocate,* May 19, 1896.

manhood suffrage. Of course, in many parishes Negroes had regularly been denied a free ballot by extra-legal means; but to change the law itself required either a constitutional amendment or a new constitution. The legislative session of 1894 decided to try the former. As the Governor recommended, a bill was passed which offered to the voters, at the next state election in 1896, an amendment which would restrict the franchise to adult males who "shall be able to read the Constitution of the State in his mother tongue, or shall be a bona fide owner of property . . . assessed to him at a cash valuation of not less than $200." [3] An ominous proviso was attached. If the proposed amendment was approved by the voters, then the subsequent legislature, in 1896, was specially empowered to rewrite this suffrage amendment, and after the solons made whatever changes they saw fit, it would then become part of the constitution, without resubmission to the people.

Hardy Brian spoke for the Populist leadership when he castigated the whole proposal as "infamous, damnable and hell born." Though Brian exaggerated when he predicted that the legislature might raise property requirements to a level of $10,000, some degree of upward revision was, unquestionably, the end in view. *Nation* magazine thought that the clause for legislative rewriting in the suffrage amendment to be "the most extraordinary way of changing a constitution ever proposed." [4]

The amendment passed the House of Representatives 74 to 9, and was approved by the Senate 27 to 0 (Populist Senator Brian was absent). Of the three People's Party men in the House, two voted against it, and the other was not present. The Populist legislators supported instead a reform of the

3 *House Journal,* 1894, pp. 835–36.
4 Natchitoches *Louisiana Populist,* May 17, 1895; *Nation,* LXII (April 30, 1896), 334.

state's election laws, based upon an Australian (secret) ballot; but their bill was tossed about from one committee to another, and finally buried.[5] Governor Foster insisted, and the overwhelming Democratic majority in the legislature backed him up, that any thought of reform at the polling place should wait until the "standing menace" of ignorance was relieved of the possibility of voting.[6]

This time, however, the Bourbons had gone a bit too far. Important segments of the Democratic press, along with many conservative propertied citizens, agreed with the Populists to the extent of urging ballot reform and condemning the proposed method of suffrage restriction. The Alexandria *Louisiana Democrat* blasted the assembly which passed the amendment as "the worst legislature" in the state's history, Warmoth and Kellogg's sorry regimes notwithstanding. The paper warned: "There must be a change and speedily, or the people, so long defrauded, will reassert their political rights even if it entails revolution and bloodshed. They have long been suppliants, on bended knees at the throne of power. Their just demands have been periodically scorned with the utmost contumely. Patience and forbearance will cease to be virtues, and more stringent measures will be resorted to. A word to the wise ought to be sufficient." [7]

Even the Colfax *Chronicle* attacked the suffrage proposal as "bristling with injustice and harshness." Editor Goodwyn made the telling observation that Louisiana should at least have provided school houses before she set about punishing ignorance and poverty.[8] But angriest of all, among the whites at least, were the Populists. Hardy Brian described the suf-

---

[5] *House Journal*, 1894, p. 836; *Senate Journal*, 1894, p. 361; *Calendar of the House of Representatives of the State of Louisiana*, June 28, 1894, p. 45.

[6] *Senate Journal*, 1894, p. 340.

[7] Alexandria *Louisiana Democrat*, June 27, 1894, quoted in *ibid.*, 418–19.

[8] Colfax *Chronicle*, January 4, 1896.

frage amendment as a "stepping stone to perpetually place this government in the hands of the rich, depriving the poor of any rights except to eke out their lives in hovels." [9] On the other hand, it received unstinted praise from the men who had once been the mainstay of the Burke-McEnery machine. A most avid proponent was Hearsey of the *Daily States,* who said that he favored anything that might keep "ignorant negroes and whites" from participating in government. The fact that the Pelican State had the highest number of white as well as black illiterates was not forgotten by either side in the controversy.[10]

Significantly, Democratic politicians and editors in the parishes of great cotton plantations unanimously applauded Governor Foster's words that "this force of brute numbers" must be eliminated from the body politic.[11] In a way, the cotton barons were making a sacrifice. For suffrage restriction would somewhat reduce their influence in political affairs. Ever since Reconstruction, the disproportionate representation in Democratic nominating conventions of such parishes as Tensas and Bossier had been based almost entirely upon illiterate and propertyless—and sometimes nonexistent—Negro registrants. Yet the planters were realistic men. They apparently were reaching the conclusion that the potential danger of the Negro vote now outweighed its previous advantages. Hearsey's bland explanation, that ballot box fraud "has become tiresome" for the planters, did not accurately state the case.[12] Fictitious or real, the black voter was never a boring subject.

Populist influence steadily grew among Negroes during the critical time of 1894–96. Around Bastrop, black men who had

9 Natchitoches *Louisiana Populist,* May 17, 1895.

10 New Orleans *Daily States,* quoted in Colfax *Chronicle,* January 4, 1896. See also, Lake Charles *Commercial,* quoted in Franklinton *New Era,* August 30, 1894.

11 Baton Rouge *Daily Advocate,* May 19, 1896.

12 New Orleans *Daily States,* quoted in *ibid.,* December 5, 1897.

not attempted to vote in a dozen years began to make inquiries as to the location of the registrar's office. Negro Populists in Baton Rouge were reported by the *Daily Advocate* to be making the nights "hideous" with their "yells and howls." The registrar in Opelousas kept himself locked in jail to avoid the crowds of blacks who clamored to be added to the rolls. While in Grant and Natchitoches parishes, a peculiar fusion of Democrats and white Republicans was effected in hopes of stopping the rush of Negroes into the Populist camp, but it was to little avail; the "colored Populists" of Grant even committed outrages upon members of their race who attended an anti-Populist rally.[13]

There was derision at the sight of white Populists in the uplands holding picnics and inviting their Negro neighbors to come and eat with them; scorn was heaped upon an audience of South Louisiana whites who "howled [themselves] hoarse" in approval of a speech advocating political rights for black men; nonetheless, such un-Southern happenings surely frightened the Bourbon Democrats.[14] Racial animosity seemed to be losing its grip upon numerous farmers who had earlier been among the staunchest advocates of white supremacy. "We can no longer depend upon the solidarity of the white race," grumbled the *Tensas Gazette*. The alternative, therefore, was "either a limitation of the suffrage, or a continuation of the present methods," which would "mean strife, bloody riots, and the degradation of society." [15] To the planter mentality, giving up their manipulated thousands of

[13] Bastrop *Clarion-Appeal*, quoted in Lake Providence *Banner Democrat*, March 7, 1896; Baton Rouge *Daily Advocate*, March 4, 1896; Opelousas *Courier*, February 29, 1896; Colfax *Chronicle*, May 4, 1895; Natchitoches *Louisiana Populist*, November 1, 1895. See also, letter from Mark Brazeale, in Colfax *Chronicle*, March 28, 1896.

[14] Colfax *Chronicle*, October 17, 1891; August 5, 1893; Opelousas *St. Landry Clarion*, March 7, 1896.

[15] St. Joseph *Tensas Gazette*, March 13, 20, 27, 1896.

Negro votes was infinitely preferable to a class conflict in which poor whites and blacks were allied against them.

The People's Party—the "P.P.," as some Democrats preferred to call it—made a serious effort to capture two Louisiana congressional districts in 1894. The silver issue had, by that time, replaced the subtreasury plan as the favorite agrarian panacea for economic ills. The depression which began in 1893 focused attention even more on the demand for an expanded currency. By promoting "free and unlimited coinage of silver," Populist leaders hoped to lure inflationist-minded Democrats into the third-party camp, and they also anticipated increased campaign contributions from the wealthy silver mine owners of the West. This appeal was blunted by the fact that most of the Democratic Party members in the South also jumped aboard the silver bandwagon. In Louisiana, as in other agricultural states, a Democratic silver movement commenced by 1894. But Governor Foster, and most of the inner circle of state party leaders, refused to pander to inflationist sentiment; they continued to adhere to President Grover Cleveland's conservative gold standard policies. And Foster's chief journalistic organ, the *Daily Advocate,* opined that the national depression would have a "salutary effect," in that "it will enforce economical methods upon the people." [16]

Populist congressional candidates in the Fourth and Fifth districts, where the third party was strongest, played the silver theme as best they could. Alexis Benoit, a liberal Monroe businessman and legislator who had recently converted to Populism, ran against Congressman Boatner, a gold standard advocate, in the latter district. Bryant W. Bailey, who campaigned for the seat of Fourth District Congressman Henry

16 Romero, *Louisiana Historical Quarterly,* XXVIII, 1167; Baton Rouge *Daily Advocate,* January 4, 1894. See also, Hicks, *The Populist Revolt,* 198–204, 301–20.

W. Ogden, was hurt by the fact that Ogden had yielded to majority opinion and "hoped and prayed" for the cause of free silver.[17]

Bailey, an earnest young man of twenty-eight, was "a strict member of the Baptist Church" at Winnfield. His education amounted to a few months spent in the inadequate Winn Parish schools. He had been a third-party man since 1890, when he began working under Hardy Brian as associate editor of the *Comrade*. During the summer of 1894, after Brian moved to Natchitoches, Bailey became editor of the Winnfield paper. Bailey also owned a moderate sized farm. He was able to purchase the *Comrade* from the Farmers' Union stockholders, whereas Brian had been editor but not owner. Goodwyn of the *Chronicle* at first scoffed at Bailey, calling him a "simpering dolt." [18] But it soon appeared that the youthful Populist was a powerful stump speaker. "Bellowing Bailey" or "Bazoo Bailey" became the Democratic nicknames for him.

At each place Bailey spoke, he invited local Democrats to come up and engage him in debate. While at Coushatta, his challenge was accepted by an elderly Bourbon who refused to believe that any post-1877 issue had relevancy. The old gentleman, according to a Populist account, "foamed and stewed over the 'wah,' . . . and . . . tore his shirt over the old twaddle of 'negro domination.' " [19] Indeed, Bourbon memories of the past became increasingly vivid whenever the status quo was questioned.

Bailey and Benoit also challenged their Democratic opponents to submit to a "white primary." The two Populists

17 West Monroe *Alliance Forum*, quoted in Natchitoches *Louisiana Populist*, September 21, 1894; Chambers, *A History of Louisiana*, II, 204. Former Congressman Newton C. Blanchard of the Fourth District went to the United States Senate in 1893.

18 Natchitoches *Louisiana Populist*, September 7, 1894; Colfax *Chronicle*, September 8, 15, October 27, 1894.

19 Natchitoches *Louisiana Populist*, October 19, 1894.

agreed to withdraw from the race if they were beaten by a vote
of the white adult males of their respective districts; the Democrats, naturally, were supposed to make the same pledge.
This Populist proposal was logically inconsistent with their
stated adherence to the principle of universal manhood suffrage, and none realized it better than the Populists themselves. As Hardy Brian wrote, they were in this instance "compelled by the intolerant course of the party in power to adopt
the same narrow policy." [20] The Populists were confident
that they had a majority of whites in the North Louisiana districts on their side, and they were equally certain that the
Democratic planters along the rivers were preparing, as in
the past, to fraudulently count the votes of their helpless
thousands of Negro sharecroppers.

Nevertheless, the third party still stood firm against any
constitutional suffrage restriction. And, equally important,
nearly all Louisiana Populists always defended the right of
the black man to vote as long as his ballot would be freely
cast and honestly counted. In the Pelican State, many Populists put free elections above the cause of free silver.[21] No
other native white political movement had ever sought genuine political equality for the Negro. "The People's party,"
one of its Alabama leaders said in later years, "brought to
the South . . . the only democracy the South has ever
known." [22]

As anticipated, the Democrats turned down Bailey's and
Benoit's suggestion for a white primary in the congressional
races of 1894. When the votes were tallied in the general
election, Bailey was credited with 5,932 ballots against 12,257

20 *Ibid.*, June 21, 1895.
21 J. A. Tetts to Marion Butler, October 3, 1896, in Marion Butler Papers,
Southern Historical Collection, University of North Carolina Library.
22 Joseph Columbus Manning, *The Fadeout of Populism: Pot and Kettle in
Combat* (New York, 1928) , 5.

for Ogden. The *Comrade* editor carried six of the twelve parishes in the district, and despite the wide margin, a study of the returns—and Democratic admissions, for that matter—supports the Populist contention that the election was stolen for Congressman Ogden. In five of the six parishes carried by Ogden, no opposition party commissioners were allowed at the polls. In Caddo, where Bailey was beaten 2,097 to 66, a Northern visitor asked a Democratic official to estimate the number of votes which would be cast at a certain precinct. "Just as many . . . as we need," was the laconic reply.[23] In Rapides Parish, nearly a third of Ogden's 3,097 votes came from a single Negro precinct, while in De Soto Parish the blacks reportedly were told that midnight visits would be paid to their cabins if they tried to vote for Bailey. A Shreveport newspaper which had supported Ogden termed his total "outrageous," and conceded that Bailey "was honestly and fairly elected." [24] But another Democratic organ of that city treated the lopsided returns with levity: "B. W. Bailey; where is he, up a pine tree?" chortled the *Daily Caucasian*.[25]

Benoit, in the Fifth District, received 4,549 votes in the official returns, against 14,755 for Congressman Boatner. As did Bailey, Benoit insisted that an honest count would have shown the incumbent Democrat the loser. Relatively speaking, Benoit had the weaker of the two Populist claims to victory. But he enjoyed one advantage which Bailey lacked; he possessed the necessary funds to contest the election. When Boatner returned to Washington in 1895, Benoit was at his heels to lay the case before the House of Representatives. The Monroe Populist charged gross frauds in 10 of the 15 par-

[23] *Report of the Secretary of State*, 1902, p. 577; Indianapolis *Daily Journal*, quoted in Shreveport *Progress*, November 24, 1894.

[24] Shreveport *Progress*, November 10, 17, 1894.

[25] Shreveport *Daily Caucasian*, quoted in Natchitoches *Louisiana Populist*, November 16, 1894.

ishes; in four of these, he obtained a mere 81 votes against Boatner's 7,124. In one parish Boatner's total exceeded the whole registration (which was padded to begin with) by about 1,000. The congressional committee that examined the returns agreed with the Populist's charges, but instead of seating Benoit, the committee determined that "no valid election had taken place," and the seat was declared vacant.[26]

Boatner had to return and face a new election. Benoit was again the opponent. Typical of conservative reaction in the Fifth District was that of the Rayville *Beacon,* which thought that Boatner was entitled to the remainder of the term because "to oppose him would be tacitly admitting that the election was a fraud, which we cannot afford to do." Predictably, the official returns of the special election of June 10, 1896, sent Democrat Boatner back to Congress. Benoit contested again, but this time the investigating committee did no more than cut Boatner's legal majority down from above 6,000 to 802.[27]

Elsewhere in the state in 1894, the People's Party obtained a majority in two southeastern parishes, but fell far short of electing a congressman. Its candidate in the Sixth District, M. R. Wilson, carried backland Livingston and Washington parishes over Congressman Samuel M. Robertson. But the Sixth District, as a whole, voted Democratic by 7,981 to 2,230. Populist Wilson almost carried big St. Landry Parish, and his supporters insisted they would have won it except for the fact that their three strongest precincts had been closed on election day through Democratic machinations.[28] In the southwestern Third District, Populist John Lightner offered

---

26 *House Documents*, 56th Cong., 2nd Sess., No. 510, pp. 519–20. See also, Robert Ray to William E. Chandler, February 12, 1896, in Chandler Papers.

27 Rayville *Richland Beacon*, May 9, 1896; *House Documents*, 56th Cong., 2nd Sess., No. 510, p. 526.

28 *Report of the Secretary of State*, 1902, p. 578; Natchitoches *Louisiana Populist*, July 12, 1895.

only feeble opposition to the Democratic incumbent, whose most serious antagonist was the Republican nominee, Judge Taylor Beattie. "John Lightning," as amused Democrats called him, polled most of his 641 votes from Calcasieu and Vermilion parishes. Independent "workingmen's" candidates, Populist supported, ran in the New Orleans congressional districts in 1894; but they were denied representation at the polls and only a handful of votes were officially reported for them.

Louisiana Populism emerged from the 1894 congressional campaigns frustrated but not yet discouraged. Third-party leaders were positive that they had elected two congressmen in North Louisiana, and the reeking frauds perpetrated by the oligarchy in the cotton parishes were at last beginning to repulse many middle-class Democrats; a number of the latter were said to be expressing an interest in Populism.[29] But the picture was quite dark in South Louisiana. Seemingly, outside of St. Landry and Vermilion parishes, almost no impression had been made upon the mass of French Catholic voters; Lafayette and St. Martin parishes, for example, reported not one Populist ballot in 1894.

The fact that the Brians, Bailey, and most third-party activists were Baptist in religion apparently did much harm to the Populist cause among rural Cajuns. Some Democratic journals in the southern parishes used the religious difference as a means of undermining Populism. Catholics around Baton Rouge were told that the Reverend Brian and his son were members of a secret and militant anti-Catholic organization; this information, the *Weekly Truth* archly suggested, ought to be of interest to those members of the Mother Church who might be sympathetic to Populism. In reply, Hardy Brian vehemently denied that he or his father, or the third party,

[29] Natchitoches *Louisiana Populist,* October 19, 1894, August 23, 1895.

were "in any sense opposed to Catholicism." [30] In Natchitoches Parish, which unlike most of North Louisiana had a large Catholic minority, John Scopini, an active Populist and a Catholic, decided to publicly warn his fellow parishoners about the falsehoods which "low down, thieving Democrats" were telling about the Protestant Populist leadership.[31]

Although they had thus far failed to create a viable statewide organization, Louisiana's Populists had some basis for believing, by 1895, that they were on the threshold of success. For one thing, the third-party revolt was now formidable in several other Southern states. North Carolina's Populist-Republican fusionists took over all branches of that state's government in 1894–96 and their legislature sent Marion Butler to the United States Senate; and fusion tickets in Alabama and Georgia had obtained more than 40 percent of the vote. Nationally, the third party had rolled up almost 1,500,000 votes in the November races of 1894, which was 42 percent above Weaver's total two years before. The achievements of the party elsewhere, it was supposed, would redound beneficially in Louisiana.[32]

Worsening economic conditions also encouraged agrarian radicalism in all parts of the South. The great depression of the 1890's dropped the value of cotton and sugar ever lower. Middling cotton prices, which had hovered around ten cents per pound at the beginning of the decade, plunged to six cents by late 1893. November of 1894 brought the lowest price recorded by the New Orleans cotton exchange in half a cen-

30 Baton Rouge *Weekly Truth,* August 4, 1894; letter from Hardy L. Brian, in New Orleans *Times-Democrat,* quoted in Baton Rouge *Daily Advocate,* August 3, 1894.

31 Letter from John Scopini, "a Catholic," in Natchitoches *Louisiana Populist,* October 11, 1895.

32 Hicks, *The Populist Revolt,* 333–39; Haynes, *Third Party Movements,* 281; Natchitoches *Louisiana Populist,* January 18, 1895.

tury—four and seven-eighths cents.[33] Consequently, the share-croppers and small farmers of northern and central Louisiana began to experience privation as bad or worse than that suffered during the depression of the 1870's. "None can tell if we have reached rock bottom," one agriculturist wrote early in 1895. "I fear if there is nothing done to alleviate the suffering among the people, that we will have a revolution. . . . The people are restless." [34] A Democratic newspaper admitted, by the following year, that Democrats in the poorer parishes were "as scarce as dollars." [35]

The sugar planters of South Louisiana were also feeling the sting of depression. Domestic prices for raw sugar fell from almost six cents per pound in 1889 to an average of three cents by 1894. From 1890 until 1894, however, the decline in sugar value was cushioned by a two cents per pound bounty provided by the Republican-sponsored McKinley tariff. Louisiana planters received, in four years, a total of thirty million dollars from the federal government.[36] But President Cleveland's return to office in 1893 spelled trouble for the bounty. The Democratic Congress passed, and Cleveland signed, the Wilson-Gorman Act of 1894, which repealed the two cent bounty; it substituted instead an ad valorem duty on foreign sugar which, because of the current low prices, was deemed insufficient protection by the planters. The marvelous windfall of the bounty was ended. Four of Louisiana's Democratic representatives in Congress, hoping to appease the sugar interests, had voted against the Wilson-Gorman

33 Boyle, *Cotton and the New Orleans Cotton Exchange*, 183; New Orleans *Times-Democrat*, quoted in Colfax *Chronicle*, November 17, 1894.

34 Letter from "Old Guard," in Natchitoches *Louisiana Populist*, January 11, 1895.

35 Alexandria *Town Talk*, quoted in Natchitoches *Louisiana Populist*, January 3, 1896.

36 Sitterson, *Sugar Country*, 303, 328; *Proceedings of the Sixth Annual Session of the Louisiana State Agricultural Society*, 6–7.

Bill, but both senators had, with some reluctance, supported it.[37] And the planters were furious at the Democratic Party. A sizable number of the Louisiana sugar planters had always voted Republican in national elections. But reaction to the Wilson-Gorman tariff caused a majority of the state's larger producers to announce their intention "of voting the Republican ticket in all national matters in the future." On September 17, 1894, at Washington Artillery Hall in New Orleans, the planters organized the National Republican Party. State Democratic leaders were appalled. "This," said Hearsey's *Daily States*, "is the maddest movement that was ever made in politics." [38]

A serious division within the ranks of the state's politico-economic elite had now taken place. The newly organized National Republicans (soon to be called the "Lily Whites") were willing to cooperate with the Kellogg and Warmoth factions of the "Regular" Republicans, at least to the extent of electing Republican protectionists to Congress from the First and Second districts and especially the Third District. There was little indication that the planters intended, at first, to meddle with the Democratic status quo on local and state matters. But this step was not long in coming. The National Republicans' three congressional candidates were all beaten in the 1894 election, and fraud was largely, if not wholly, responsible for their defeats. In some sugar country localities, Democratic commissioners had suddenly moved the polling places from towns to inaccessible swamps.[39]

Rebellion against the Democratic Party did not often go

---

37 *American Economist,* XIV (August 3, 1894), 53, (September 14, 1894), 126.
38 *The Louisiana Planters: A Formidable Revolt Against the Free Trade Democracy* (Boston, 1894), 9–17; New Orleans *Times-Democrat,* October 18, 1894; New Orleans *Daily States,* quoted in *Chautauquan,* XX (November, 1894), 229.
39 Uzee, "Republican Politics in Louisiana," 149–50; *American Economist,* XIV (November 2, 1894), 213.

unpunished in Louisiana. The planters may have thought that their status gave them immunity, but they were wrong. Governor Foster, though himself a sugar planter, was plainly angered by the conduct of his wealthy neighbors who had drifted away from Democratic orthodoxy. Suddenly, the hitherto lenient tax assessments on certain sugar lands were revised upward. John N. Pharr, of Foster's home parish of St. Mary, complained in 1896 that his taxes had shot up about 20 percent within the last two years. Many other growers were similarly penalized for their heresy.[40]

Their grievances against the ruling Democrats drew the Populists and sugar planters together as the state election of 1896 approached. Both relished the prospect of unseating Governor Foster. Both deplored the proposed suffrage amendment: the Populists, mostly because it would wreak havoc among the illiterate poor whites; the National Republicans, because their black laborers were always willing to vote any ticket not labeled Democratic. And, not least important, each was strongest where the other was weakest. For the "little one to five bale farmers" who were said to make up the body of North Louisiana Populism would not ordinarily support wealthy Republicans from the lower parishes, while the Populists, for their part, had failed to make an impression upon sugar land voters in the previous elections. Moreover, the National Republicans had money to finance campaigns, which made the prospect of union more tempting to the upcountry agrarians. As one cynical but truthful Bourbon remarked, "the Populist wampum was distressingly short."[41]

Three-way negotiations, involving the Warmoth wing of the Regular Republicans, the "Lily White" National Re-

40 Plaquemine *Iberville South,* March 14, 1896; Baton Rouge *Daily Advocate,* March 12, 1896. See also, Romero, *Louisiana Historical Quarterly,* XXVIII, 1169–70.

41 Shreveport *Evening Judge,* February 12, 1896.

publicans, and the Populists, commenced in the late summer of 1895. Both Regular and National Republican emissaries were dispatched to the People's Party state meeting at Alexandria in August of 1895. The Populists made no public commitment on fusion at that time; they simply issued a manifesto urging "the good people of Louisiana to proceed at once in forming such a compact organization as will prevent . . . outrages of their rights of suffrage." [42] A Democratic organ in Shreveport, horrified at the Populist manifesto, remarked that "they even go so far as to say that they are in favor of voting the negro honestly. . . . Think of this, Louisianians! Are you willing to go this far with them?" [43]

In November of 1895, the People's Party executive committeemen again met with National and Regular Republicans, and this time a public statement was made regarding their plans for cooperation in the state election the following spring. Both Republican groups agreed that if the Populist Party's nominating convention, scheduled for January 8, 1896, would select a state ticket which would be "representative" and one that was made up of men who opposed the suffrage amendment, then the Republicans would support it. The Populists sealed the bargain by affirming their hostility to said amendment and by promising a ticket "liberal and broad gauged." The agrarian leaders added that demands for silver coinage and honest elections were to be major planks in their platform. Louisiana, as a prominent New Orleans Republican predicted, would see "pretty lively times" when the April election came near.[44]

42 Henry Clay Warmoth to William E. Chandler, February 4, 1896, in Chandler Papers. Daniel, "The Louisiana People's Party," 67–68; Natchitoches *Louisiana Populist*, August 16, 1895.

43 Shreveport *Evening Judge*, August 9, 1895.

44 Natchitoches *Louisiana Populist*, December 6, 1895, January 17, 1896; H. Dudley Coleman to William E. Chandler, November 2, 1895, Chandler Papers.

Andrew Augustus Gunby, Monroe attorney and newspaper publisher, was considered as the most likely Populist nominee for governor. Gunby had been known as a "fretful porcupine" in the Democratic Party for many years. He endorsed the third party's program as early as 1892, and his increasing affinity for Populism eventually prompted the "one hundred planters" who controlled the Democratic organization—and the election returns—in Ouachita Parish to formally denounce him as "unworthy of the notice of decent people." [45]

It developed that neither did the Republican sugar planters care for Gunby's liberal notions. On January 2, 1896, six days before the Populist nominating convention, the "Lily White" Nationals violated the spirit of their pledge to the agrarians by assembling at the Hotel Royal in New Orleans and nominating E. N. Pugh, a conservative Ascension Parish planter, for governor. The planters' intentions were clear. They hoped to stage a coup by presenting the Populist convention with a ready-made candidate. But, as the *Daily Advocate* noticed, the People's Party men had no taste for this proffered "sugar teat." [46]

The Populist nominating convention, meeting at Alexandria, opened and closed on notes of mingled outrage and confusion. Virtually none of the delegates present were willing to accept Pugh. But preparations to nominate Gunby stopped when the Monroe publisher, though pledging himself to support the third party's ticket, asked that his name not be presented before the convention. This Populist gathering, according to a cruel but perhaps accurate Bourbon commentator, included among the delegates "many old hacks with lightning rods praying to get struck"; but none of the hopefuls, such as Thomas J. Guice, had either the money to help

[45] Shreveport *Evening Judge*, September 22, 1895; Natchitoches *Louisiana Populist*, January 17, 1896; Lake Providence *Banner Democrat*, April 25, 1896.
[46] Baton Rouge *Daily Advocate*, January 7, 1896.

finance a state campaign or a broad reputation upon which to draw contributions and votes.[47]

Out of desperation, party leaders put the name of state chairman Andrew Booth before the convention. Booth himself instigated the move. The "hayseed from New Orleans," as Booth was sometimes described, received the gubernatorial nomination without opposition. Candidates for other state offices were also selected, and no sugar planter was included. Later that day, to the "utter mortification and surprise" of Hardy Brian and the other convention managers, the nominee privately asked their help in "preparing the convention" to accept his resignation as head of the ticket so that Pugh, the Republican, might take his place.[48]

Booth's apparent treachery made the third-party leaders furious. They at once told the story to the convention, whereupon Booth was informed that his unconditional resignation as the nominee and as state chairman would be promptly accepted. However, he refused to comply. Booth insisted that until such time as Pugh were nominated, he was the legally designated Populist candidate for governor. Faced with this wretched situation, the convention adopted a resolution empowering the fifty-three members of the central executive committee of the Louisiana People's Party to fill any vacancy which might occur on the state ticket through resignations "or otherwise [*sic*]." [49]

The Populist executive committee met on January 23 and replaced Booth and almost every other member of the improvised Alexandria ticket. Shortly before, a compromise with the National Republicans had been reached. Though none revealed the details, it was obvious that the mutually awkward

---

47 *Ibid.*, January 10, 1896.

48 Natchitoches *Louisiana Populist,* January 17, 1896. See also, Shreveport *Evening Judge,* February 12, 1896.

49 Natchitoches *Louisiana Populist,* January 17, 1896.

situation had been resolved by an arrangement in which the People's Party would select all the nominees, but the positions of governor, auditor, and attorney-general must be filled from the ranks of the sugar planters. In return, the planters whom the Populists selected for these three posts must espouse all planks in the agrarians' platform and, with the help of other wealthy National Republicans, were to furnish the bulk of the campaign funds for the crusade to unseat Foster. The gubernatorial candidate chosen by the Populist committee was John N. Pharr of St. Mary Parish.[50]

Pharr, whose political history included plunges into the Whig, Democratic, Prohibition and Republican parties, was one of the largest sugar planters of St. Mary and one of Louisiana's wealthiest men. Sixty-seven years of age in 1896, his real estate and manufacturing equipment was valued at over $700,000; his bank accounts probably ran Pharr's total worth to considerably above $1,000,000.[51] But his advocacy of silver coinage and other Populist demands, temporary though it might be, met enthusiastic reception in the poverty-stricken uplands. In fact, some Republicans thought of him as more of a Populist than anything else.[52] And a sudden blossoming of Populist newspapers indicated that Pharr's ample purse had come to the assistance of the state's struggling third-party journalists.

One of the potential strengths of the Louisiana People's

[50] Besides Pharr, the sugar planters on the fusion ticket were: H. P. Kernochan, for auditor; and L. F. Southon, for attorney-general. The other four nominations went to Populists: J. B. Kleinpeter, for lieutenant governor; J. W. McFarland, for secretary of state; John Pickett, for treasurer (he was the incumbent) ; G. A. Cooke, for superintendent of education. New Orleans *Times-Democrat,* January 22–25, 1896.

[51] Recapitulation and Valuation of the Properties of John N. Pharr, April 5, 1898, in John N. Pharr Papers, Department of Archives, Louisiana State University. Unfortunately, the collection of Pharr papers is skimpy and contains little of a political nature.

[52] Letter from J. R. G. Pitkin, to an addressee whose name is illegible, March 20, 1896, in Chandler Papers.

Party lay in its colorful and numerous press. Beginning with the Winnfield *Comrade* in 1890, approximately fifty Populist weekly newspapers were published in over twenty-five parishes at one time or another by 1900. As might be expected, many of them were ephemeral sheets, coming to life during a particular campaign and then dying for want of advertisers and paying subscribers. Grant Parish led the list with seven Populist newspapers during the decade, followed by St. Landry and Calcasieu with four, and Catahoula and Natchitoches parishes with three apiece. Two People's Party journals appeared in each of the following parishes: Lincoln, Livingston, Ouachita, Rapides, Sabine, Webster, and Winn. Fourteen other parishes contained one each. Most of these were published in remote villages, some of which have probably never since had any kind of newspaper; but of the state's larger communities, all except ultraconservative Shreveport included at least one People's Party journal.[53]

Bourbons tended to discount the influence of the People's Party editors. These "little fly up the creeks," opined one Democratic paper, spoke for nobody "except themselves and their tape worms. And it is doubtful even if they correctly represent the sentiments of the latter."[54] But in fact the copies of, and quotations from, the Populist newspapers which have survived give every appearance of having mirrored the opinion of the party's rank and file. In almost every case, the men listed as editors also ran for political office or served on state party committees.

Hardy Brian, state legislator and editor of the Winnfield *Comrade* (1890–94) and the Natchitoches *Louisiana Populist* (1894–99), stood at the forefront of the Pelican State's

---

53 A list of all Louisiana Populist newspapers to which some reference was discovered is contained in the appendix.

54 Baton Rouge *Daily Advocate*, quoted in Shreveport *Evening Judge*, October 4, 1895.

third-party journalists. The latter paper—its title was shortened to *Populist* in 1898—attempted for a time to act as the official state organ of the People's Party. However, as early as 1895 Brian was forced to admit that he had failed to attract much of a statewide readership. Even so, his list of subscribers, though not large, probably exceeded that of any other Populist newspaper in Louisiana. Brian was a talented, if sometimes scurrilous, newspaperman. He had the ability to retort in kind to Bourbon abuse. At one election, he compared Democratic voters to "a sow returning to her wallow, a dog to his vomit." He wrote of President Cleveland as "bovine necked, big bellied Grover, our most excellent majesty and tub of fat who reigneth in Washington." And although at heart a nonviolent man, Brian once or twice urged his fellow partymen to go to the polls armed, and if the Democrats were caught in the act of stealing votes: "Kill them on the spot!" [55]

John Tetts's Robeline *Battle Flag* was another frequently quoted Populist organ. Democrats sometimes referred to it as the "Bloody Flag." In the same shop was published the *New Era*, a children's weekly made up by Tetts's three daughters: Eunice, Lillian and Ollie. The *New Era* was supposed to entertain, give moral instruction, and incidentally sow Populistic doctrines among young people. As had always been his lot, Tetts continued to meet frustration and failure. He became secretary of the state People's Party in 1896; then he ran for the legislature in Natchitoches Parish but lost by four votes when the Democrats refused to count the returns from his home precinct.[56] Pressed by creditors he was unable to pay, Tetts had to close his newspaper office later that year.[57]

[55] Natchitoches *Louisiana Populist*, September 28, 1894, March 29, August 23, December 20, 1895, September 4, 1896.

[56] Shreveport *Evening Judge*, October 22, 1895; Shreveport *Sunday Judge*, April 26, 1896; Natchitoches *Louisiana Populist*, May 1, 1896.

[57] J. A. Tetts to Chaplin, Breazeale, and Chaplin, April 8, 1896, in Chaplin, Breazeale, and Chaplin Papers, Department of Archives, Louisiana State University. See also, Natchitoches *Louisiana Populist*, September 4, 1896.

For a time, in 1896–97, he wandered about the state trying to arouse interest in reviving the nearly defunct Farmers' Union; his efforts were in vain, and the Union which he had founded held its last state meeting in August of 1897. Now past fifty, Tetts attempted to make a new beginning as a Populist editor. He moved to Sabine Parish in 1898 and began issuing the Many *Sabine Free State,* which shortly folded. As the twentieth century began and Populism died, Tetts joined the Republican Party. In 1902 he was selling books in the town of Many.[58]

The most radical of third-party voices in Louisiana was that of the New Orleans *Issue.* Unlike the rural agrarian press, the *Issue* disdained any farmer who hired tenants or laborers, and urged both urban and country Populists to investigate the doctrines of socialism and "aye, even communism." Vulgarity, too, was no stranger to the New Orleans weekly. Commenting upon the Populist notion that the Democratic and Republican parties would someday merge into one conservative organization, the *Issue* suggested that the two were "already snoozing in the same bed. . . . What we object to is the fornicabuggery [*sic*] part of it. They ought to get married and save themselves . . . the disgrace." The paper also remarked that Louisiana's working people seemed not as intelligent as bees, for bees were smart enough to kill the parasitic drones in their hives.[59] It may be taken for granted that this was one Populistic journal which obtained no financial help from Pharr or any sugar planter during the 1896 fusion campaign.

After the Populists on January 23 announced him as their gubernatorial choice, John Pharr—the "Old Swamper," as his supporters affectionately nicknamed him—then received

58 Natchitoches *Louisiana Populist,* September 25, 1896, July 30, 1897, February 4, 1898; *Report of the Secretary of State,* 1902, p. 542; Many *Sabine Banner,* August 28, 1902.

59 New Orleans *Issue,* October 4, 13, 1894, July 13, 1895.

the nomination of the National Republicans and the Regular Republicans. Former Governor Warmoth was chiefly responsible in getting the Regular's endorsement for Pharr; but some Regulars, including William P. Kellogg and Negro legislator Thomas A. Cage, refused to go along with the fusion ticket and actually worked for Governor Foster during the campaign.[60] The sugar planter National Republicans were, however, solidly behind Pharr.

The Democrats, eager to create dissension among Republican ranks, reminded Negroes that Pharr was one of the sugar planters who had ejected laborers from their plantation cabins during the great strike of 1887. This was true. On the other hand, the charge that Pharr was the champion Negro-flogger of South Louisiana, that "scores of old gray-headed negroes . . . can testify to the terrors of the bullwhip wielded by his lusty arms," that "several have went [*sic*] to their happy hunting ground through Pharr's manipulations"—these may be dismissed as lurid specimens of the Bourbon imagination.[61]

Fusion candidate Pharr was scarcely a believer in genuine equality for the black man, but neither was he a racist of the Bourbon variety. His position, if nothing else, led him to give absolute endorsement of the Negroes' right to vote and to secure justice in the courts. This was enough to prompt some Democrats into calling "John N (igger) Pharr" and his allies the "Populist-negro social equality ticket." [62] Another Demo-

---

[60] Warmoth to Chandler, February 4, 1896, in Chandler Papers; Uzee, "Republican Politics in Louisiana," 154–55.

[61] Colfax *Chronicle*, March 14, 1896; Lake Providence *Banner Democrat*, April 18, 1896.

[62] Baton Rouge *Daily Advocate*, March 1, 1896; Natchitoches *Louisiana Populist*, February 14, April 10, 1896; Shreveport *Evening Judge*, February 16, 1896. In one of his campaign speeches, Pharr stated: "I was reared with the negro and worked side by side with him for twenty odd years. I never found him other than a good laborer and as honest as most other men. If he has cut a bad figure in politics, we are to blame for it," Quoted in Perry H. Howard, *Political Tendencies in Louisiana* (Baton Rouge, 1957), 98–99.

cratic analysis of the fusion party described its component parts as: "The wild-eyed bilious pop, the odoriferous coon and the pampered and succulent sugar teat." [63]

Bourbon Democrats did not register much surprise at the coalition of poor whites and Negroes. After all, they held both in about equally low esteem. What did stun them was the action of the wealthy sugar men. "Truly the picture is awful!" exclaimed the *Iberville South*. "To think that any number of the Southern planters . . . should now go over . . . to the coons and to a small body of communists in the northern corner of the State, is more than astounding!" To the White Castle *White Castilian*, this was the worst "mongrel ticket" in Louisiana's history.[64] Major Hearsey was nearly at a loss for words as he ruminated over the "utterly improbable" political combination of "hayseed and canejuice . . . and malodorous nigger wool." He tried to point out to the sugar planters that they had no more in common with "white trash" Populists than they had with their black laborers.[65]

For once, the Democratic oligarchy of Louisiana confronted the distinct possibility of defeat. Unhappiness over Governor Foster's platform, which evaded the silver vs. gold controversy and endorsed the suffrage amendment as a means to "insure the control of affairs to the intelligence and virtue of the State," was not confined to Populist and Republican ranks.[66] As one suspicious Democrat wrote, Foster's next legislature might take a sweeping and arbitrary view of who ought to be disfranchised as "poor white trash." [67] The *St.*

---

[63] Baton Rouge *Daily Advocate*, February 2, 1896.

[64] Plaquemine *Iberville South*, February 1, 1896; White Castle *White Castilian*, quoted in *ibid.* See also, Opelousas *St. Landry Clarion*, January 11, 1896.

[65] New Orleans *Daily States*, quoted in Plaquemine *Iberville South*, February 1, 22, 1896.

[66] Shreveport *Evening Judge*, December 20, 1895.

[67] Many *Sabine Banner*, quoted in *ibid.*, December 30, 1895. Soon afterward, the *Sabine Banner* renounced the Democratic Party and turned Populist.

Tammany Farmer, a supporter of the amendment and a believer that "wealth and intelligence" had a natural right to
rule, gloomily admitted that it was impossible to "convince
the poor and humble that they should aid in their own political degradation." [68] The seriousness of the crisis prompted one change in tactics by Foster. Shortly before the April
election, Democratic leaders began soft-pedaling the suffrage
amendment and ultimately dropped it from the platform entirely.[69] Its defeat was thus made certain.

The Fosterites had additional reason to worry because of
the situation in New Orleans. A recently organized "Citizens'
League," headed by prominent business, professional, and social leaders of the city, was placing an independent ticket in
the municipal and legislative election which was to be held
the same day (April 21) as the gubernatorial contest. Most
of these civic reformers had four years earlier been active in
the Anti-Lottery League. Among them were Walter Denis
Denegre, Charles Janvier and John M. Parker. Special encouragement to the Citizens' League came from Secretary of
State Thomas S. Adams, who had recently broken with Foster and who, for a time, was even talked of as a possible Populist nominee for governor in 1896. The reform organization
was powerful enough to forestall the customary ballot box
stuffing in at least half the city's precincts. As to the Foster
vs. Pharr state election, the Citizens' League was officially
neutral; but indications were that most of its members
planned to vote for Pharr. Mayor John Fitzpatrick, whose
corrupt machine was the prime target of the reformers, was
a political ally of Governor Foster.[70]

[68] Covington *St. Tammany Farmer,* March 28, 1896.
[69] *Ibid.;* Shreveport *Progress,* April 25, 1896,
[70] Henry C. Dethloff, "Populism and Reform in Louisiana" (Ph.D. dissertation, University of Missouri, 1964), 254, 256–61; New Orleans *Times-
Democrat,* March 31, 1896; George M. Reynolds, *Machine Politics in New
Orleans, 1897–1926* (New York, 1936), 27.

No one had more at stake in the outcome of the 1896 state campaign than did the black population. Even in the most "bulldozed" cotton parishes, Democratic landlords seemed to be having an unusual amount of difficulty in discouraging Negro participation in the approaching election. "The poor, ignorant, deluded negro has gone into spasms over the name of Pharr," groused a Bourbon leader of Morehouse Parish.[71] In East Carroll, where more than 90 percent of the inhabitants were black, the *Banner Democrat* listed the names of local Negroes who were "brewing up trouble" by talking for the fusion ticket and advised them to "leave politics severely alone . . . if they want to live in this parish." Then, in the paper's next issue, it observed that "you might as well talk to a brick wall as to try and make the nigger believe who his best friend is." [72] Black people, however, well understood which of the two gubernatorial candidates had sponsored the "sufferings amendment," as some of them called it. While downstate, in the New Orleans area, a recently established Negro newspaper, the *Daily Crusader,* promoted the Pharr cause with noticeable effect.[73]

Whatever else might be said about the Democrats, they at least were not hypocritical about their plans for election day. The oligarchy was in trouble. A grass-roots rebellion had cost Foster the support of thousands of white farmers who had voted for him in 1892; New Orleans could no longer be considered as safely Democratic; the economic depression, combined with the Governor's known predilection for the gold standard, increased his unpopularity; nevertheless, the incumbent administration still absolutely controlled the

71 Bastrop *Clarion-Appeal,* quoted in Lake Providence *Banner Democrat,* March 7, 1896.

72 Lake Providence *Banner Democrat,* March 28, April 4, 1896.

73 Farmerville *Gazette,* April 22, 1896; New Orleans *Daily Crusader,* quoted in Natchitoches *Louisiana Populist,* March 6, 1896.

election machinery in about a dozen plantation parishes, and intended to make the most of it. The following statement from a leading North Louisiana Democratic daily was not intended for humor. It was simply frank: "It is the religious duty of Democrats to rob Populists and Republicans of their votes whenever and wherever the opportunity presents itself and any failure to do so will be a violation of true Louisiana Democratic teaching. The Populists and Republicans are our legitimate political prey. Rob them! You bet! What are we here for?" [74]

Hearsey of the *Daily States,* whose maledictions against the "carpetbag, scalawag and nigger buzzards" helped keep up the fighting spirit among his planter-subscribers, prophesied that even if Pharr did obtain an official majority of the vote, the "better element" of Louisiana would be willing to start a "bloody revolution" to keep him out of office.[75] The *Daily Advocate* also approved the possibility of a right-wing revolt; but if war should come, the official journal of the state government added, John Pharr would be wholly responsible. Because "this ignorant and low bred boor proceeds from place to place scattering his fire-brands among the rabble and inciting the baser passions of the populace." The *Times-Democrat,* scolding Pharr because he went about the state "preaching the good qualities of negroes," feared that his speaking tour alone "will mean something very like a revolution before he gets through." [76]

Speakers for the fusion ticket were, however, permitted to talk at New Orleans, Baton Rouge, and most of the other larger communities of the state. There were some untoward incidents. When Pharr appeared at the Opera House in the

[74] Shreveport *Evening Judge,* December 15, 1895.
[75] New Orleans *Daily States,* quoted in Lake Providence *Banner Democrat,* February 1, 1896, and in Bayou Sara *True Democrat,* April 18, 1896.
[76] Baton Rouge *Daily Advocate,* March 4, 1896; New Orleans *Times-Democrat,* quoted in Opelousas *Courier,* March 7, 1896.

town of Plaquemine, a vile smell made it almost impossible
for his audience to remain. The *Iberville South*'s reporter attributed this to the body odor of the many Negroes present,
but the actual cause was a hydrogen sulfide stink bomb,
tossed in by Democratic rowdies.[77] The town of Shreveport
presented a special problem. It was such a bastion of reaction
that Pharr wisely cancelled a speaking engagement there, perhaps because of a report that the board of health planned to
throw him and his "political menagerie" into the municipal
pest house.[78]

Although the men on Pharr's state ticket escaped bodily
harm, individual acts of reprisal were carried out against local fusionists. One Populist candidate in East Baton Rouge
Parish was shot, and another had his barn burned; there
also, two Negroes were killed as a result of political troubles.
The printing shop of a Populist newspaper in Minden was
wrecked.[79] In the town of Washington, the editor of the
People's Party Tribune, while being informed that he was
"a crippled cur" and his paper a "Populist snot rag," was also
told that only the fact that he sat in a wheelchair saved him
from physical punishment.[80] Most troubled of all parishes
was St. Landry, where fusionist efforts to register more Negroes resulted in several shootings; Governor Foster dispatched state troops, equipped with rifles and one Gatling
gun, to the scene. But in this instance the soldiers took no
aggressive action. One of the officers in the militia sent to
St. Landry indignantly told a reporter that local Democrats
had "unmercifully whipped" Negro women with barbed wire
in order to discourage Populist-Republican activities.[81]

77 Plaquemine *Iberville South,* April 18, 25, 1896.

78 Shreveport *Sunday Judge,* March 15, 1896.

79 Natchitoches *Louisiana Populist,* February 28, 1896; Baton Rouge *Daily
Advocate,* April 12, 1896; Farmerville *Gazette,* April 29, 1896.

80 Opelousas *St. Landry Clarion,* February 15, 1896.

81 New Orleans *Daily Picayune,* April 15, 1896; New Orleans *Daily States,*
April 21, 1896.

The bitter passions unleashed by the campaign helped give the state another unenviable niche in the record books of violence. In 1896 Louisiana recorded twenty-one lynchings. This was not her all-time peak figure, but for that year it exceeded the combined total for every other state and territory west of the Mississippi River, and it accounted for one-fifth of all such murders in the United States.[82] The fact that the Pharr platform had an anti-lynching plank especially provoked the *Daily States,* which maintained that the fusionists thereby "inferentially approved" of white women being raped. According to this source, Pharr's supporters were also on dangerous religious grounds when they tried to promote racial good will, because "the infallible and irreversible law of Almighty God . . . has planted the race prejudice between the white and the black." Never before, not even in the heady days of McEnery and the Lottery, had Hearsey's paper been so blatantly racist, or so influential. More than any other man, Major Hearsey was credited with setting the tone for the Democratic campaign in the state election of 1896.[83]

Hardy Brian remarked shortly before the April 21 election that it would take "a gigantic piece of stealing" to count Pharr out, and the Democrats proved equal to the challenge.[84] The official returns showed Governor Foster as the victor over Pharr, 116,116 to 87,698. Excluding the twelve alluvial parishes which Democratic commissioners firmly controlled, and where the fusionists were denied representation at the polls, Pharr ran ahead of Foster, 84,278 to 82,401.[85] Of the twelve parishes where the worst frauds occurred, six in particular aroused the ire of Populists and Republicans:

82 Work (ed.) , *Negro Year Book . . . 1918–1919,* p. 374.

83 New Orleans *Daily States,* quoted in Opelousas *Courier,* January 4, March 21, 1896. See also, Plaquemine *Iberville South,* May 23, 1896.

84 Natchitoches *Louisiana Populist,* March 20, 1896.

85 *Senate Journal,* 1896, p. 22; *Report of the Secretary of State,* 1902, p. 563.

	Foster	Pharr	White Adult Males Census of 1890 [86]
Bossier	3,464	58	1,005
Concordia	3,013	80	609
East Carroll	2,635	0	310
Madison	1,803	0	340
Tensas	1,968	0	401
West Feliciana	3,093	1	613
Totals	15,976	139	3,278

Registered white voters were in a majority in thirty-two of Louisiana's parishes. Pharr carried twenty-five of these, and he also ran first in four predominately Negro parishes of South Louisiana. Governor Foster carried only seven white parishes and won in twenty-three where Negro voters outnumbered whites. As to the suffrage amendment which Foster had initially sponsored, it was defeated in virtually every parish.

Of the three urban localities of Louisiana, Foster narrowly won New Orleans, 26,330 to 21,683, but obtained a runaway majority in Shreveport (Caddo Parish), 3,210 to 227. Pharr took the parish which included Baton Rouge, 4,859 to 1,470. Since East Baton Rouge Parish was heavily Negro, and factional fights among the Democrats allowed black men to vote freely there in 1896, the latter figures indicate what the fusion ticket would probably have accomplished had honest elections been held in other Negro parishes. Also, it is worthy of notice that in places where the fusion ticket won handily, local Democratic leaders did not accuse the opposition of fraud. The major charge hurled against the Populists and Republi-

---

[86] *Report of the Secretary of State,* 1902, p. 563; *Compendium of the Eleventh Census, 1890,* I, 782–83. The other six parishes which had only Democratic commissioners, and which turned in highly suspicious returns, were: Caddo, East Feliciana, Iberville, Jefferson, Rapides and St. Martin.

cans was that they were trying to let Negroes cast a free ballot.[87]

Not since Reconstruction had the people of Louisiana confronted a crisis as dangerous as that which developed between April 21 and the convening of the new legislature on May 14. Immediately after election day, Governor Foster ordered state troops to Natchitoches and St. John the Baptist parishes. In Natchitoches, hundreds of armed and furious white Populists were threatening to assault the parish seat of government, where Democratic election supervisors had refused to count the ballots from Negro Populist precincts; but news of the militia's approach scattered the farmers. The trouble in St. John began when Negro fusionists seized a ballot box which they believed had been stuffed by white Democrats. After two white men were killed, Governor Foster sent in a field artillery unit of the state militia. Many Negroes organized for an attack upon the troops, but the mob ultimately dispersed.[88] These events, anxious citizens across the state believed, were only the beginnings of trouble. Even the staid *Daily Picayune* envisioned "war and rapine, and . . . blood from the Arkansas line to the Gulf of Mexico," if the Populists and Republicans did not submit to the announced returns.[89]

The fusionists maintained that Pharr had beaten Foster in actual votes cast by at least twenty thousand.[90] Few Democratic spokesmen bothered to deny that fraud had taken place, and some were rather proud of their work in surmounting majority opinion. Their justification for stealing the election was most succinctly expressed by a Bastrop Democrat who

87 Baton Rouge *Daily Advocate*, February 27, March 4, April 26, 1896.

88 Natchitoches *Louisiana Populist*, May 1, 1896; Donaldsonville *Daily Times*, April 24, 1896; Uzee, "Republican Politics in Louisiana," 160.

89 New Orleans *Daily Picayune*, quoted in Shreveport *Evening Judge*, May 8, 1896. See also, Opelousas *St. Landry Clarion*, May 2, 1896.

90 Clipping from Monroe *Bulletin*, May 16, 1896, in Pharr Papers.

boasted that "a vast majority of the very best people" stood
behind the "brave young Governor." [91] As another Bourbon
explained, the opinion of property, intelligence, and virtue
must take precedence over the wishes of the "corrupt mass." [92]

Both fusionists and Democrats issued bloodthirsty mani-
festoes shortly after election day. Hardy Brian, who had succeeded Booth as party chairman, called upon "the white men
of the state" to assemble in Baton Rouge and, if legal means
failed, to use violence to see that Pharr obtained legislative
recognition as the rightful governor.[93] The Democratic proclamation was couched in the language of, and likely was
authored by, Henry J. Hearsey; it depicted the "monster, hor-
rid, formless and crowned with darkness" which was threatening to overthrow orderly Democratic government and elevate to power the "great horde of ignorant blacks who yearn
for social equality." And "woe betide" those who might attempt to prevent Foster's second inauguration; for cost what
it may, "this land shall not be a Hayti or San Domingo." [94]

Indeed it did look for a time as if a civil war within the
state was building up. Nine thousand Populists from North
Louisiana's hills were said to be preparing to march upon the
state capitol; and what the *Daily Advocate* described as "a boat
load of sugar-teats" from downstate, equipped with muni-
tions of war "sufficient to accomplish the successful bombard-
ment and siege of Baton Rouge" lay at anchor in the Mississippi. Democratic stalwarts in the capital city and the Florida
Parishes organized into paramilitary units and made plans to
defend the Foster government. As had happened during the

91 Bastrop *Clarion-Appeal,* quoted in Baton Rouge *Daily Advocate,* June
30, 1896.

92 Baton Rouge *Daily Advocate,* July 1, 1896.

93 Natchitoches *Louisiana Populist,* May 8, 1896.

94 "Address of the Democratic State Central Committee," in Shreveport
Evening Judge, May 6, 1896.

critical spring of 1877, many country people were neglecting their crops because of the political excitement.[95]

But the fusionists, as most of their leaders realized, did not have the guns or the organization to seize the State House by force of arms. Their only real hope lay in the possibility of a legislative investigation into the election returns. For over sixty members of the General Assembly had been elected in opposition to the Foster Democracy. Populists in the new legislature numbered eighteen, the Citizens' League twenty-seven, the Republicans thirteen, and there were about four independents.[96] Although this still left the Democrats with a slight legislative majority, the chance for enough defections among them to swing the balance of power to Pharr seemed, for a moment, to be good. Even a representative from East Carroll, who along with Foster had benefitted from the 2,635 to 0 vote in that parish, decided as a matter of conscience to vote with the Populists and Republicans.[97]

On May 14, a joint session of the legislature refused, by a vote of eighty-six to forty-eight, to investigate the returns. A number of Citizens' League solons, who were primarily interested in obtaining a new city charter for New Orleans,

[95] Colfax *People's Demands*, quoted in Baton Rouge *Daily Advocate*, May 5, 1896; Baton Rouge *Daily Advocate*, May 7–14, 1896; Covington *St. Tammany Farmer*, April 25, 1896.

[96] Donaldsonville *Daily Times*, April 28, 1896; Natchitoches *Louisiana Populist*, July 10, 1896; Uzee, "Republican Politics in Louisiana," 46, 48; Dethloff, "Populism and Reform in Louisiana," 282. There were two People's Party men in the Senate and sixteen in the House of Representatives. The senators were: J. P. Patton, of Winn; M. R. Wilson, of St. Landry. The representatives were: J. W. Bailey, Jr., of St. Landry, Henry Breithaupt, of Catahoula; J. M. Brown, of Natchitoches; J. E. Bullard, of Sabine; Patrick Donahay, of St. Landry; C. L. Gunby, of Union; I. D. Hogan, of Jackson; D. E. James, of Winn; Josiah Kleinpeter, of East Baton Rouge; R. P. LeBlanc, of Vermilion; S. J. Meadows, of Claiborne; T. W. Pipes, of Lincoln; A. L. Stewart, of Grant; W. L. Truman, of St. Landry; J. W. Williams, of Vernon; J. W. Young, of Acadia.

[97] St. Joseph *Tensas Gazette*, May 22, 1896; Lake Providence *Banner Democrat*, May 23, 1890.

abandoned the fusionists on the final vote. The rumored Populist army of nine thousand did not arrive, the sugar planters' "Pharr Man-of-War" in the river weighed anchor and departed, and nearly all the armed men in and around the State House were Democrats. Only a fistfight or two in the streets of Baton Rouge marred the restoration of quiet to the city.[98]

A few days later Governor Foster delivered his second inaugural address, in which he spoke again of the need for "some action" in the direction of suffrage restriction and promised that "the rich man in his palace and the poor man in his humble home shall be protected," as far as it was within the power of the state to do so. After the inaugural ceremony, a grand ball was held in the Governor's Mansion, where a "vast concourse of the elite from every parish" had gathered. The first set was danced by Governor Foster and Mrs. Samuel D. McEnery.[99]

98 Dethloff, "Populism and Reform in Louisiana," 288–91; Baton Rouge *Daily Advocate*, May 15, 1896; Franklinton *New Era*, May 21, 1896.
99 Baton Rouge *Daily Advocate*, May 19, 1896.

Bourbonism Triumphant

T H E   S T A T E   electioin of 1896 and the legislative session which followed broke the back of Louisiana Populism. The General Assembly, during the month of June, compensated for the defeat of the suffrage amendment by passing complex registration and election laws which were designed, as a source close to Governor Foster implied, to reduce the votes of the uneducated of both races.[1] Within one year the new laws were to be in effect. Significantly, the same legislative session refused to increase the state's tiny appropriations for public schools. Relative to that issue, the *Daily Advocate,* which had recently been purchased by Major Hearsey, pointed out that "the education of a bad citizen will increase his power for evil and make him a worse citizen." [2]

Also approved by the 1896 legislature was an administration bill which would place before the shrunken electorate, early in 1898, the question of holding a constitutional convention. By that time, mostly because of the registration law, at least 90 percent of the blacks were to be off the rolls, along with tens of thousands of poor whites. The convention bill, passed over the objections of all but one Populist and most Republican legislators, provided that if the voters agreed to

[1] Baton Rouge *Daily Advocate,* July 3, August 19, 1896, August 14, 1897.

[2] *Ibid.,* February 12, 1898. See also, Opelousas *St. Landry Clarion,* June 13, 1896.

the calling of a convention, then the work done by the elected delegates was to be final—the new constitution would not be submitted to the people for ratification.[3]

A consummation of the wedding between McEnery Bourbonism and the Nicholls-Foster patrician class had visibly taken place at the General Assembly's session of 1896. Fear of the large number of opposition solons—although the Citizens' Leaguers did not consistently vote with the Populists and Republicans—drove the Fosterites and McEneryites to act in total harmony. A chief beneficiary of this union was the new United States Senator whom the legislature selected. With Governor Foster's backing, "that noblest Roman of them all, . . . that peerless Democrat and sturdy champion of the plain people," Samuel D. McEnery, was elevated to the national Senate.[4] In July the legislature adjourned. The Governor, wearied by the tumult of the past few months, departed for a lengthy vacation in the Dakotas. Hardy Brian remarked, hopefully: "If the Indians will only scalp him they will be gratefully remembered by our people." [5]

The presidential election and congressional races of 1896 aroused little enthusiasm among the dwindling forces of Louisiana agrarianism. The state Democratic regime, finally realizing the inevitability of the free silver tide in the national party, sent a silverite delegation to the Chicago convention which nominated William Jennings Bryan.[6] The People's Party convention at St. Louis also endorsed Bryan, in an effort to unify all inflationists behind a single presidential candi-

3 *House Journal*, 1896, pp. 393–94; Edwin Aubera Ford, "Louisiana Politics and the Constitutional Convention of 1898" (M.A. thesis, Louisiana State University, 1955) , 69–99.

4 Baton Rouge *Daily Advocate*, May 28–29, 1896. See also, Romero, *Louisiana Historical Quarterly*, XXVIII, 1184.

5 Natchitoches *Louisiana Populist*, July 29, 1896.

6 Baton Rouge *Daily Advocate*, June 16, 1896; New Orleans *Daily Picayune*, August 5, 1896.

date. This action dismayed many Southern Populists, to whom the idea of any kind of fusion with the hated Democrats was repugnant to the extreme. But Northern and Western third-party men, whose primary enemy had been Republicanism and who in the past had locally fused with Democrats in the manner that Southern agrarians had with Republicans, engineered Bryan's nomination.[7] The Louisiana delegation at St. Louis, "for the sake of the great People's party . . . and to show our sincerity for free coinage of silver," went along with the decision of the majority and voted for Bryan.[8]

The Populists' St. Louis convention did, however, select a man of their own party, Tom Watson, as their vice-presidential nominee. In several states, including Louisiana, the People's Party approached Democratic leaders with a proposition that a joint ticket be issued in the November election, one in which Watson's name would appear with Bryan's. To the surprise of many, the Pelican State's Democrats agreed to give the Populists half the electors for second place on the national ticket.[9] North Carolina's Populist Senator Marion Butler complimented Louisiana's third-party leader Hardy Brian by writing that "there is no State in the Union where we have done as well as you have done." [10]

Yet from the third-party standpoint nothing of value had really been accomplished in Louisiana by this partial fusion with the Democrats. Allowing the agrarians half of the vice-presidential electors in 1896 was the only concession the Bourbon Democracy ever made to the Populists, and it was done with the palpable intent of enticing them back into the Demo-

---

[7] "The Populists at St. Louis," *Review of Reviews*, XIV (September, 1896), 265–66. See also, Robert F. Durden, "The 'Cow-bird' Grounded: The Populist Nomination of Bryan and Tom Watson in 1896," *Mississippi Valley Historical Review*, L (1963), 397–423.

[8] Natchitoches *Louisiana Populist*, August 7, 1896.

[9] H. L. Brian to Marion Butler, September 25, 1896, in Butler Papers.

[10] Marion Butler to H. L. Brian, September 30, 1896, *ibid.*

cratic fold. Numerous Populists loathed doing business with the Bourbons under any conditions, or for any reason. From Monroe, A. A. Gunby warned his fellow party members that "when you dance with a bear watch your partner." [11] Only the great allure of Bryan and free silver made the uneasy Populist-Democratic association possible.

Although fusion had been arranged at the national level, Populist congressional candidates ran against Democratic incumbents in four of Louisiana's districts in 1896. All four Populists were thoroughly beaten. The new registration and election laws had not yet become effective; the plantation parishes sent in their customary fictitious landslides for the Democratic candidates. B. W. Bailey, in the Fourth District, received 4,726 out of approximately 15,000 votes in the official total; Alexis Benoit, in the Fifth, obtained 4,870 votes out of about 15,000 reported. The Populist candidate in the Third District had a mere 195 ballots, and only 924 Populist votes were counted in the Sixth District.[12]

The important registration law went into operation on January 1, 1897. It required no property qualifications and, strictly speaking, had no restrictions on illiterates; on the other hand, certain "information" had to be recorded on the registrar's rolls. If the prospective voter could not give this information to the satisfaction of the registrar, then that person was not allowed to vote.[13] A Lincoln Parish Populist sadly estimated that his party's strength was being cut "at least two-thirds" by Democratic registrars.[14] The *Daily Advocate*

11 Monroe *Bulletin,* quoted in Natchitoches *Louisiana Populist,* October 9, 1896. See also, Tetts to Butler, October 3, 1896, in Butler Papers.

12 *Report of the Secretary of State,* 1902, p. 579.

13 Monroe *Bulletin,* quoted in Natchitoches *Louisiana Populist,* January 8, 1897; Natchitoches *Louisiana Populist,* January 7, 1898; Colfax *Chronicle,* quoted in Shreveport *Progress,* January 1, 1898.

14 Ruston *Progressive Age,* quoted in Baton Rouge *Daily Advocate,* December 12, 1897. See also, Opelousas *People's Tribune,* quoted in Natchitoches *Louisiana Populist,* January 7, 1898.

gleefully noted that the new registration was "death on niggers and the kind of Pops who will be inclined to vote [with
Negroes]." [15] Ignorant white Populists, the *Iberville South*
agreed, "are no better than negroes" and thus deserved the
same fate of disfranchisement.[16] Many literate small farmers,
who probably would have been allowed on the rolls, decided
not to bother with a trip to the registrar's office. As one of
them wrote, their candidates had been counted out so regularly and so overwhelmingly that they were tired of "going to
the election and losing valuable time without any valuable
result." [17]

A force of nature also contributed to the political apathy
which was settling upon the poorer whites by 1897. The
northern parishes had been hit by a catastrophic drought.[18]
Hunger on an unprecedented scale was described from many
areas, and even people who had once been in "comfortable
circumstances" were reported as traveling "on foot from house
to house soliciting . . . a cup of molasses with which to appease
the hunger of their starving children." [19] The situation was
worst in the Populist parishes of Winn, Jackson, and Lincoln,
where over twenty thousand individuals were said to be "in
a destitute condition." Reliable observers wrote that other
thousands in Vernon and Sabine parishes were "without
food" and "almost naked." [20] The *Louisiana Populist* angrily
commented that "this is not India, but Louisiana." [21] A hurriedly organized Louisiana State Relief Committee provided
some help and kept down the death toll, and under these dire

15 Baton Rouge *Daily Advocate,* December 12, 1897.

16 Plaquemine *Iberville South,* December 4, 1897.

17 Letter from "Fifth Ward," in Natchitoches *Louisiana Populist,* May 15,
1896.

18 Shreveport *Progress,* January 16, 1897; New Orleans *Daily Picayune,*
February 3, 1897.

19 Baton Rouge *Daily Advocate,* January 31, 1897.

20 *Ibid.,* February 3, 21, 1897.

21 Natchitoches *Louisiana Populist,* February 26, 1897

circumstances all but the most reactionary among the Bourbon elite approved of such aid. In Union Parish, however, the "best people" objected because the food relief "demoralized labor." [22] Fortunately, by the summer of 1897 the rains had come, and grain and vegetables as well as cotton were being raised in the uplands. But having gone through so much hardship and discouragement, fewer and fewer persons in the old heartland of Populism had any time for politics.

In August and again in November, 1897, the Populists held state conventions at Monroe and at the latter gathering issued a platform which upbraided the Democrats for attempting to limit manhood suffrage and sharply criticized the call for a constitutional convention. The new Populist platform did, however, advocate a poll tax as a prerequisite for voting. Whether they intended this as a means of restricting Negro participation in politics is not entirely clear; they declared that "every man twenty-one years old . . . who discharges all the duties of citizenship, including the payment of a poll tax, shall have the right of suffrage in Louisiana." [23] The difficulty in interpretation arises from the fact that the state was already supposed to have a compulsory poll tax on all adult males, whether they voted or not, dating from the Constitution of 1879.[24] If the Populists simply intended this tax to be enforced, it would have disfranchised no one, white or black. But if payment was to be made optional, and only upon registration to vote, it would have served to keep most poor Negroes away from the ballot box. In all probability, the People's Party leaders were being deliberately vague on this point, hoping to catch the support of those on both sides of the question of Negro voting. Hardy Brian stoutly insisted

22 Farmerville *Gazette,* quoted in Baton Rouge *Daily Advocate,* March 30, 1897.
23 "State Platform," in Natchitoches *Louisiana Populist,* December 31, 1897.
24 *Constitution of 1879,* Art. 208.

that most Populists were "in favor of manhood suffrage as against $ $ suffrage." [25]

Even though they were opposed to the holding of a constitutional convention as proposed by the legislature, the Populists believed that they must offer a slate of delegates for the election which would decide upon the convention and its personnel. Included on the Populist ticket were a number of Republicans. These latter were not the sugar planter National Republicans but rather the white leaders of the Regular or, as it was coming to be called, the "Negro wing" of the Republican Party. Indeed the Populists' former allies, the sugar planters, had by this time come to generally endorse the idea of Negro disfranchisement. Thus the new coalition of Populists and Regular Republicans stood as the only political organization which spoke at all for the interests of the black man.[26] Democrats laughed at the combination, but they were puzzled by it. What had the Populists to gain by drawing closer to the Negro, at this late date? [27] Black voters had been hurt worst of all by the new registration.

One Populist spokesman, A. A. Gunby, admitted what was obvious. With or without the Negro, they could not stop the convention or elect many of its delegates. "Still," he wrote, "we are in favor of fighting wrong to the bitter end." [28] Probably that was the key to the riddle. As Populist ranks thinned, those who remained, realizing the hopelessness of the struggle and finding the Bourbon fist more oppressive than ever, were ready to make a last, valiant protest. Hardy Brian, the state

[25] Natchitoches *Louisiana Populist,* August 27, 1897. Henry C. Dethloff's dissertation, "Populism and Reform in Louisiana," suggests that the Populists did in fact approve of Negro disfranchisement. Some undoubtedly did. But most of the evidence points in the opposite direction. Most Populist leaders seemed to believe that the Democratic oligarchy was as eager to disfranchise poor whites as it was Negroes.

[26] Plaquemine *Iberville South,* November 27, 1897.

[27] Baton Rouge *Daily Advocate,* November 23, December 2, 7, 1897.

[28] Monroe *Bulletin,* quoted in Natchitoches *Louisiana Populist,* January 8, 1897.

party chairman, went so far as to say that the "better than thou" Louisiana aristocracy would not rest content until it owned slaves again. "The whole effort to qualify suffrage," he said, was aimed toward that goal.[29]

The election for the constitutional convention, on January 11, 1898, proceeded according to Democratic plans. The official ballot was almost four feet long, 252 candidates were listed, and voters were allowed no more than three minutes in the booth.[30] Among those too confused to finish voting was an associate justice of the Louisiana Supreme Court.[31] Fewer than 50,000 ballots were reported statewide: 36,178 for the convention; 7,578 against. B. W. Bailey, editor of the *Comrade,* was the only Populist to gain election as a delegate. Bailey did little at the sessions but cast negative votes, and he refused to sign the completed document.[32]

Not without reason did the president of the convention describe it as "little more than a family meeting of the Democratic party of the State of Louisiana." [33] This presiding officer was Ernest B. Kruttschnitt. His more famous uncle, Judah P. Benjamin, had personified the Whiggish coalition of planters and urban conservatives in antebellum Louisiana.[34] Kruttschnitt continued the family tradition into the Bourbon peri-

29 Natchitoches *Louisiana Populist,* August 27, 1897.

30 *Official Journal of the Constitutional Convention of the State of Louisiana,* 1898, pp. 3–6; Baton Rouge *Daily Advocate,* January 8, 1898. The 252 names included the 92 listed as candidates for "delegates at large," and the remainder ran from individual parishes. No single ballot would list over 100 names. But to add to the confusion, many of the candidates were listed twice.

31 New Orleans *Daily Item,* quoted in Natchitoches *Louisiana Populist,* January 14, 1898. The Judge was Joseph A. Breaux of New Iberia.

32 *Official Journal of the Constitutional Convention of the State of Louisiana,* 1898, pp. 4, 384. Six poor white hill parishes voted against the calling of the convention, and the only other parish to do so was St. James, which despite the new registration still had a Negro voting majority. For the official returns, see Baton Rouge *Daily Advocate,* January 27, 1898.

33 *Official Journal of the Constitutional Convention of the State of Louisiana,* 1898, pp. 8–9.

34 Shugg, *Origins of Class Struggle,* 136, 155; Simon I. Neiman, *Judah Benjamin* (Indianapolis, 1963), 49–73.

od. Especially did he glory in the fact that the product of the convention, by legislative arrangement, was not to be submitted to the voters for ratification. "We have absolute and despotic power," Kruttschnitt told the assembled delegates. "The people [have] protected themselves against themselves." [35] Fittingly, Major Hearsey of the *Daily States* was awarded the printing contract for the convention.[36]

What emerged from the convention of 1898 was virtually the Constitution of 1879 drawn up anew, with the addition of suffrage restriction. Even the six mill limitation on state taxation was retained. As to suffrage, voters now had to demonstrate the ability to read and write in their native language, or, as an alternative, show a property assessment of not less than $300.[37] Supposedly, the "grandfather clause," as it was termed, allowed a loophole for poor whites. For those who had voted prior to the advent of Radical Reconstruction in 1867, or whose father or grandfather had so voted, were exempt from the above requirements.[38] Mississippi's new Constitution of 1890 and that of South Carolina of 1895 had also been worded so as to disfranchise the Negro, but neither had used the ingenious "grandfather clause."

The intent of Louisiana's grandfather clause may be questioned. Only three and a half months were allowed for the registration of those who could qualify under it. Many prominent Democrats took the view that the clause was merely an "evasion," and at any rate, the United States Supreme Court

35 *Official Journal of the Constitutional Convention of the State of Louisiana,* 1898, p. 379.

36 *Ibid.,* 11.

37 *Constitution of 1898,* Art. 197.

38 *Ibid.* Besides the "grandfather clause" exception, naturalized citizens were also permitted to vote without literacy or property qualifications. The Democratic machine in New Orleans benefitted from the votes of naturalized citizens, and used its considerable influence at the constitutional convention to protect them from disfranchisement. See J. L. Warren Woodville, "Suffrage Limitation in Louisiana," *Political Science Quarterly,* XXI (1906) , 177.

would, they thought, soon declare it invalid. Both of Louisiana's national senators put themselves on record to this effect.[39] Yet about forty thousand individuals did register under the "grandfather clause." One hundred and eleven of them were not white.[40]

By 1900 the number of white voters, though far below what it had been in 1896, had climbed back to approximately the same figure that had been registered in the 1880's. The real havoc had been wreaked with black voters: only 5,320 were still on the rolls in 1900, which was less than one-twentieth their previous number.[41] Of course, most of those disfranchised had not lost much, since the bulk of Negro registrants had not been permitted a free ballot at any time since Reconstruction. And those planters who had derived political benefits from the fraudulent counting of the votes of their sharecroppers were now able to console themselves with an article in the Constitution of 1898 which made it mandatory that "in all political conventions in this State the apportionment of representation shall be on the basis of population." [42] Thus, until the spread of the party primary system in the twentieth century, the planters had not given up much, after all.

The demoralized remnants of the Louisiana People's Party entered nominees in both the congressional races of 1898 and the gubernatorial election of 1900. In 1898, their candidate who polled the highest vote was Hardy Brian in the Fourth District. But Brian obtained a mere 1,476 and carried only Grant and Winn parishes.[43] With the false Negro vote removed, Democratic totals in the Fourth and other districts fell

---

39 Shreveport *Evening Journal*, March 13, April 6, 1898; *Nation*, LXVI (May 19, 1898), 374; William A. Mabry, "Louisiana Politics and the Grandfather Clause," *North Carolina Historical Review*, XIII (1936), 306.

40 *Report of the Secretary of State*, 1902, p. 558.

41 *Ibid.*, 552–53, 556–57.

42 *Constitution of 1898*, Art. 200.

43 *Report of the Secretary of State*, 1902, p. 580.

below the level that Populist candidates had attained four or even two years previously; even so, the Bourbon party still won by margins of three to one, or better. "The great bulk" of what had once been the Populist Party, said Hardy Brian, "stayed at home in sullen despair." They felt that "it was no use, the Democrats would count them out." [44]

In the 1900 contest for the governorship, Donelson Caffery, Jr., a conservative gold standard Democrat who was at odds with the Foster administration, accepted the nomination of both the People's Party and the "Republican-Fusion ticket," the latter being made up of G.O.P. remnants within the state.[45] Running on the Populist ticket, Caffery obtained 4,938 votes and failed to carry a single parish; on the separate fusion ticket, his state total was 9,277, and he won only St. James Parish. The victorious Democratic gubernatorial candidate, William W. Heard, obtained 60,206 votes statewide.[46] Surveying the ruins of Populism in 1900, A. A. Gunby attributed his party's decline to a smothering of spirit as well as the restrictions on suffrage. "Apathy," he wrote, "seized the majority and they are willing that the minority should rule." [47] Never again would the People's Party run candidates in Louisiana elections.

Bourbonism once again ruled serenely. The Negro had been removed as a direct political factor. White agrarianism had seemingly been crushed. "The people are thoroughly cowed," observed one man who had been associated with the third-party movement in the upland parishes. "They are," he added, "under complete subjection. They will bow the knee, receive the yoke and pass on, hewers of wood, drawers of wa-

[44] Natchitoches *Populist,* November 11, 1898. The title of Brian's paper was shortened that year.

[45] Franklin *St. Mary Banner,* March 10, 1900; Shreveport *Evening Journal,* April 16, 1900; *Nation,* LXX (January 18, 1900), 42–43.

[46] *Report of the Secretary of State,* 1902, p. 564.

[47] Monroe *Bulletin,* quoted in Shreveport *Evening Journal,* April 22, 1900.

ter, beasts of burden; without spirit, without complaint, without resentment." [48] Yet the most fitting epitaph for Louisiana Populism was composed by Hardy Brian. In March of 1899, in the last issue of his newspaper, he wrote: "We refused to take up the gun [and] so we lost. . . . The fight will be won some day, but by [unchristian] methods." [49]

Brian's parting words drew little attention. Neither was much notice given, later that year, to the futile effort of a Winn Parish man to be elected, with a Populistic platform, to the state legislature. His name was H. P. Long, Sr.[50] Huey and Earl were the names of two of his small children.

48 Shreveport *Progress*, April 2, 1898.

49 Natchitoches *Populist*, March 10, 1899. Brian prepared to leave Natchitoches after the March 3 issue of his paper was destroyed by C. V. Porter, who worked for the Bourbon Democratic newspaper in town, the *Enterprise*. The affair was kept out of the city papers, "owing to Mr. Porter having lately been appointed District Attorney." Colfax *Chronicle*, March 11, 1899.

50 Colfax *Chronicle*, December 9, 1899–April 14, 1900.

Appendix

For the majority of Louisiana's Populist newspapers no surviving copies, not even fragments, exist. The only complete file extant is that of the Natchitoches *Louisiana Populist,* which for several years attempted to act as the official state journal of the party. But many others that were published are partly evident in the *Louisiana Populist,* and to a greater extent in a thorough search of the files of the leading Democratic newspapers of the state during the 1890's. A partial list is also given in James S. Penny, "The People's Party Press During the Louisiana Political Upheaval of the Eighteen-Nineties" (M.A. thesis, Louisiana State University, 1942).

The list below designates the parish and town of publication, the name of the paper, and the dates of known Populist affiliation. (One of them, the New Iberia *Enterprise,* was a journalistic freak; it was jointly owned by Populists and Democrats and had rival editorial pages.) Not included in the list are the Republican newspapers which happened to support fusionist candidates at one time or another. Neither are included certain independent-minded journals, such as the Shreveport *Progress,* which occasionally leaned toward the People's Party but never openly joined it.

Grant Parish: Colfax *Ocala Demand* (1891–92) ; Colfax *New Era* (1892–93) ; Colfax *People's Demands* (1895–98) ; Montgomery *Mail* (1892–93) ; Pollock *News* (1896–97) ; Pollock *People's Demands* (1898–99) ; Pollock *People's Voice* (1899–1900) .

St. Landry Parish: Opelousas *People's Tribune* (1896–98) ; Washington *People's Party Tribune* (1895–96) ; Washington *Post* (1896) ; Washington *Advocate* (1896) .

Calcasieu Parish: Lake Charles *Patriot* (1894–95) ; Lake Charles *New Road* (1895–98) ; Oberlin *Calcasieu Reformer* (1895–97) ; Jennings *Record* (1896–98) .

Catahoula Parish: Trinity *Farmers' Advocate* (1895–96) ; Olla *Signal* (1895–97) ; Olla *Free Silver Advocate* (1898–99) .

Natchitoches Parish: Natchitoches *Louisiana Populist* (1894–99) ; Robeline *Battle Flag* (1892–96) ; Robeline *New Era* (1895) .

Lincoln Parish: Ruston *Caligraph* (1892) ; Ruston *Progressive Age* (1892–99) .

Livingston Parish: Springfield *Star* (1893) ; Springfield *Bee* (1896) .

Ouachita Parish: Monroe *Bulletin* (1896–1900) ; West Monroe *Alliance Forum* (1894) .

Rapides Parish: Alexandria *Age of Reason* (1896) ; Alexandria *Louisiana Reformer* (1896) .

Sabine Parish: Many *Sabine Banner* (1896) ; Many *Sabine Free State* (1898) .

Webster Parish: Minden *New Forum* (1896) ; Minden *Banner of Liberty* (1896–98) .

Winn Parish: Winnfield *Comrade* (1890–1900) ; Winnfield *Southern Sentinel* (1898) .

Acadia Parish: *Louisiana Mentor,* probably published at Crowley (1893–94) .

Bienville Parish: Arcadia *Alliance Forum* (1894–96) .

Caldwell Parish: Columbia *Caldwell-Watchman* (1894) .

Cameron Parish: Lakeside *Review* (1892–96) .

Claiborne Parish: Homer *Alliance Farmer* (1892–94) .

De Soto Parish: Grand Cane *Beacon* (1896) .

East Baton Rouge Parish: Baton Rouge *Capitol Item* (1896–98) .

Iberia Parish: New Iberia *Enterprise* (1897–98) .

Jackson Parish: Jonesboro *Jackson Parish Appeal* (1896) .

Orleans Parish: New Orleans *Issue* (1891–96) .

Tangipahoa Parish: Amite *People's Call* (1895–96).

Union Parish: Farmerville *Herald* (1895–96).

Vermilion Parish: *Southern Record,* probably published at Abbeville (1896).

Vernon Parish: Leesville *People's Friend* (1891–97).

Essay on Authorities

Only the sources which proved most valuable are discussed here. The footnotes in each chapter will show the numerous other works and items of lesser importance that were utilized.

MANUSCRIPTS AND DOCUMENTS

Most of the collections of papers investigated are on deposit at the Department of Archives, Louisiana State University. Regrettably, few of the Bourbon leaders and none of the agrarian reformers of Louisiana left papers of real substance. Particular letters of significance do, however, appear in several collections. The Gay Family Papers provide insights into the lives of a politically active and wealthy sugar planter family. The Bosley Family Papers reveal the economics of a typical cotton plantation. Useful for political and social developments within the 1877–1900 period are the Breda Family Papers, the Ellis Family Papers, and the voluminous correspondence of the legal firm of Chaplin, Breazeale, and Chaplin. Disappointing because of their scantiness are the Pharr Family Papers and the E. A. Burke Papers.

The Library of Congress provided two collections with important correspondence dealing with Louisiana affairs: the William E. Chandler Papers, and microfilm copies of portions of the Rutherford B. Hayes Papers. The Marion Butler Papers in the Southern Historical Collection at the University of North Carolina yielded letters from several Louisiana Populist leaders, and the manuscript history "The Farmers Alliance" by C. W. Macune was microfilmed for my use by the University of Texas Library. Also consulted was an interesting but undated manuscript in the Tulane University Library, Covington Hall's "Labor Struggles in the Deep South."

Among state government documents, the most invaluable were the journals of the General Assembly for the period 1877–1898: the *Official Journal of the Proceedings of the House of Representatives of the State of Louisiana,* and the *Official Journal of the Proceedings of the Senate of the State of Louisiana.* Through these documents the legislators' positions on issues could be traced. An available source for parish voter registration and election statistics during the late nineteenth century is the compendium included in the *Report of the Secretary of State to His Excellency W. W. Heard, Governor of the State of Louisiana,* 1902. Data on public schools can be found in the various reports of the state superintendent of education. Most useful to me was the *Biennial Report of the State Superintendent of Public Education,* 1892–93. Insights into the attitudes of the rural elite are to be found in the *Proceedings of the State Agricultural Society,* published annually as a state document from 1887 to 1897. The State Agricultural Society was a semi-official organization largely made up of well-to-do planters and planter-politicians.

The federal *Tenth Census, 1880* and the *Eleventh Census, 1890* provided a wealth of statistical information on rural and urban Louisiana. Other federal documents were frequently consulted which dealt in whole or in part with Louisiana political or racial disturbances in the years after Reconstruction. These consisted of, in addition to the *Congressional Record,* various *House Miscellaneous Documents, House Executive Documents, Senate Executive Documents,* and *Senate Reports.*

NEWSPAPERS AND PERIODICALS

In undertaking to recreate the flavor of Louisiana society and politics in the years from 1877 to 1900, the newspapers of the state furnished the most important single type of source. The files of well over fifty were used, many extensively. Most are available on microfilm at the Louisiana State University Library; others are to be seen in bound volumes at the Tulane University Library or the Library of Congress. Of all newspapers, the New Orleans *Daily Picayune* was searched most thoroughly for the entire period. Not only was it usually more judicious editorially than the bulk of the state's press, but its pages were replete with noteworthy clippings from papers in the country parishes. The rural press—and everything outside of New Orleans in that period should be considered rural—was, despite its lamentable racism and partisanship, as a rule surprisingly well edited. The Colfax *Chronicle*, the Opelousas *Courier*, and the Natchitoches *People's Vindicator* were outstanding sources of information on the conservative Democratic viewpoint. Even more significant was the Baton Rouge *Daily Capitolian-Advocate* (the title was shortened to *Daily Advocate* in 1890), because it was for most of this period the official journal of the state government. As such, it was a consistent barometer of the opinions of the ruling oligarchy. Much of the rural press, including the *Daily Advocate* and the Shreveport newspapers, frequently echoed the editorial opinions of the ultra Bourbon and racist New Orleans *Daily States*.

Although there were many newspaper voices of protest in Louisiana during the late nineteenth century, their circulation was generally smaller, and fewer of their files have survived. Approximately fifty Populist papers were published in the state between 1890 and 1900, but only the files of the Natchitoches *Louisiana Populist* are completely extant. Two Negro newspapers of which copies are preserved give at least some indication of the problems and attitudes of the state's black population: the *Weekly Louisianian* and the *Weekly Pelican*, both published in New Orleans.

Out-of-state newspapers offered worthwhile sources of information on particular events and were also indicators of national opinion about Louisiana matters. Among those used were the New York *Times*, the Cincinnati *Enquirer*, the Galveston *Daily News*, the St. Louis *Post-Dispatch*, and the Philadelphia *Journal of United Labor* (later retitled the *Journal of the Knights of Labor*).

Several periodicals with national circulations devoted considerable space to developments in Louisiana. Most vital for the agrarian viewpoint was the *National Economist,* the interstate magazine of the Farmers' Alliance movement. Among the general readership periodicals, the *Nation, Harper's Weekly,* the *Forum,* the *Arena,* and the *North American Review* provided articles of special interest. Along with these, various articles in learned journals, including the *Journal of Southern History,* the *Mississippi Valley Historical Review,* and the *Louisiana Historical Quarterly* proved indispensable.

UNPUBLISHED MONOGRAPHS

A number of theses and dissertations were consulted and cited which deal with aspects of life in late nineteenth-century Louisiana. Some were of especial help. Useful for events leading up to the restoration of "white home rule" is William Edward Highsmith, "Louisiana During Reconstruction" (Ph.D. dissertation, Louisiana State University, 1953). Clarence Howard Nichols, "Francis T. Nicholls, Bourbon Democrat" (M.A. thesis, Louisiana State University, 1959) has detailed information on the first post-Reconstruction state administration. On the Republican opposition to the Bourbon Democracy, an illuminating source is Philip D. Uzee, "Republican Politics in Louisiana, 1877–1900" (Ph.D. dissertation, Louisiana State University, 1950). Allie Bayne Windham Webb presents the tortured history of black suffrage in "A History of Negro Voting in Louisiana, 1876–1906" (Ph.D. dissertation, Louisiana State University, 1962). Curley Daniel Willis, "The Grange Movement in Louisiana" (M.A. thesis, Louisiana State University, 1935) gives essential data on the rise and decline of that early agricultural organization. For some of the activities of the notorious Lottery, I am indebted to John T. White, "The History of the Louisiana Lottery" (M.A. thesis, Tulane University, 1939). Certain facets of the Negro Exodus of 1879 were brought to my attention by Earl Howard Aiken, "Kansas Fever" (M.A. thesis, Louisiana State University, 1939). Margaret M.

Williams draws an unflattering picture of politics and education in "An Outline of Public School Politics in Louisiana Since the Civil War" (M.A. thesis, Tulane University, 1938). Although not directly concerned with Louisiana, Martin M. LaGodna, "Kansas and the Ocala Convention of 1890: Groundwork of the People's Party" (M.A. thesis, Florida State University, 1962) proves enlightening as to the origins of Populism. A pioneer effort to describe the Populist movement in Louisiana is Lucia Elizabeth Daniel, "The Louisiana People's Party" (M.A. thesis, Louisiana State University, 1942). A more recent analysis of the same subject by Henry C. Dethloff, "Populism and Reform in Louisiana" (Ph.D. dissertation, University of Missouri, 1964) has considerable merit, but it ignores the repressiveness of the Bourbon oligarchy and fails to take into account the distinctiveness of the Populist reform effort.

CONTEMPORANEOUS ACCOUNTS AND GENERAL STUDIES

Of all books used which were written during the period, two dealing with the Farmers' Alliance movement were the most valuable. Much of the early history of the Louisiana Farmers' Union could not have been unearthed had it not been for the clues provided in these obscure accounts: W. Scott Morgan, *History of the Wheel and Alliance, and the Impending Revolution* (Hardy, Ark.: published by the author, 1889), and Nelson A. Dunning, *The Farmers' Alliance History and Agricultural Digest* (Washington: Alliance Publishing Company, 1891). Almost as useful for information on Louisiana agrarianism were two local histories for which no author or editor is listed: *Biographical and Historical Memoirs of Louisiana*, 2 vols. (Chicago: Goodspeed Publishing Company, 1892), and *Biographical and Historical Memoirs of Northwest Louisiana* (Nashville: Southern Publishing Company, 1890). Other contemporary accounts of special worth for political, racial, or social developments include: George Washington Cable, *The Negro Question* (New York: Charles Scribner's Sons, 1890), Albert

M. Gibson, *A Political Crime: The History of the Great Fraud* (New York: W. S. Gottsberger, 1885), Julian Ralph, *Dixie: Or Southern Scenes and Sketches* (New York: Harper and Brothers, 1896), and Henry Rightor, *Standard History of New Orleans, Louisiana* (Chicago: Lewis Publishing Company, 1900).

Several modern works on Louisiana, the South, and American agrarianism deserve mention because of their utility to me. Roger W. Shugg, although dealing with an earlier time in Louisiana, gave me inspiration and insight in his *Origins of Class Struggle in Louisiana: A Social History of White Farmers and Laborers during Slavery and After, 1840–1875* (Baton Rouge: Louisiana State University Press, 1939). My research would have been vastly more difficult were it not for the regional perspectives offered in C. Vann Woodward's classic study, *Origins of the New South: 1877–1913* (Baton Rouge: Louisiana State University Press, 1951). I am also indebted to Woodward for his *Reunion and Reaction: The Compromise of 1877 and the End of Reconstruction* (Boston: Little, Brown, 1951). Still of some value in untangling the events surrounding the end of Reconstruction is Garnie W. McGinty, *Louisiana Redeemed: The Overthrow of Carpet-bag Rule, 1876–1880* (New Orleans: Pelican Publishing Company, 1941). John Samuel Ezell devotes considerable attention to the Louisiana Lottery in *Fortune's Merry Wheel: The Lottery in America* (Cambridge, Mass.: Harvard University Press, 1960). Worthwhile because of its data on cotton prices during the nineteenth century is James E. Boyle, *Cotton and the New Orleans Cotton Exchange: A Century of Commercial Evolution* (Garden City, N.Y.: The Country Life Press, 1934). The economic history of the sugar parishes comes in for careful study in J. Carlyle Sitterson, *Sugar Country: The Cane Sugar Industry in the South, 1753–1950* (Lexington: University of Kentucky Press, 1953). Irwin Unger's masterful work on *The Greenback Era: A Social and Political History of American Finance, 1865–1879* (Princeton, N.J.: Princeton University Press, 1964) allowed me to better comprehend the relationship of Louisiana Greenbackism to the inflationist movement at the national level. For the Farmers' Alliance and Southern Populism, the detail and analysis available in Theodore Saloutos, *Farm-*

er Movement in the South: 1865–1933 (Berkeley and Los Angeles: University of California Press, 1960) was of inestimable benefit. The old study of the People's Party by John D. Hicks, *The Populist Revolt: A History of the Farmers' Alliance and the People's Party* (Minneapolis: University of Minnesota Press, 1931) is still the standard work, but it should be supplemented by Norman Pollack's interpretations and collection of readings, *The Populist Mind* (Indianapolis: Bobbs-Merrill Company, 1967).

Index

Abbeville, La., 189
Acadia Parish, 42n
Acklen, Joseph H., 48, 80
Adams, Henry, 90–91
Adams, Thomas Scott: early career of, 167–68; appointed secretary of agriculture, 201; tries for Democratic gubernatorial nomination, 202–204; opposes independent action, 207; resigns as head of Farmers' Union, 230; breaks with Gov. Foster, 258; mentioned, 161, 196, 197, 211, 216, 219, 220, 221, 231n
Adams County, Miss., 33
Agricultural Wheel, 148, 151, 152
Agriculture: post-Reconstruction conditions, 34–47 *passim;* vocation of majority, 35; plantation system's survival, 35, 38–39, 53; amount of land tilled, 37; cotton production, 35–36, 40–44 *passim,* 46; sugar production, 35–39 *passim;* corn production, 36; livestock production, 36, 43; sweet potato production, 36; rice production, 136. *See also* Land values
Alabama, 98, 122, 241, 245
Alexandria, La., 166, 216, 217, 219, 249, 250, 251
Alexandria *Farmers' Vidette,* 219–20
Alexandria *Louisiana Democrat,* 236
American Federation of Labor, 212
American (Know Nothing) Party, 72
Anderson, Thomas C.: member of returning board, 8; arrest and trial, 32–33
Anti-Lottery League: organized, 169; captures Farmers' Union, 201–204; mentioned, 216, 220
Antioch Church, 146
Arcadia, La., 159, 166, 189
Arkansas, 40, 122, 148
Arnaud, Aurel, 192–93
Ascension Parish, 39n, 164, 175, 250
Australian ballot, 236
Avoyelles Parish, 159

Backbone Railroad (New Orleans, Baton Rouge, and Vicksburg Railway Company), 49–51, 206
Bailey, Bryant W.: candidate for Congress in 1894, 239–40, 241–42; editor of *Comrade,* 240; candidate for Congress in 1896, 271; at 1898 constitutional convention, 275
Baptist Church: against Lottery, 104; religion of Populist leaders, 244–45
Barbour, Fannie, 38
Bastrop, La., 95, 190, 237, 264
Bastrop *Morehouse Clarion,* 127, 190
Baton Rouge, La.: becomes state capital, 101; segregation in, 101; mentioned, 13, 32, 40, 64, 65, 79, 95, 129, 155, 163, 164, 167, 189, 203, 204, 209, 238, 244, 260, 263, 265, 267
Baton Rouge *Daily Advocate,* 168, 189, 205, 224, 228, 232, 238, 239, 250, 260, 265, 268, 271–72